AMC
JAVELIN, AMX
& MUSCLE CAR RESTORATION
1968-1974

Scott Campbell

CarTech®

CarTech®

CarTech®, Inc.
838 Lake Street South
Forest Lake, MN 55025 USA
Phone: 651-277-1200 or 800-551-4754
Fax: 651-277-1203
www.cartechbooks.com

© 2015 by Scott Campbell

All rights reserved. No part of this publication may be reproduced or utilized in any form or by any means, electronic or mechanical, including photocopying, recording, or by any information storage and retrieval system, without prior permission from the Publisher. All text, photographs, and artwork are the property of the Author unless otherwise noted or credited.

The information in this work is true and complete to the best of our knowledge. However, all information is presented without any guarantee on the part of the Author or Publisher, who also disclaim any liability incurred in connection with the use of the information and any implied warranties of merchantability or fitness for a particular purpose. Readers are responsible for taking suitable and appropriate safety measures when performing any of the operations or activities described in this work.

All trademarks, trade names, model names and numbers, and other product designations referred to herein are the property of their respective owners and are used solely for identification purposes. This work is a publication of CarTech, Inc., and has not been licensed, approved, sponsored, or endorsed by any other person or entity. The Publisher is not associated with any product, service, or vendor mentioned in this book, and does not endorse the products or services of any vendor mentioned in this book.

Edit by Wes Eisenschenk
Layout by Monica Seiberlich

ISBN 978-1-61325-453-0
Item No. SA318P

Library of Congress Cataloging-in-Publication Data Available

Written, edited, and designed in the U.S.A.
Printed in U.S.A.

Front Cover: One of the most rewarding experiences you can have is re-assembling your car with restored, factory-correct parts. With fresh paint on the 1970 Javelin, author Scott Campbell begins to put his car back together.

Title Page: This 1973 Javelin shows all the signs of being a great restoration candidate. The car featured the 360 with an auto on the console, Fresh Plum paint, white vinyl roof, and a white interior. (Photo Courtesy Michelle Kiffmeyer)

Back Cover Photos

Top Left: Carefully position the axle over the leaf springs. Raise the springs until the center bolt aligns with the hole in the spring perch, bolt the axle to the springs, and then lift everything together to install the rear shackles. Protect the axle and springs from coming in contact with each other or the garage floor.

Top Right: An original lower radiator hose removed from a 1968 AMX displays the part number and early-style "AM" logo in white. Lower radiator hoses commonly contain a spring to prevent collapsing. As with the top hose, it was secured with Wittek tower-style hose clamps at either end.

Middle Left: The rivet heads can be drilled without spinning. A spinning rivet quickly cuts a large hole through the door tag making it impossible to reinstall it with original-style rivets.

Middle Right: AMX over-the-top racing stripes were part of the performance Go Package, but could be deleted upon request. They were not available on cars equipped with the 290 V-8. After applying vinyl stripes, park outside in bright sunshine for a couple of days to set the glue and allow any small bubbles to disappear.

Bottom Left: Just like the panels they attach, bolt head markings differ from year to year. Label and bag all of the attaching hardware as it is removed so it can be reused in the same position. If assembling a car that was purchased disassembled, be sure that any visible fasteners are the same type with uniform markings.

Bottom Right: As with the quarter panel, trim the outer wheelhouse back until clean metal is reached. Reproduction outer quarters are made in two sections (front and rear); complete one half of the job at a time. Keeping half of the original quarter in place temporarily allows for perfect alignment of the replacement panel.

CONTENTS

Acknowledgments 4
Introduction 5

Chapter 1: Finding Your Project Car 7
Model Year Rundown 7
Where to Look 15
Vehicle Identification Number 15
Door Tag Codes 16
AMX Dash Number 17
Engine Casting Numbers 17
Popular Options 18
Red Flags 18
Play it Safe 21

Chapter 2: Creating a Game Plan 23
Driver, Show Car or Street Machine 23
Complete or Partial Restoration 24
Time and Space Requirements 24
Making a Budget 25

Chapter 3: Getting Started 26
Your Work Area 26
Tools and Equipment 26
Safety First! 29
Cleaning and Inspection 30
Disassembly 35
Storing the Parts 39
Replacement Parts Sources 40

Chapter 4: Body Repair 41
Evaluating Condition 41
Paint Removal 42
Bolt-On Panels 44
Structural Rust Repair 46
Outer Body Rust 51
Surface Rust 57
Collision Damage 58
Door Hinges 58
Panel Adjustment 60
Block Sanding and Prep 62

Chapter 5: Painting Your Car 64
Interior Body Paint 64
Cutting in the Color 70
Exterior Body Paint 74
Caring for Paint 77

Chapter 6: Engine and Transmission 78
Inspection 78
Removal 80
Disassembly 82
Painting and Detailing 82
Transmission 84

Chapter 7: Engine Compartment 86
Refinishing Small Parts 87
Cowl and Firewall 88
Engine Installation 93
Engine Accessories 94
Cleaning Tip 101

Chapter 8: Undercar Components 102
Suspension System 104
Steering System 114
Driveshaft 116
Braking System 116
Exhaust System 117
Wheels and Tires 118
Brake Lines and Fuel Lines 120
Restore or Over-Restore? 121

Chapter 9: Interior 122
Interior Removal 122
Window Glass 127
Dash and Console 128
Seats 131
Seat Belts 133
Door Panels 134
Steering Wheel 135
Interior Refinishing 137

Chapter 10: Trunk 138

Chapter 11: Body Trim and Finishing 144
Rubber Parts 144
Bumpers 145
Moldings and Trim 147
Grille and Lights 149
Vinyl Top and Stripes 152

Chapter 12: Performance Upgrades 155

Chapter 13: Presentation and Showing 162
Detailing 162
Presentation 166
Car Show Props 167

Chapter 14: Care and Storage 168
Driving and Parking 168
Weather Conditions 168
Storage Tips 169

Chapter 15: Future Collectibility 171

Conclusion 174
Source Guide 175

Acknowledgments

When I was asked to undertake this project, I knew it would be no small feat. An AMC restoration book had never been produced, and even though I do this type of work every day, I don't even pretend to know everything about the subject matter. For this reason, I immediately contacted some of the most respected members of the AMC community, people who have disassembled, documented, and restored some of the finest original AMC muscle cars in the world. These calls and messages led to the formation of a "secret" Facebook group dedicated to the project, where we could discuss topics in detail, compare findings, and generally form a consensus of what is most correct, despite the subtle variations that exist between cars assembled within the same year, or even the same month.

For their invaluable assistance and free sharing of restoration information, I would like to extend a special thanks to Tom Benvie, Brooke Pitt, Steve Parson, Ross Peterson, Joe Roberts, Kevin Shope, and Ian Webb. The combined knowledge that these gentlemen possess could easily fill ten books! So many additional people helped in other ways, often not even knowing that their answers to my random questions were actually for the book. Others offered their cars as subject matter for photos that were needed. My sincere thanks to all of you as well.

Several AMC project cars are prominently featured, and my gratitude goes to their owners because some work was actually delayed a bit to produce photos for the book. Thank you to Will Cook, Russell Barnes, Nevada Johnson, David DiPiero, and Rich Rider. Entrusting your awesome AMC muscle cars to me was the only way that writing this book was even possible.

Thanks also to B & B Auto and Wayne's Collision, both of Medina, Ohio, for indulging my impromptu photo shoots as bodywork was in process and paint was applied. It is a privilege to have a choice of body shops nearby capable of producing consistent show-quality work.

Finally, I would like to thank my wife and children for the time that this project took me away from them, and my neighbors for not complaining when my lawn wasn't cut quite as often this year!

Introduction

Following its inception in May 1954, American Motors Corporation capitalized on its image as a builder of practical, economical cars; Rambler sedans and station wagons were engineered to get you from point A to point B as efficiently as possible without a lot of drama. But, along the way, something happened.

As early as 1957, American Motors was dabbling in V-8–powered performance cars; the Rambler Rebel was among the fastest domestic cars produced that year. And by the late 1960s, following the success of the Pontiac GTO and Ford Mustang, among others, little AMC found itself right in the thick of things, producing several high-performance models including the 343-powered Rogue, 390 Javelin SST, and Hurst SC/Rambler.

Even more incredible is that American Motors fielded a competitor to the Corvette with its two-seat AMX sports car! But despite their best efforts, and due in large part to the increasing costs of gasoline and auto insurance, the original muscle car era began to wind down and AMC once again found itself building small, practical cars along with Jeeps and a few models engineered by Renault.

A rare sight indeed, this 1969 AMC Hurst SC/Rambler is a perfect candidate for a top-flight restoration. This project car comes from central Minnesota and had spent many years out in the elements before finding a new home in 2005. (Photo Courtesy Michelle Kiffmeyer)

This is likely the reason that so many people have overlooked AMC's performance models for so many years. To most people, "American Motors" meant Gremlin or Pacer; when the conversation turned to muscle cars, American Motors was generally left out completely. Only recently have mainstream collectors cast an eye toward the products of American Motors. But because most AMC cars were produced in much smaller numbers than comparable GM, Ford, or Chrysler models, demand for some of them has already outstripped the number of surviving examples.

The red, white, and blue 1970 Javelin SST Trans-Am edition is one example; only 100 cars were

INTRODUCTION

originally produced and few survive. Another hot collectible in recent years has been the 1971 Hornet SC/360; only 784 units were originally produced and fewer than 200 are known to exist today.

Low production combined with decades of limited collector interest has done little to raise the bar on AMC restorations. A lack of easily accessible restoration information hasn't helped either, especially in the days before the Internet. Although GM, Ford, and Chrysler muscle cars have long enjoyed a strong aftermarket, as well as specialized periodicals and restoration support, AMC owners have had to make do with scarce, often conflicting or confusing information and relatively few reproduction parts. The result is a lot of amateur restorations using mismatched or incorrect parts pirated from various AMC models or years.

With the price of AMC muscle cars finally on the rise, there is an urgent need for a concise, easy-to-follow blueprint for accurately restoring an AMX, Javelin, or other AMC performance model. That is the mission of this book. However, because the value of a restored AMC car generally trails that of a comparable GM, Ford, or Chrysler model, it is not difficult to spend much more on a restoration than the car will ever be worth, at least in our lifetime. That is one reason I do not profile a 1,000-point rotisserie makeover, ending up with a car that is too perfect to even drive.

The other reason, of course, is that AMC workers did not stand the body shells upright to carefully paint the underside! You will discover how these cars were originally built so that you can accurately duplicate their factory-new appearance. You also won't be bogged down seeing every step involved in rebuilding an engine or transmission. That book has already been written. In fact, if you're doing a stock rebuild, everything you need to know for assembling the drivetrain is in the AMC Technical Service Manual (TSM) that corresponds to the model year of your particular car.

Since there is no need to rewrite the TSM, this book is intended to complement it; it fills in the details needed to *restore* a car rather than just *repair* one. In these pages you will find the nuts and bolts information needed to perform a real-world rolling restoration with the goal of it being a show-quality, stock-appearing, *drivable* car that you will be proud to own and display for many years to come. But first, you will find useful information designed to help you find, evaluate, and purchase a project car.

I cover the disassembly process, some basic as well as more advanced restoration steps, the reassembly phase, and final detailing. All major systems are covered: body and paint, mechanical, and interior. Some aspects of a high-quality restoration require hands-on training followed by months or even years of practice in order to hone your skills, but having a better understanding of these operations will give you a greater appreciation of what you might pay someone else to do. Who knows? You may be inspired sufficiently to get your hands on some equipment and give it a try yourself. The more you can do, the less you will spend.

A variety of AMC models and years were used to illustrate this book to present as much original restoration detail information as possible. The two primary vehicles featured are a Matador Red 1968 AMX with a 290 V-8 and automatic and a Bittersweet Orange 1970 base model Javelin with a 390 V-8 and 4-speed transmission. These two cars provide a nice cross section of 1968–1970 restoration information.

Although the main focus of this book is the early two-seat AMX and similar four-passenger Javelin, most of the restoration information can be applied just as easily to second-generation 1971–1974 Javelins and Javelin AMXs, as well as Hurst SC/Ramblers, Rebel Machines, Hornet SC/360, and even 1972 and newer V-8–powered Gremlins, AMC's "mini muscle car." All AMC cars built during the muscle car era were assembled using the same basic procedures and assembly sequence. Whenever possible, photos of original unrestored parts and other details are included, rather than replacement parts or parts that are already refinished.

When restoring any car you find that some things go even easier than expected, and naturally there are some setbacks along the way as well. No major project is without a few of those! However, in the end all of the trials and challenges that are part of restoring an AMC muscle car will be worth it because car show spectators will stroll past the rows of common Mustangs and Camaros just to check out something a little different. Let's get started!

CHAPTER 1

FINDING YOUR PROJECT CAR

You've decided that it's time to find a muscle car project of your own, and your desire for something less expensive, or a little more uncommon than a Ford, Chevy, or Mopar, has pointed you in the direction of American Motors. If you haven't already chosen a favorite model there are several great muscle cars to consider.

Model Year Rundown

American Motors began to get serious about performance cars following the introduction of the modern V-8 engines late in 1966. Although the 343-powered 1967 Rogue was a great performer, American Motors upped the ante for the next model year.

1968

Featuring a Carter AFB 4-barrel carburetor, forged crankshaft and connecting rods, the high-compression AMX 390 V-8 was the company's largest and most powerful engine to date. Also arriving for the 1968 model year was the sporty Javelin pony car and the two-seat AMX sports car, which was introduced mid-year in late February.

The new Javelin was a Mustang competitor, and as such it was compared directly to Ford's offering in AMC's print advertising. Available in only one body style, a semi-fastback, the Javelin offered the choice of a thrifty 6-cylinder or powerful V-8 engine coupled to either a manual or automatic transmission. The Javelin SST was a more upscale version with nicer interior appointments including fully reclining seats, as well as full wheel covers and additional exterior brightwork. Following the mid-year introduction of the AMX, the 390 V-8 became the Javelin's top engine option.

With the new AMX sports car, American Motors had an image changer on its hands. Available only with a 4-barrel, high-compression V-8, dual exhaust, traction bars, and

Although it looks fairly rough, this 1968 AMX provided a wealth of original information both before and during its teardown. Driven for years, even through Ohio winters (note the snow tires!) and then parked for decades in a barn, this one-owner, 66,000-mile car was nonetheless deemed worthy of a complete restoration.

CHAPTER 1

The Javelin was AMC's entry in the pony car field. But, unlike the Ford Mustang and Chevrolet Camaro, it was available in only one body style: a semi-fastback coupe. Introduced in late 1967 as a 1968 model, the Javelin's first generation ran through 1970, as seen here. Clean examples can still be found at a reasonable price, although high-performance and limited-edition variants have steadily increased in value.

The 1968–1970 two-passenger AMX sports car was the first AMC model to enjoy mainstream collector interest. Every one built featured a high-compression 4-barrel V-8, bucket seats, and dual exhaust. AMX production for all three years totaled just 19,134 units. This 1968 model features the optional Trendsetter side exhaust system as well as the Go Package, which was a popular performance option group for the AMX.

a pair of fully reclining bucket seats, the new AMX was intended to be a "halo car," lowering the median age of visitors to AMC showrooms; in that role it was a major success. Sales success, however, was not realized. Although high volume was never planned for the AMX, one advertisement stated that just 10,000 units were planned for the first year. Actual production fell short of even that goal. A two-passenger muscle car was not a good fit for everyone, but many Javelin sales could certainly be attributed to customers who had been lured into AMC dealerships by the hot new AMX.

1969

The 1969 model year saw the continuation of both the Javelin and AMX models with only detail refinements. Additional wood-grain trim was added to the center dash panel and door armrests, and the Javelin received a slightly different grille and smaller "Javelin" scripts for the hood and upper quarter panels. New paint colors were offered along with additional colors for the AMX Go Package stripes.

The big news for 1969 was the introduction of the Hurst SC/Rambler collaboration between American Motors and Hurst Performance of Warminster Township, Pennsylvania. It was a compact Rogue hardtop (in its final season), equipped with the AMX 390 V-8 engine, 4-speed transmission, a functional forced-air induction hood scoop (the first for American Motors), subframe connectors, torque link traction bars, and other performance modifications.

Often regarded as the swan song for the Rambler name, the 1969 Hurst SC/Rambler featured two distinctly different paint schemes, although both were patriotic red, white, and blue. Because only 1,512 units were produced, an SC/Rambler was a rare sight when new, unless you happened to be at the dragstrip!

Also new and exciting was the mid-year introduction of the Big Bad Colors option for both the AMX and Javelin. Available in Big Bad Orange, Big Bad Green, and Big Bad Blue, this option featured high-impact colors, even applied to the front and rear bumpers. The front bumper required an additional molding along the leading edge to complete the bright grille opening. Big Bad bumper moldings are rarely found for sale today. Optional rear bumper guards were also painted to match, if ordered, and Go Package–equipped AMXs painted in the Big Bad Colors were limited to black

FINDING YOUR PROJECT CAR

The 1969 Hurst SC/Rambler combined AMC's compact Rogue hardtop body with an AMX 390-ci V-8, backed by a BorgWarner 4-speed transmission. Available in two distinctly different paint schemes, the only other option was an AM radio. Combined production was just 1,512 units making it very collectible today. But beware of clones because many SC/Ramblers had been driven to their deaths, or allowed to rust beyond repair. This is an example of the flashier "A" paint scheme.

or white only for the over-the-top stripe colors.

Other AMC models also received the Big Bad paint colors in 1969, but without the body-color bumpers. This included the Rebel Raider, a special edition sold in the New York region.

1970

Both the Javelin and AMX received a significant makeover for the 1970 model year, the final season for the AMX as a two-seater. The car's interior was completely new, including the dash, door panels, and seats, which were now high-back buckets that no longer reclined. A functional ram-air hood was at last optional for both models, as well as a distinctive Shadow Mask paint scheme for the AMX only; the hood, fender tops, and perimeter of the side glass were painted in a low-gloss black, separated by a silver pinstripe.

With the Rogue body discontinued, American Motors turned to the newly restyled intermediate Rebel for another special edition, "The Machine." Larger but more powerful than the Hurst SC/Rambler, and with its 340-hp 390 V-8 The Machine didn't disappoint. It could be ordered with an optional, console-shifted automatic transmission. The first 1,000 units were finished in a red, white, and blue motif with reflective racing stripes; after that, any production Rebel color could be ordered sans racing stripes. Unique to the Machine was a lighted tachometer incorporated into the back of the functional forced-air induction hood scoop.

Model year 1970 was a pinnacle year for special edition Javelins, including one named for SCCA Trans-Am series driver Mark Donohue. Built to commemorate Donohue's (as well as AMC's) success in the series, the Mark Donohue–edition Javelin SST was a 360 or 390 V-8–powered model featuring an AMX ram air hood as well as new fiberglass ducktail spoiler that was developed in cooperation with Donohue. The spoiler included a sticker placed on the passenger side bearing Donohue's signature. No code found in the car's VIN or door data plate indicates this option; a factory-built Mark Donohue Javelin can only be

"The Machine" represented AMC's intermediate-size muscle car for 1970, using the newly restyled Rebel hardtop body. Unique features included a hood scoop–mounted tachometer, and reflective stripes on 25A-coded cars that were painted white with blue hood and lower bodysides. Any standard Rebel color was available for the Machine, but without the distinctive stripes.

CHAPTER 1

The 1970 Rebel Machine was the only AMC to feature a hood-mounted 8,000-rpm tachometer, complete with the brand-new AMC logo. Mounted into the back of the hood scoop, the tach was lighted for easier nighttime viewing. Heat and vibration have taken their toll on many of these tachs, but repairs to the mechanism or wiring are often possible.

Reflective red, white, and blue racing stripes add interest to the rear view of a 25A-coded Rebel called the Machine. Red, white, and blue accent stripes were also applied to the lower part of the grille. Reflective "The Machine" stickers were found on the front fenders, trunk lid, and dash of every Rebel Machine.

verified as authentic by having original paperwork.

Not to be confused with Pontiac's Firebird variant, the 1970 Javelin Trans Am was a limited edition AMC vehicle that featured a unique paint scheme of Frost White, Matador Red, and Commodore Blue, along with a pedestal-mounted rear spoiler. Built as a marketing tool to promote AMC's involvement in Trans-Am racing, these were equipped exactly the same, including the SST package and 390 V-8 backed by a 4-speed transmission. Production was limited to just 100 cars and many of the Trans Am Javelins remain unaccounted for today.

All three Big Bad Colors were continued for 1970, but became a regular color option without the

Model year 1970 was a good one for the AMC Javelin, which had freshened exterior styling, a completely new interior, available ram air induction, and limited production special edition models that included the Trans Am and Mark Donohue editions. The Big Bad Colors option was continued for 1970, but without the body-color bumpers seen in 1969.

A base model 1970 Javelin with a 390 V-8 and 4-speed transmission makes for an extremely unusual combination because most highly optioned Javelins were SST models. This is a classic "before" shot as the car still wears its weathered original paint and stripes. The original vinyl top is almost completely missing.

FINDING YOUR PROJECT CAR

Limited to just 100 units, the 390-powered 1970 Trans Am edition Javelin SST is a rare and valuable muscle car from American Motors. Although some are documented as destroyed, roughly three quarters of the original run remain unaccounted for. In the early days some were repainted in solid colors, so who knows where the next one will surface?

The Big Bad Colors option included a choice of bright orange, green, or blue, with matching painted bumpers used in 1969 only. For 1970 (shown) the Big Bad Colors became a regular color option with no other special features. Every AMC fan has his or her favorite Big Bad color!

unique painted bumpers. Big Bad–painted 1970 Rebels (including The Machine), Hornets, and Gremlins can be found as well as AMXs and Javelins. The AMX Shadow Mask option was available in conjunction with the Big Bad Colors, and made for a striking combination.

1971

Despite lobbying by AMC design chief Richard Teague, the two-seater AMX was discontinued for the 1971 model year. Now, instead of having two unique body styles and wheelbases, The AMX and Javelin lines were combined into a larger and more radically styled Javelin AMX that featured a raised-profile fiberglass hood, along with front and rear spoilers. Optional on the AMX model only was an attractive T-stripe for the hood and front fender tops that was

For the 1971 model year, the AMX and Javelin lines were combined into the four-passenger Javelin AMX. Standard Javelins were also available sans the rear spoiler, raised-profile fiberglass hood, and AMX interior appointments. Available with a choice of V-8 engines ranging up to a 401-ci, the 1971–1974 AMX featured a polarizing new styling that included distinctive front fender humps. Collector interest in this generation has been building for several years, driving prices upward.

CHAPTER 1

Javelin and Javelin AMX models for 1971–1972 feature a simulated twin-hatch effect stamped into the roof panel. When a vinyl top was ordered it only covered the dual front sections of the roof as shown here. A smooth roof panel was used in 1973–1974, so the optional vinyl top now covered the entire roof and upper quarter panels, extending all the way to the back of the car.

The restyled 1971 Javelin was longer and wider, but continued a version of the full-width taillight treatment used in the previous years. Javelin taillights were similar for 1972, but added a chrome grid overlay that resembled the standard 1972 grille. A single backup light was centered in the taillight assembly from 1970 to 1972 for Javelin and AMX models.

Intended to fly under the radar of insurance companies that had become weary of insuring traditional big-block muscle cars, the 1971 Hornet SC/360 was a potent combination of light weight and a powerful 360-ci engine. Understated in appearance compared to AMC's earlier special editions, the SC/360 found only 784 buyers, making one a rare sight today. Cars equipped with the optional Go Package included a 4-barrel carburetor and functional forced-air induction hood scoop.

available in a choice of colors. Less expensive base model Javelins and upscale Javelin SST models were also available, and shared the curvy new styling. Interior design was also new for 1971, and featured a wraparound driver's cockpit and molded plastic interior side panels.

Gone for 1971 was the 390 engine, replaced by an internally larger 401-ci V-8. Also gone was the Rebel line; it received new front-end styling to become the new Matador. Just a handful of Matadors were produced with an understated Matador Machine performance package. It had no external stripes or graphics, and was promoted only minimally in AMC sales materials.

AMC's special edition muscle car for 1971 was based on the compact Hornet line that had been launched the previous year. Named the Hornet SC/360, it was intended to fly under the radar of the auto insurance companies that had been raising premiums for traditional big-block muscle cars. Available in any Hornet color, the standard SC/360 had a 2-barrel, 360-ci engine with 3-speed standard floor shift. Optional was a 285 hp, 4-barrel Go Package version with functional ram air hood scoop, as well as a 4-speed manual or automatic transmission.

1972

Model year 1972 was largely a carryover for the Javelin and Javelin AMX. Both models received new taillight lenses, and the non-AMX cars now sported a sturdy-looking egg crate grille. The outer wire-mesh grille for the Javelin AMX was now blacked out instead of silver. An attractive new side C-stripe was available for the SST. Inside, the optional center console was slightly redesigned and the dash switches were now chrome with universal symbols.

An interesting variation was the new Pierre Cardin interior for the Javelin and Javelin AMX. Developed for American Motors with the cooperation of the well-known fashion designer, the package included wildly striped seats and headliner, special door panel inserts, and a chrome-plated badge for each front fender. Gone for 1972 was the Hornet SC/360 model as well as the Matador Machine package.

American Motors created a new performance category for 1972 by installing a 304-ci V-8 in the subcompact Gremlin model introduced two years earlier. Even with a standard 2-barrel carburetor, the V-8 Gremlin X was a solid performer, requiring rear axle torque links to prevent axle wind-up and wheel hop. The short-wheelbase 1968–1970 AMX and compact Hurst SC/Rambler were

The Pierre Cardin edition Javelin was developed in cooperation with the famous fashion designer, and featured wild graphics for the seats, door panel inserts, and headliner. A Pierre Cardin logo also appeared on each front fender. Although definitely not for everyone, the option did sell well enough in 1972 to be continued for the 1973 Javelin as well. A limited number of Javelin AMX models also received the Pierre Cardin interior.

the only other models so equipped. Especially when combined with the newly available Levi's interior option, which featured seats and door panels trimmed in simulated blue denim, a V-8 Gremlin X is a rare and desirable collectible today.

If a stock V-8 Gremlin wasn't enough, one AMC dealership in Mesa, Arizona, was busy converting 304-powered Gremlins into 401-powered Gremlins! Randall American built a limited number of XR-401 Gremlins, most of which saw

When searching for an AMC muscle car project don't overlook a V-8–powered Gremlin X, built from 1972 to 1976. With a 2-barrel 304-ci engine in the lightweight Gremlin body, it can be classified as a mini muscle car, and one that surprised its share of unsuspecting challengers back in the day. This is a 1974 model.

CHAPTER 1

Much like the Chevrolet muscle cars modified by Yenko, or the Dodges tuned by Mr. Norm's Grand-Spaulding Dodge, the AMC faithful turned to Randall American of Mesa, Arizona, for levels of performance not available from the factory. Starting with 304-ci Gremlins, the dealership transplanted 401-ci engines to create the Randall 401-XR, capable of high-13-second elapsed times on the quarter-mile. With just over 20 produced from 1972 to 1974, and fewer known to survive, a documented Randall 401-XR is the most sought after variation of AMC's mini muscle car. (Photo Courtesy Randall AMC)

Brand new for 1973 were separate, quad taillights for Javelin and Javelin AMX models. Often referred to as "TV" taillights because of their shape, they were carried over for 1974 models as well. Watch for rust perforation around these lights because of the rubber seals that can trap water against the tail panel.

Another change for 1973 Javelin and AMX models were handsome, new solid-rubber bumper guards for the front and rear. These replaced the longer chrome and rubber guards used earlier. Because of bumper regulations in certain states, some 1974 models used a much larger version, which was functional but less attractive.

dragstrip duty from day one. Today, original, documented XR-401 Gremlins command a strong premium over other factory H-coded V-8 Gremlins built through 1976.

1973

Model year 1973 saw yet another new grille for the standard Javelin (the SST trim level was discontinued after 1972), as well as handsome new quad taillights for all Javelin models. The roof panel was now smooth without the T-top effect of the 1971–1972 cars, and the optional vinyl top now covered the entire roof and upper quarter panels. Front and rear bumper guards were new, made of solid rubber instead of chrome-plated steel with rubber inserts. New side stripes for the Javelin were designed to accentuate the car's curvy flanks.

Inside all models, the front bucket seats were new and much slimmer, now without the hard plastic backs used since 1970. The distinctively-styled Pierre Cardin interior option was continued for 1973, which means that there are early- and late-style Pierre Cardin seats.

1974

Model year 1974 was the last one for the Javelin and Javelin AMX. Changes to both models were minimal. The front seat release levers were relocated from the center of the seat back to the lower corner. The three-spoke sport steering wheel center now included an "AMC" logo instead of "American Motors" spelled out. Both models offered an optional 401-ci V-8 right to the end. With the impending discontinuation of the Javelin line, the 1974 model year was extended to the end of the calendar year, with production of the Javelin AMX continuing even after AMC's supply of fiberglass hoods was depleted. For this reason, some very late-production 1974 Javelin AMXs were assembled with a standard steel hood.

Where to Look

If you have set your sights on a particular model, the next step is to begin the search for a suitable restoration candidate. Here is where things have changed dramatically over the past couple of decades. No longer is it necessary to wait for the Sunday classifieds or a monthly copy of *Hemmings Motor News* to find collector cars for sale (although the print edition of *Hemmings* is still a great place to look). Your search can now begin immediately with websites such as Craigslist, eBay Motors, the online *Hemmings Classifieds,* and others.

If you are looking for a particular year and model you can bookmark several of these sites, then narrow your search criteria to eliminate any unsuitable listings. Check them regularly; you will be surprised to see how many AMC muscle cars come up for sale each week.

Even Facebook is useful for locating collector and project cars as well as obsolete parts that are not advertised anywhere else. Although not as searchable as other sites, joining one or more appropriate Facebook groups can provide a variety of car listings and links on a daily basis.

Many cars listed on eBay remain unsold after the conclusion of the auction or "Buy It Now" listing. Some cars are listed with an unrealistic reserve just for exposure or to test the market. Even if a car has apparently been sold, a short message to the seller can't hurt since deals can fall apart, and you could be the next interested party in line.

Craigslist is another excellent resource for locating project cars, and there are websites that allow you to check all of Craigslist, not just one local listing at a time. Don't rule out the local newspaper classifieds either. Interesting projects have also been found at local auctions and estate sales.

Networking with local car guys can also produce results. Even though the "Javelin" in the neighbor's shed may turn out to be a four-door Hornet, any lead is worth investigating. For many car enthusiasts, hunting for rare muscle cars is just as much fun as restoring and driving them!

Vehicle Identification Number

Now that you have found a potential project car, you need to be armed with the knowledge to decode its vehicle identification number, or VIN. As required by federal law, American Motors installed a VIN plate readable through the driver-side lower corner of the windshield beginning with cars built on January 1, 1968. Earlier cars, and most of the 1968 models, have a stainless steel VIN plate located on the top of the passenger-side spring tower under the hood.

AMCs also have a hidden hand-stamped partial VIN on the driver-side front frame rail, hidden behind the steering box. This number includes only the engine code and final six sequential characters of the VIN, and can *only* be viewed with the steering box removed.

Every AMC muscle car has a hidden partial VIN hand stamped on the driver-side front frame rail. This identification number includes only the engine code and final six sequential characters of the VIN. Often lightly stamped, this number cannot be seen without first removing the steering gearbox, so some disassembly is required for inspection. If this number does not match the last seven characters of the car's VIN tag and title exactly, there is a serious problem and the car should be avoided.

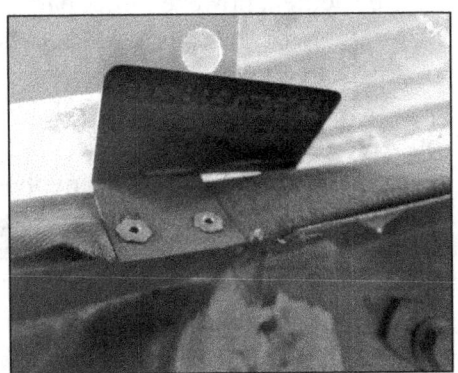
Federal law required a VIN plate readable through the windshield beginning with cars produced on January 1, 1968. These earliest number tags were riveted directly to the cowl before installation of the dash assembly. Most 1968 AMC models also have a polished stainless steel VIN plate spot welded to the top of the passenger-side spring tower. Visible only with the hood open, the spring tower tag was phased out during the 1968 model run.

CHAPTER 1

For 1969 and newer cars the VIN plate was set into the top of the dash rather than being attached directly to the car's body. Although it looks neater, there is a greater possibility of loss, or a VIN tag being swapped to a different car if the dash was replaced with a used one. Decades ago these were inexpensive used cars so there was often little concern for keeping things in order.

The AMC door tag, when original to the car, can often be used to gauge the production date as well as to confirm how the car was originally equipped. Trim and paint codes can be checked in the AMC Technical Service Manual (TSM) that corresponds to the car's model year. If the door tag is not affixed with star-shaped rosette rivets it has been removed, so inspect the car carefully before considering a purchase. Similarly, a tag that appears to be brand new may be a reproduction that does not exactly match the original.

There is no simple way to inspect this number on a car that is fully assembled, but it can't hurt to ask the seller for a look anyway. Your request may be denied, however, since partial disassembly of the steering system is required. Every VIN found on the car and title must match exactly. If any of these numbers do not agree, it is a serious problem that could involve prior accident damage or even theft. Such a car may be difficult or impossible to register, so be very cautious.

Door Tag Codes

If the title and VIN check out, another source of original build data is the aluminum tag affixed to the trailing edge of the driver's door. This plate provides the body and model numbers, as well as paint and trim codes for the car as it was originally produced. The last entry on the door tag is the build sequence number, which can be used to approximate the week a particular car was assembled. But be aware that over the years many damaged doors were replaced with a door from a salvage yard, and the original tag was rarely transferred to the replacement door. For this reason an AMX today may have a door tag with a Javelin model code. Know the correct codes for the car you are inspecting *before* you look at it because an incorrect door tag devalues the car from a collector's standpoint.

Because in almost every case the door tag numbers do not correspond to the car's VIN it is not illegal to replace a damaged or missing tag, or create a new reproduction tag to match one that is badly corroded. If a door tag appears to be much newer than the rest of the car it is likely a reproduction. If it is not attached by star-shaped rosette rivets it has been removed at some point and may not be original to the car.

Take this into serious consideration if the car in question has a desirable paint color such as Big Bad Orange, or a leather interior. Always check under the carpet and behind

An additional label was installed on the driver's door of 1970 and newer AMC cars. However, decades later it is not uncommon to find it in poor condition or even missing altogether following a repaint. When present, this gray-colored label includes the car's build date (month and year only) as well as the complete VIN. An original label in good condition should be carefully protected when restoring the car.

the dash instruments for evidence of the car's factory-original paint color. Many collectors prefer the patina of an original door tag that has never been disturbed because the possibility exists that a shiny new tag may not be an exact duplicate of the original.

Beginning with the 1970 model year a gray-colored label was also affixed to the edge of the driver's door that includes the complete VIN, plus the month and year that the car was assembled. Replacements can generally be created by a skilled print shop using sharp photos of an original label. Because this decal includes the car's specific VIN and build date, new replacements are generally unavailable.

AMX Dash Number

Nearly every 1968–1970 AMX has a dash-mounted plate containing a "production number" that actually doesn't correspond to the VIN or sequence numbers. This plate was really nothing more than a marketing gimmick, but made the AMX one of the first numbered limited editions. However, the first few hundred AMXs were assembled with a simple "AMX" plate instead of a number, and some of the lowest number plates were held back by American Motors for potential celebrity buyers.

Most low and even numbers, such as "AMX 01000" were never even installed, but were instead kept as souvenirs by AMC employees. Because these numbers continued uninterrupted throughout the 1968–1970 production run, many late-1970 cars carry plates with numbers that are several thousand higher than actual AMX production. If an original, one-owner AMX still has its original plate it will provide a very

The 1968–1970 AMX dash-mounted production number was really nothing more than a sales gimmick intended to make the cars seem more exclusive. The location of this plate started on the glove box, moved to the center speaker cover during the 1968 model year, then returned to the glove box door for 1970 when the plates were larger with red and blue accents. Numbering continued over the three-year production run with some late cars bearing numbers that are thousands higher than actual AMX production.

general idea of when the car was built within the model year, but that's all.

Engine Casting Numbers

An old joke in AMC circles describes a "numbers matching" car as one with the same engine size cast onto both sides of the block. That's because unlike engines of other manufacturers, AMC V-8 engines are not coded to the car's VIN. This means that, in most cases, there is no way to positively prove that an engine or transmission is original to the car. But it also means that a badly damaged or missing engine can be replaced with a similar one without adversely affecting the car's value.

The only exceptions were cars built for sale in Georgia and Tennessee, where the law required all new motor vehicles to have the engine and transmission coded to the car in which they were installed. For this purpose the car's sequence number from the door tag, plus the two-digit model year were hand stamped on the engine and transmission.

One other caveat involves the 390-ci V-8, because it was the only engine size carried over from 1969 to 1970, when better-breathing cylinder heads and other significant upgrades increased output from 315 to 325 hp. Be sure that when inspecting a 1970 model that the 390-ci engine is correct for the car's model year.

AMC blocks, heads, and other components have a multitude of casting numbers and date codes, but the first ones to check when inspecting a project car are the aforementioned numerals spelling out the engine's displacement. These large numerals can be easily seen on both sides of the block, right behind the motor mounts.

A trained eye can recognize the more rounded 1968–1969 "390" compared to the narrower digits found on a 1970 390 block. Some replacement blocks, however, were cast without any size identification at all, but these are fairly uncommon.

A small aluminum tag attached to the front of the passenger-side valve cover also identifies the engine size, its build date, and any factory overbore information. Many tags were lost, however, when aftermarket valve covers were installed, or swapped with covers from a different car altogether. Check also on the back of the driver-side valve cover in case they were switched side-to-side. If the tag is present, and appears to agree with the engine size as well as the car's approximate build date, consider it a bonus because correct replacements are becoming hard to find!

CHAPTER 1

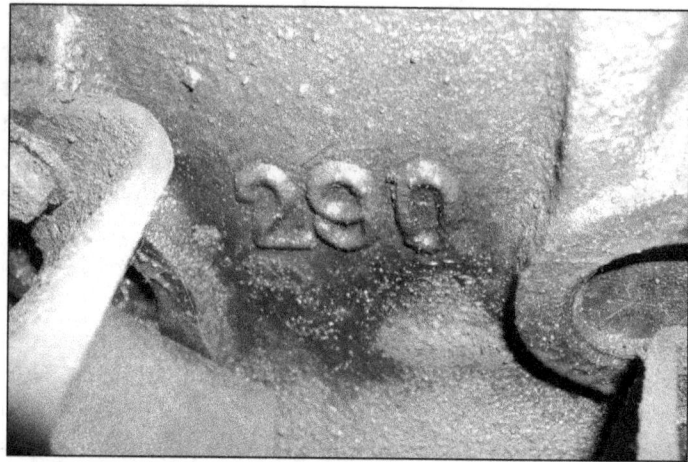

Most AMC V-8 engine blocks have the displacement cast into both sides of the block behind the motor mounts in large numerals. Using a flashlight, these numbers can be checked from underneath with the engine installed. A 1970 390 block has numerals that are narrower than a 1968–1969 390 block, which has numerals that look like this 290 casting. This is good information to have when inspecting a car for purchase.

The V-8 valve cover identification tag was originally mounted to the front of the passenger-side valve cover. It identified the engine size (X indicates 390 ci here) and included the build date code and overbore information if applicable. Many of these tags were lost forever with the installation of aftermarket valve covers. Because they are not being reproduced at this time, having a nice original is desirable for an accurate restoration.

Popular Options

Most of the desirable performance and appearance options and equipment on an AMC muscle car are permanently documented between the car's VIN plate and door tag. If you have found an original Big Bad Blue 1969 AMX with saddle leather seats, a 390 V-8, and console-shifted automatic transmission, the code for each of these options is unmistakably embossed for your inspection, and any missing equipment is a bargaining chip for negotiating a lower purchase price. However, many other important options are not coded to the car, including air conditioning, electric windshield wipers, AM/FM radio, rear bumper guards, and the high-performance Go Package.

Equipment included with the Go Package varied by model, but typically consisted of front disc brakes, heavy-duty suspension and cooling systems, Twin-Grip rear axle, and Space Saver spare tire, among other items. Much of the Go Package equipment could be ordered separately and is often added later during rebuilds and restorations. These items can only be documented as original to a car by having copies of the factory build order or window sticker price.

The 1970 Mark Donohue–edition Javelin is known for its unique rear spoiler with signature decal, and is the only AMC special edition muscle car that cannot be documented by the VIN or door tag codes. Although all 2,501 cars were built within a certain date range, original paperwork is the only proof of authenticity for these desirable models, and many cloned or tribute cars already exist.

Red Flags

I have previously covered the possibility of non-matching numbers and door tag replacement. Here are a few more items to consider before you make a purchase.

Title

One potential obstacle to project car ownership is a vehicle offered for sale without a title. Many states did not require paper titles when these cars were new, but in most cases there are legitimate ways to secure a title. Be sure to check the laws in your state before considering such a purchase. A car with a title branded as "rebuilt" or "salvage" should be avoided as this status generally cannot be removed and will negatively impact future resale value, regardless of how nice the car appears.

Rust

Another potential deal breaker is structural body rust. All AMC cars are of unit-body construction so it's never as easy as lifting the shell to roll a new frame underneath. The

Fender gussets, known in the AMC world as troughs, are U-shaped channels designed to strengthen the front end of the car and provide additional crash protection. Despite being sealed to the fender with rubber flaps, they frequently filled up with dirt and sand causing them, and the fender above, to rust out. Mice seem to find these sealed compartments inviting as well; nests are often found in gussets that haven't rusted away.

If you can see rust holes on the inner or outer rocker panel, you can be sure that the center section is rusted away as well. The rocker panels along with the subframe rails are the main support for an AMC unit body, so rust perforation is more than cosmetic. Because of their three-piece, welded construction, replacement of the entire rocked panel is necessary if serious corrosion such as this has occurred.

Surprise! If you can see evidence of previous rust repairs be prepared to find something like this. Shoddy rust repairs are fairly common and generally require a lot of extra work to repair correctly. Bubbled or cracked body filler is a tipoff that rust has returned. Expect the worst where rust is concerned. It always looks worse once the paint and body filler are stripped away.

When inspecting a 1968–1970 AMX be sure to check the floorpans underneath both seats. This area is prone to rust damage because of an underlapping seam that was not sealed properly. As the car was driven, dirt and water collected underneath the carpet, allowing rust to take hold. Javelin models have no seam here and are less likely to have corrosion problems in this area.

subframe and rocker panels are the body's main support, so examine these components carefully, especially the inner part of the rockers underneath the car. If rust-through is found it will be the first repair that is needed so plan accordingly, or keep looking for a car with better bones.

Other areas of concern are the floorpans, trunk floor and drop-offs, taillight panel, driver-side A-pillar, and at the lower corners of the rear window. A deteriorated vinyl top can also cause serious rusting of the car's roof panel. Luckily not every AMC tended to rust in the same areas so solid replacement sections can generally be found. But if the project

CHAPTER 1

Although this quarter panel is badly rusted, it has never had any repairs so you can see the extent of the rust damage. Although it may look worse, a project car like this is actually a better bet than one that has been quickly patched up and painted for resale. A car sold in primer may also hide many ills so expect to completely redo any bodywork that has already been completed. If a vehicle is described as "ready for paint," it rarely is; use this information when negotiating your project car purchase.

Even in humid climates not every AMC car of the same year and model rusts in the same areas. That's good news because donor cars are still available that can provide good sheet metal for use in restorations. As an example, despite having serious rust elsewhere, this AMX survives with a nearly perfect original trunk pan.

in question is rusted in *all* of these places you should probably keep looking, unless the car is something really special or has a great deal of sentimental value.

Although not as serious, rust damage can also be found at the leading edge of the hood, on the fender tops, lower corners of the doors, and the rear lip of the trunk lid. It's simple enough to replace these bolt-on parts once you track down new old stock (NOS) or better quality used replacements. None of these parts have been reproduced in steel, and likely never will be. However, lower quarter panel sections, trunk drop-offs, the rear valance panel, and partial floorpans have been reproduced for Javelin and AMX models. Be sure to purchase the best-quality reproduction panels that are available from fulltime AMC parts vendors because lesser-quality reproductions also exist, and the difference in quality is significant.

Accident Damage

During your inspection process it is also important to check for previous accident damage. Serious panel misalignment or body filler in places that rust is unlikely to occur are tip-offs. American Motors rarely used shims in building cars so finding shims can be another indicator of repaired collision damage. Check the front frame rails, and behind the front bumper and grille for damage to the core support and radiator extension panels. Something as simple as a missing grille bracket could indicate that the front substructure is out of shape. Pull up the trunk mat to check the floor, and inspect the back of the taillight panel for evidence of a rear-end collision. It seems that few muscle cars have survived without some type of accident damage, even if it's only minor.

Disassembled Cars

Another situation with the potential for disaster is buying a project car that has already been disassembled. These cars generally cost less, but there's a reason. Although it can be helpful for inspecting the body for rust damage, a disassembled car may actually hide faults such as poor panel alignment that may not be revealed until the doors and fenders are installed much later. Crucial parts may also be missing, and, unless all of the hardware is carefully bagged and labeled, you will spend hours locating and sorting fasteners. It is always best to start with the nicest, most complete project car that you can find, preferably one that is still assembled and can be driven.

Modifications

Modified muscle cars are plentiful and frequently found for sale. These cars may look great and be reasonably priced, but don't be dazzled by shiny wheels and other custom parts if your goal is a stock-appearing restoration. Many original equipment parts including air cleaners, carburetors, emissions control systems, radios, and steering wheels are becoming harder to find and may be very expensive.

Another potential liability is incorrectly painted stripes. No matter how nice the paint job is, the removal of painted stripes will likely necessitate at least a partial repaint of the car.

Play it Safe

One final caution involves purchasing a vehicle sight unseen. It is a common practice these days to conduct a nationwide search for a project car and having it delivered is

Purchasing a disassembled project car has advantages and disadvantages. The cost is generally lower, and inspecting the body for rust is easy, but other problems may not be evident, and unless you are very familiar with a particular model, missing parts and hardware can cause headaches later on. Reassembling a car is always easier if you are the one who disassembled it.

Starting with a complete, unaltered project car is preferable to buying one that has been disassembled already, or quickly fixed up for resale. A project that can be driven is even better, although if the car is not roadworthy you may still be able to run the engine and check the transmission. Be sure to test all of the electrical components and accessories before beginning the teardown.

Modified muscle cars, or ones missing a lot of original parts can frequently be found for sale at swap meets and car corrals, often at a bargain price. They can be a great value for building a street machine or race car, but if you want a stock-appearing restored muscle car buy the nicest most complete car that you can find. Once all of the custom or missing parts are replaced you may end up spending more than the cost of a much better car.

CHAPTER 1

AMC offered its 1969½ SC/Rambler in both A (right) and B (left) paint schemes. Among the cosmetic differences, the "A" cars featured a blue arrow centered on the car "directing" airflow into the hood scoop. (Photo Courtesy Mark Fletcher Collection)

American Motors catapulted itself into the muscle car wars with the debut of the AMC Javelin. Par for the course was adding special paint schemes such as this; Big Bad Green was offered in 1969 and 1970. (Photo Courtesy Mark Fletcher Collection)

as easy as making a phone call; it's also fairly inexpensive even if the car isn't drivable. However, if it can be arranged, always have someone local to the car inspect it for you, because photos usually make a vehicle look much better than it actually is.

Helpful people who frequent the online AMC forums may be willing to check out your potential purchase for free or for expenses only. If this isn't possible just assume the car will be in worse condition than described. This way you will never be disappointed, and you may even be pleasantly surprised when your new muscle car project arrives in the driveway.

Here is one of the rarest color combos found on any AMC. This 1969 Javelin features Big Bad Green paint with parchment bucket seats and GlennGerry fabric. Not pictured is the tan dash and carpet. (Photo Courtesy Mark Fletcher Collection)

CHAPTER 2

CREATING A GAME PLAN

Far too many automotive restoration projects are started and never finished. The unfortunate cars involved are frequently sold in boxes for pennies on the dollar, or parted out then sent to the crusher. Although usually well intentioned, many restorations are doomed from the beginning because of a serious lack of planning. For this reason this chapter may well be the most important one in the entire book!

Now that you have chosen and located a suitable AMC muscle car project, steps should be taken that will affect the final outcome of the restoration, and virtually guarantee its success—before a single bolt is removed. Perhaps the most important part of any large project is to form a game plan. This means that you must decide the scope of the project, plan your level of personal involvement, estimate the amount of time and space that is required, and set up a reasonable budget for completing the restoration to your satisfaction, and (you hope) on schedule.

Driver, Show Car or Street Machine

In the chapters that follow, choices are occasionally provided that correspond to the type of restoration that you have chosen for your particular project. The first category is *daily driver,* a term that is pretty much obsolete in the AMC world since most of these cars left the daily driver ranks quite some time ago. Increased collectibility and a dwindling supply of replacement body parts have elevated the status of any AMC muscle car to that of a valued collectible used only occasionally.

So, for the purpose of this book, a frequently driven AMC is considered a *weekend driver,* one you may take to cruise-ins, a local car show, or drive into town with the family to get some ice cream. These cars are generally a lot of fun to own because they are rarely trailered, and you need not consult the local five-day weather forecast before deciding if it will even leave the garage!

Next up is a *show car,* which, by definition, is one that is reserved for display at car shows and other similar events. These are frequently over-restored to a level that is even *better* than original; a show car is used sparingly and stored carefully when not being driven, if it is driven at all. These cars generally receive a more thorough restoration with the underside of the car receiving just as much attention as the top. For this

The 1969 Hurst SC/Rambler proved to be a formidable "swan song" offering from AMC. With a 390-ci, 4-speed transmission and 3.54 posi "Traction Lock" rear end, many a big-block foe was loaded onto the trailer when squaring off against a SC/Rambler. (Photo Courtesy Mark Fletcher Collection)

Show cars are typically too nice or too valuable to drive regularly. Many are competing to advance in concours judging, so they must be trailered to any event where they will be displayed. In years past some arena-type show cars could not even be started because they had no fluids that could leak. Today most owners and enthusiasts have gotten away from having a complete trailer queen, preferring instead a car that can at least be driven onto the show field.

A street machine can be just as nice as a stock-class show car, but without any concern for originality. Want a blower sticking through the hood? No problem! Non-stock cars are judged for execution and cleanliness only, with no deduction for incorrect parts, so anything goes. Friends who have built an AMC street machine may be a good source for rare original take-off parts that can be used for your restoration.

reason they are generally trailered to shows because even careful driving would subject the car to stone chips and wear.

Restrictions set by classic vehicle insurance companies, as well as limits for use set by individual states when applying for historical or collector license plates may also determine how much you are able to drive your AMC muscle car once it is finished. If you plan to drive your car to work on a regular basis be sure to license and insure it appropriately to avoid any possible problems down the road.

The final category is *street machine*, which can be just as detailed as a show car, but without the concern for original, date-coded, or factory appearing components. When building a car that will not be judged in stock class competition, anything goes because the car is graded only for build quality and cleanliness. There is no need to source era-correct hose clamps or bolts with factory-correct head markings when building a street machine, and that can mean a big savings of time and money.

Deciding which type of car you want to have at the end of the project is the decision that you should make before you begin.

Complete or Partial Restoration

Another choice that is crucial to the success of your project is deciding on the level of restoration to be performed. If your project is in sound mechanical condition and your goal is a nice weekend driver, you may prefer to keep driving the car while you restore it, one system or section at a time. You may have the car painted first, then upgrade the interior, have the chrome parts replated, and so on as time and funds allow until the project is completed to your satisfaction. Most of this can be accomplished without taking the car off the road for extended periods of time, or you can do it exclusively in the off-season.

A show-quality restoration is best accomplished all at once so everything is fresh and new at the same time. For this reason a show car generally requires a larger investment, and a minimum of one year in the shop instead of on the road. Once finished, a show car also requires special handling and storage procedures to maintain its "just finished" appearance.

Yet another choice is a partial restoration, the perfect solution for a clean, original car that doesn't require an extensive amount of work. A car like this may only need under-hood detailing, some paint touch-up, or upholstery work.

Factory original cars are a treasure, so be sure to examine your project carefully and consider all of your options before deciding on a complete restoration.

Time and Space Requirements

Don't believe what you see on those automotive reality television shows. Even a partial restoration can take months or even years depending on the amount of time dedicated to it. With only evenings and weekends to work on your project, some months pass with little progress to show for

CREATING A GAME PLAN

the hours spent working on the car. Don't become discouraged after setting an unrealistic deadline for completing your restoration, and don't cut corners just to finish it on time. There will still be car shows and cruise-ins when your project is finished regardless of when that happens to be!

Having adequate room to work is another important factor in the success of your project. A disassembled car takes two to three times more space than an assembled one, and that doesn't include the workspace. A minimum requirement for any restoration is a two-car garage, assuming that there is additional indoor space available elsewhere for parts storage.

Renting additional space for storing parts, or even to house the car once it's finished may be a workable solution for someone without enough garage space. However, expect to pay well over $100 per month for only enough space to park one car, and that gets you only a concrete floor and a door. Liability concerns generally preclude any repairs or restoration work from being performed at a rented storage facility. Also be sure that any cars or valuable parts stored in other locations are insured against theft, fire, and other loss, just as they should be when stored at home.

Making a Budget

After deciding on the type and level of restoration best suited to your particular situation, the next step is to form a realistic budget for successfully completing the project in the time allowed. Your budget needs to include the car itself if you don't already own it, storage or workspace if you are planning to rent it, tools and equipment that need to be purchased, all parts and supplies, plus any labor for work that is done by others.

Start by checking current prices online for the equipment and parts that you know will be needed. Fulltime AMC vendors such as American Parts Depot and Kennedy American have online catalogs that can be used to check pricing for reproduction parts. Don't forget to include shipping charges and state sales tax if applicable. Check eBay or the AMC forums to get an idea of pricing for some of the obsolete parts that are not being reproduced.

Pricing for used parts varies greatly even within the same AMC show or swap meet. Although the going price for a solid front fender may appear to be $250, keep looking for a better price; you can generally go back and purchase the more expensive one later if needed. However, you won't be able to return it if you find a less expensive one. For the purpose of making your budget, estimate high for any used parts just in case bargains never appear.

Ask friends or fellow club members with similar cars how much you can expect to spend for some of the hard-to-find parts, bodywork, paint, chrome plating, and so on. Call a machine shop, and visit some local body shops if your car will be going to one. If possible drive the car or take it on a trailer to get actual estimates. But don't be surprised if more than one body shop shows little or no interest in working on an older collector car. Most body shop work schedules are dictated by the insurance companies, so late-model collision work always comes first. Be sure to ask for referrals when networking with other local car guys.

Budget high for everything, total it up, and then add 50 percent as a cushion. With this number in hand you may now decide how to disburse the funds for the restoration. It may not be practical to allocate a set amount per month for completing the project, because some aspects of the restoration will cost much more than others. Engine rebuilding or bodywork and paint require a much larger percentage of the total budget, and generally must be paid for all at once.

With some careful planning, a bit of luck, and the information in this book, you may complete your project on time and under budget, or at least not *too* far over it!

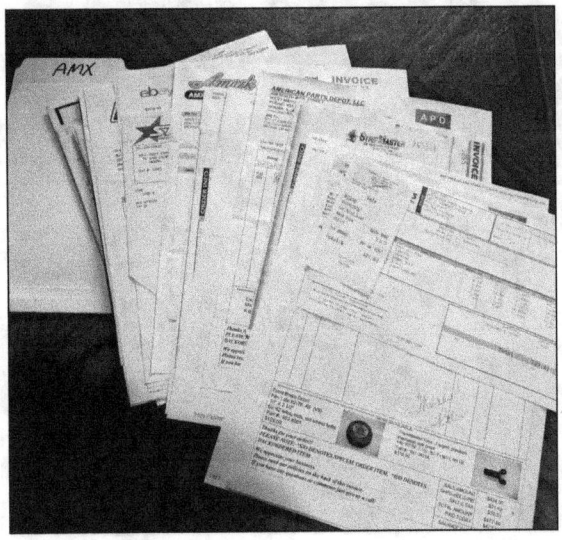

Maintain a comprehensive file for every collector car that you own. Include receipts for any service that you have done, as well as for all parts purchased for the project. Many replacement parts carry a lifetime warranty, so keeping all of your receipts together and in order by date may pay off in the future. Your receipt file also becomes a running total of roughly how much you have invested in the project to date.

CHAPTER 3

Getting Started

By now you are eager to begin unbolting parts, and it's almost time! Just be sure that everything is in order before you begin.

Your Work Area

Adequate workspace is crucial to the success of any restoration project. This includes room for the car's body, all of the parts that have been removed, all of the new parts, plus ample space to move around and work on subassemblies such as the engine, transmission, rear axle, and seats. Any parts left outside are at risk of theft or damage from the elements, so make room indoors for everything before you begin.

A large, well-lit pole building or multi-car garage with a level, concrete floor is ideal, especially if it is a dedicated workspace uncluttered with bicycles, furniture, lawn equipment, or the cars you drive every day. If you live in a climate with cold weather, a small portion of your shop or other large building can be walled off and heated during winter months. Even a temporary enclosure framed with wood and covered with clear plastic sheeting retains heat, and also contains dust or paint spray during the completion of a restoration. Building an enclosure with sturdy 2x6 rafters and a plywood deck overhead also adds considerable parts storage space to your work area.

Tools and Equipment

A good set of hand tools along with several specialized pieces of equipment are necessary for undertaking almost any large automotive project. Don't be tempted to purchase inexpensive tools that can slip and round off the head of original bolts and fasteners. Quality hand tools such as the Craftsman brand do a better job than less expensive tools, and they carry a lifetime warranty

Stripped of all bolt-on body parts, this 1968 AMX is ready for a thorough inspection, and then rust repairs can begin. Store any body parts that will be reused in a safe, indoor area. At this stage, a project car is fairly light so it can be moved around easily when needed.

GETTING STARTED

Utilize shop space to your best advantage. A wood-framed work room enclosed with clear plastic allows plenty of light to enter, retains heat in the winter, and when used with a retractable plastic curtain contains dust and paint spray. Position your air compressor on the outside where it can draw plenty of clean air. An added bonus is the storage space created overhead, so use sturdy 2x6 lumber for the rafters.

An organized toolbox saves time and improves efficiency. The time you save not having to hunt for the proper-size wrench or socket each time can be spent actually accomplishing something. Keep your hand tools clean and your air tools oiled. Quality tools last a lifetime with proper care.

against breakage. Have a good selection of flat-blade and Phillips-head screwdrivers, pliers, locking pliers, combination wrenches, 3/8- and 1/2-inch-drive socket sets, as well as other commonly used hand tools organized by size on pegboard hooks or in your toolbox drawers.

Don't let your buddies tease you about being too organized; the time that you save by not having to search for the right size wrench or socket every time really adds up over the course of a long-term project!

Air Compressor

A large air compressor with the capacity to run a variety of tools or even a glass media blasting cabinet is another necessity. Compressors come in a variety of sizes, so it is possible to have one that is either too small or too large for your needs. A good size for a home shop is a 5- or 6-hp unit with a 60-gallon tank. An air compressor this size requires a specialized NEMA 6-20 receptacle, which is a 20-amp, 250-volt outlet. If your garage or shop is not wired for this type of service any licensed electrical contractor can perform the installation or upgrade.

Selecting a compressor with a vertical tank saves precious floor space; the tank can even be left fastened to the pallet it comes with to gain additional clearance for draining condensation from the tank. Accumulated water should be drained regularly to prevent corrosion of the tank and extend air tool life. Running the air line along the ceiling and installing an inline water filter also helps to prevent condensation from reaching your tools or contaminating the paint that you spray.

Useful air-powered tools include a 1/2-inch-drive impact wrench, 3/8-inch-drive air ratchet, and cut-off tool. These are great time savers, especially for vehicle disassembly. Other air tools such as a dual-action sander or air file will become necessary as you become involved with body repair.

Blasting Cabinet

Also necessary for a successful restoration is access to a glass-bead blasting cabinet. This is an enclosure that uses compressed air and finely ground glass media to cleanly strip old paint and surface rust from bolts, brackets, external engine parts, steel wheels, and anything else that fits inside. A spotlight inside the cabinet, along with a built-in vacuum to clear the dust, allows you to monitor the progress through the tempered glass window.

The glass-bead media is constantly recycled as it falls through the surface grid. Even parts with rubber components such as motor mounts or a complete Space Saver spare tire can be cleanly stripped, because the glass media does not damage the

CHAPTER 3

Be sure that your air compressor is up to the task of running your air tools or glass-bead blast cabinet. Regular maintenance includes checking the oil level and draining the condensation from the tank every day to prevent rust. Use an inline water filter to prevent damage to your equipment or contamination when spraying paint.

A blast cabinet uses compressed air and glass-bead media to strip multiple layers of paint or heavy surface rust from small to medium-size parts. It can also be used to freshen the appearance of aluminum parts such as a power steering pump bracket or aftermarket intake manifold. Because the glass bead does not harm rubber, parts including motor mounts or a complete Space Saver spare tire rim can be stripped without damage to the rubber.

rubber parts. The glass beads do eventually wear out and become dust, which is removed by the vacuum; they must be replaced.

Just as with air compressors, blast cabinets come in a variety of sizes from small bench-top models all the way up to those large enough to be used by two operators at the same time. A practical-size blast cabinet recommended for most auto restoration tasks measures approximately 46 to 48 inches wide and 28 to 30 inches deep. After using a bead blasting cabinet you will wonder how you ever did without it.

Shop Manual

No restoration or major repair should be attempted without the benefit of a factory-issued Technical Service Manual (TSM) for your particular year and model. Also called a shop manual, these books contain a wealth of information for repairing and assembling every system on your car. Generally included are exploded views, troubleshooting information, torque specifications, wiring diagrams, and other detailed information specific to your particular car.

If you don't already have one, copies are generally available on disc

The factory-issued TSM will become your best friend during a restoration. These books contain information for servicing every system of your particular year and model. Buying a well-used copy like this one generally costs less and can be used in the garage without feeling guilty for soiling a mint-condition collectible. Check eBay; copies are also available on DVD.

for use with your garage computer. Or you can buy a less expensive, pre-soiled printed copy so you feel less guilty about adding a few greasy fingerprints!

General repair manuals such as those published by Chilton's or Haynes are useful for doing routine driveway maintenance, but are not nearly comprehensive enough for reassembling a complete car.

Camera

Another necessity in the garage these days is a good-quality digital camera. You cannot take too many photos of your project both before and during the disassembly phase. You may think that you'll remember how everything goes back together, but after six months (or even longer) many questions will arise, and consulting a set of clear digital photos can save you considerable time and frustration.

Upload your photos to a secure hosting site such as Photobucket

Welder

If you know how to weld but don't own a welder, today's MIG welding systems are fairly inexpensive. Costs are generally $1,200 or less for an excellent quality welder from Miller or Lincoln Electric, a cart, as well as a good-quality automatic-darkening helmet, gloves, and a tank of shielding gas. A setup like this makes it easy to learn basic skills for doing bodywork and other metal repairs, even if you have never tried welding before.

Be sure to practice with some scrap steel before attempting any important repairs on your restoration project. Get the feel for setting the voltage and wire speed for the particular thickness of metal that you are joining. Serious structural repairs are best left to someone with considerable welding experience, but before long, you will be taking care of most smaller welding jobs yourself.

Workbench, Etc.

Other necessities for a well-equipped shop include a workbench with a large vice, several pairs of sturdy jack stands, a good quality 3-ton (minimum) floor jack, and some short lengths of heavy-duty chain. If you don't plan to restore multiple cars, some larger pieces of equipment such as an engine hoist can often be borrowed from friends, or rented as needed. This saves the initial expense as well as having to store a lot of extra equipment that is used infrequently.

Security

Protect your tools and equipment from prying eyes. Whenever possible, position your toolbox, air compressor, or welder where they cannot be seen from the street, or viewed through a window in your garage or shop. Unfortunately, thieves are everywhere, so the less temptation the better.

Always lock your shop or storage building when you are away, and have a permanent nighttime or motion-detector outdoor security light if your building is not in a well-lit area. If the safety of your equipment is still in doubt install a security system that can be monitored remotely.

Safety First!

Throughout this book there are references to tools that can be dangerous if used incorrectly, as well as equipment that can lift heavy things, become extremely hot, or release caustic chemicals into the air that you breathe. Although not stated every time, remember to *always* practice the safety recommendations specified for the use of this equipment. This includes using safety goggles, welding gloves and helmet, dust mask, face shield, hearing protection, and a breathing respirator.

Never run an engine without adequate ventilation. Have multiple fire extinguishers within easy reach, and check them periodically to be sure they will work if needed. Automotive ramps or cinder blocks are no substitute for a floor jack and sturdy jack stands used on a level, concrete surface. Always use wheel chocks for any vehicle that could roll away, and *never* crawl underneath a car supported only by a jack! No car project is worth serious injury or death.

Always keep your work area neat, well lit, and organized. Put away any tools and sweep the floor after each work session. Never place parts, tools, or other items on the hood or roof of your project car because it's only a matter of time until something falls off and hits you on the head. Besides, you wouldn't set something on your collector car when it's finished, so break that habit now!

If you are welding, using torches, or even a body grinder, considerable heat is being generated. Don't finish working for the day and close up the shop or garage without double-checking that nothing is smoldering or left on. Localized heat created by welding can easily ignite carpet padding, sound deadener, undercoating, or even a mouse nest hidden behind the panel you are repairing. Always check your welds and other hot spots after several minutes to be sure nothing is smoking or hot to the touch. Be sure that everything in the vicinity is at room temperature before leaving for the day.

A quality MIG welding setup can be used for a variety of body jobs and other metal repairs. Using the proper settings along with a shielding gas allows you to weld anything from frame rails to thin outer-body sheet metal. With some practice you will become proficient with your MIG and amaze your friends with your welding expertise.

CHAPTER 3

Cleaning and Inspection

Now that your work area, tools, and equipment are in order, the first step of your AMC muscle car restoration is the initial cleaning, inspection, and inventory of your project. Start by giving the car a thorough hand wash using a strong stream of water to flush out all of the window channels, as well as the underbody and wheel wells. Degrease and gently rinse the engine compartment if needed and allow to air dry. Use caution with steam cleaning or pressure washing because fragile parts may be damaged or important original markings can be removed. It may take longer but it's better to use a liquid degreaser and soft parts cleaning brush followed by rinsing with clean water. Remove any clutter or extra parts from the trunk or passenger compartment. Use a shop vacuum to clean up the trunk floor, interior carpet, and seats. Deduct the value of any coins found inside from the initial cost of the car!

After washing the engine compartment take a complete series of close-up photos. This one includes the wiring harness installation, windshield washer hose tee, and even a metal retainer used to secure the main washer hose to the harness. Also note the small round seal where the windshield washer nozzle passes through the cowl.

Use a digital camera to produce a set of "before" pictures once the vehicle is clean inside and out. These photos can be used later to document the presence of original features, options, and accessories. In addition, photograph every underhood detail such as the position of original hose clamps and vacuum hoses. Take well-lit, detailed shots of the wiring harness routing and electrical connections; these photos can help later when reassembling the car. Photograph both sides of the engine compartment as well as the cowl and firewall before removing anything.

Also photograph the complete engine from several angles. Look closely for any original stickers, paint daubs, and other inspection marks that may remain in the engine compartment. Document these details so you can duplicate them later. Also notice any factory original belts, hoses, or other maintenance parts that may remain. The original markings on these items can often be duplicated on modern replacement parts if accurate reproductions are not available.

The first step for any restoration is to give the car a good hand wash outside, underneath, and under the hood. You may want to do this right on the trailer so you can reach the underbody and wheel wells more easily. After degreasing the engine, rinse it with clean water and allow it to dry in the sun. A pressure washer or even compressed air used to dry the engine compartment can obliterate valuable original details.

GETTING STARTED

This detail shot of the firewall shows the driver's side. When photographing your project car before disassembly, be sure to include the small details such as the second metal washer hose retainer shown here. These details will set your restoration apart from the others. Also pay attention to the correct original routing of hoses and wiring for an authentic appearance.

Don't overlook the direction of the upper control arm bolts, and the orientation of the power steering hoses at the steering gearbox. For maximum authenticity these details must be recreated when your project car is reassembled. That's why a photo such as this is so helpful as a reference.

Documenting an Early 1968 Car

During auto manufacturing, running changes were quite common in the late 1960s. Early-build 1968 Javelin and AMX models, particularly those assembled late in the 1967 calendar year, include many subtle differences not found on later 1968 cars. When restoring an early 1968 model, document and strive to maintain these unique features whenever possible. Also be aware when sourcing replacement parts for a later-production 1968 or 1969 model that some early-style parts may be considered incorrect by a knowledgeable car show judge and cost valuable points in a stock class concours event.

These photos are a sampling of features unique to an early-build 1968 Javelin or AMX. ■

Fresh out of long-term storage, this early-production 1968 Javelin SST contains many features unique to AMX and Javelin models built late in the 1967 calendar year. The mint green color is not original to this car.

Early-production 1968s have round mounting bosses where the diagonal supports attach to the upper core support. These were replaced by a boxed mount with captive nut found on all later cars.

AMC JAVELIN, AMX & MUSCLE CAR RESTORATION 1968–1974

Documenting an Early 1968 Car CONTINUED

The position of the battery warning label was parallel to the core support on many 1968 cars. Later, it was installed at the end of the radiator filler panel, perpendicular to the core support.

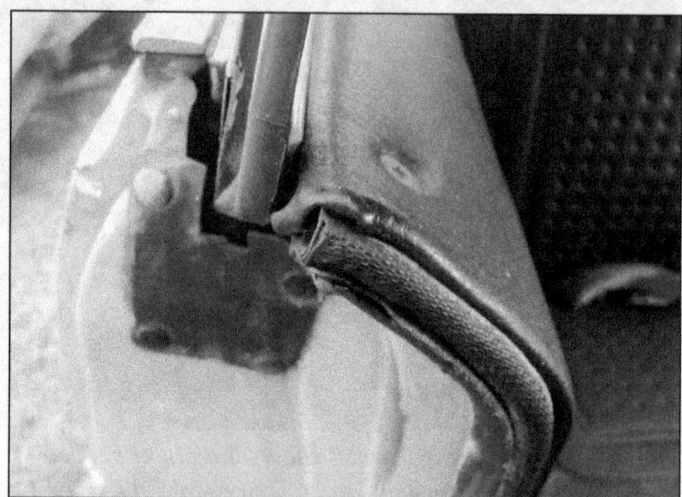

Storm strips gave a finished appearance to the pinch welds at either side of the door openings. On early cars there is no plastic cap finishing the upper end of the storm strips.

Early in the 1968 model year, front-seat shoulder belts were still optional, with only lap belts as standard equipment. Cars ordered without shoulder belts used this plug to cover the mounting holes.

The earliest 1968 models used window cranks left over from 1967 model year cars. Correct for early-production 1968s, this type was soon replaced by the newer-style window crank.

A round, body "buck" tag is attached to the passenger side of the lower core support. This tag likely contained information identifying the car before the VIN tag was attached.

GETTING STARTED

Early-style front fender braces attached at the corner of the wheel opening, but did not allow enough tire clearance. The later style used two bolts at the bottom and attached farther forward.

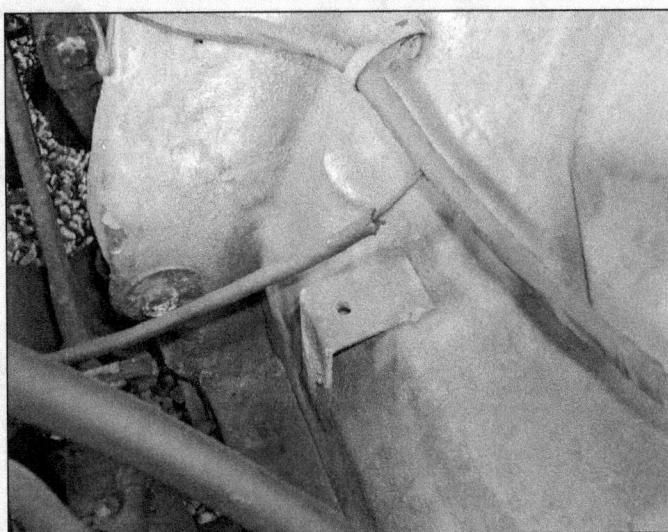
Every early-production 1968 AMX or Javelin, including cars with V-8 engines, have this bracket on the driver-side inner fender for mounting a 6-cylinder battery tray.

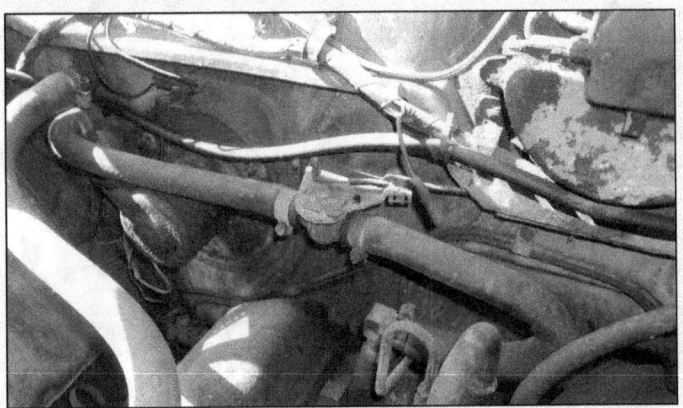
The early-style V-8 heater valve was mounted on the firewall instead of the intake manifold. After the switch to the newer type, the mounting holes on the firewall were plugged with putty.

Black plastic knobs for the light and wiper switches were only found on early 1968 models. These were upgraded to chrome-finish knobs soon after for more eye appeal.

The earliest 1968 cars had no VIN plate mounted to the top of the dash or cowl. The only VIN plate found on these cars was mounted to the top of the passenger-side spring tower underneath the hood.

CHAPTER 3

Documenting an Early 1968 Car CONTINUED

Early-production 1968 cars have a heater hose retainer bolted to the Z-shaped brace for the alternator bracket. This worm gear hose clamp is not original equipment.

Early 1968 models have black-faced gauges. As with the light and wiper switches, the gauge faces were changed to silver for more contrast. Black gauges reappeared for the 1970 AMX and Javelin.

Even the door data tags changed during the 1968 model year. Early-production tags have a black band, and later tags have revised text with a green band.

In the style of the AMX dash number plate, early-production 1968 Javelins had this nameplate attached to the glove box door. And as on the AMX, this plate was soon moved to the center of the dash.

GETTING STARTED

Disassembly

Once you have completely cleaned and photographed every important detail of your project car both inside and out, the next step is to begin the disassembly process. This procedure varies depending on the type of restoration you have planned, but for a thorough freshening much of the car needs to come apart.

Before removing a single screw, make sure you have a fine-point permanent marker and a box of resealable plastic bags on hand. Use these to identify and store all of the specialized hardware and other small parts immediately as they are removed from the car. Clear plastic snack bags work well for this purpose. If the car will be completely disassembled, expect to label and fill hundreds of bags! Additional information can also be written on the bag, or on a note included inside. Later, these bags can be sorted into different areas of the car: interior, engine compartment, suspension, and so on, and then boxed together for future use.

Save and label every fastener even if it is damaged or incorrect because it can be used later as a sampler when sourcing the correct item. If a fastener from a particular part is damaged, incorrect, or missing, write "locate one" or whatever will be needed right on the bag as a reminder to track down a replacement.

It may be helpful to photograph certain components still in place if you feel there may be confusion later. After removal, arrange these parts in their original position and then take additional photos if necessary to document their relation to one another. Armed with these photos, reassembly at a later date will be much simpler with no need to guess, or relearn how the parts originally fit together.

Unless you are planning to perform a partial, driving type of restoration, removing the engine and transmission is generally done early on. This lightens the car considerably and allows these components to be detailed individually, or delivered to a machine shop for inspection or rebuilding as necessary. Removing the drivetrain also allows greatly

If there is a chance you will not remember exactly how to reinstall something, such as this firewall steering column seal, be sure to photograph it before removal from the car. This is the beauty of digital photography: You can keep trying different angles until you have the perfect shot.

Once a difficult component is removed, it may be useful to create another photo of the parts arranged as they will need to go back together. In six months or a year when you're ready to reassemble your car consulting these photos can save time and headaches.

Before any disassembly begins, make sure you have a good supply of resealable plastic bags and a permanent marker handy. If you are working on more than one car at a time, include a short description of the car on every parts bag. This will prevent mixing up anything as you jump from project to project.

CHAPTER 3

Disconnected and stripped of most accessories, this engine is ready for removal. Be sure to remember the ground cable located at the passenger-side motor mount and the speedometer cable. Cardboard keeps bolts or any other objects from falling into the engine once the carburetor is removed.

With the front suspension and steering systems still in place, the engine and transmission must be removed from the top. Store the hood in a safe place, and use caution not to damage the firewall or upper core support. Adjusting the chain to achieve a suitable angle for the engine and transmission helps with removal.

With the engine and transmission out, it's time to remove the wiring harness, brake lines, and booster, as well as the heater fan and windshield wiper motors. The complete engine compartment can now be degreased in preparation for refinishing. Note any surface rust that must be removed, especially underneath the battery tray.

The complete engine and transmission assembly can be stored, or cleaned and detailed by resting the motor mounts on jack stands and the transmission mount on a sturdy crate. Be careful, because coolant may still be leaking from the water pump. When degreasing, take care not to get water or anything else inside the engine.

GETTING STARTED

If the front suspension and steering system will be removed for rebuilding or detailing, a great way to remove the engine and transmission is from the bottom. Simply lower the drivetrain onto a rolling cart, then lift the body. With enough overhead clearance you may not even need to remove the hood.

A great way to completely strip multiple layers of paint, body filler, or surface rust is to media blast any used body panels. A qualified shop can select an appropriate media, which cleanly removes everything down to bare steel without warping or otherwise damaging the panels. A complete car body can be media blasted if needed.

You may be in for a surprise when removing the fenders. If the gussets, or "troughs," underneath are intact they may have provided a home for mice. Because they also collect dirt and moisture, the gussets may be perforated by rust, or in extreme cases, missing altogether!

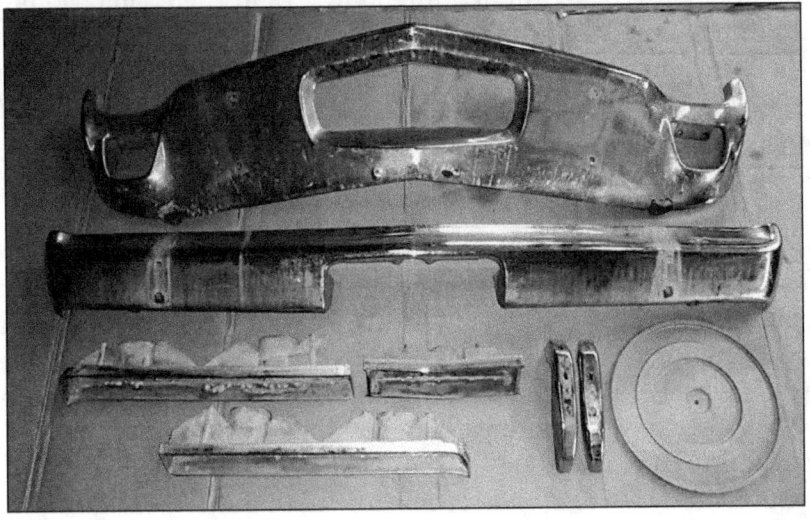

Any parts that need to be chrome plated should be removed from the car and sent out as early as possible. Several weeks or months may be required for stripping and replating chrome parts, so it's better to have them back early than to end up waiting for them when the car is otherwise finished.

 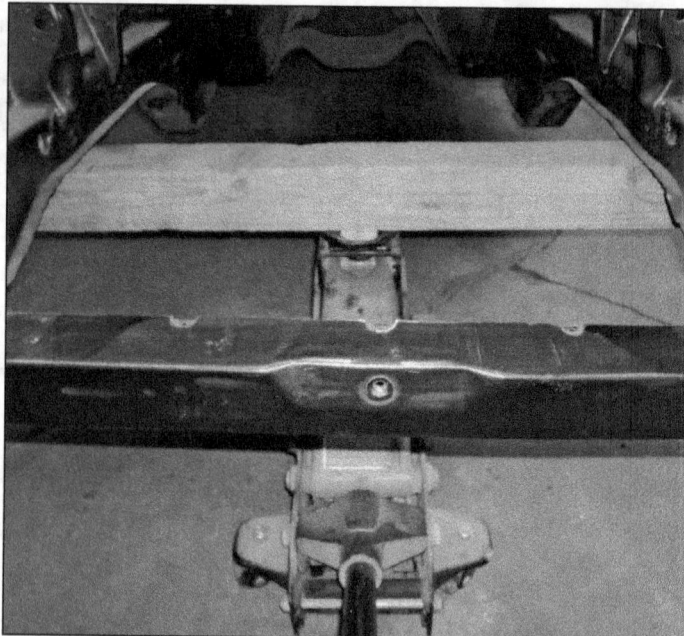

Stripped of its drivetrain, steering system, and front suspension, a car becomes difficult to move around despite its lighter weight. With the rear axle still in place, use a 4x4 beam spanning the front frame rails along with a floor jack to reposition the body shell as needed.

A small 1/2-inch-thick block of wood attached to the bottom of the beam engages the saddle of the floor jack and prevents the beam from slipping off of the jack while the car is being moved. Once the body shell is in the desired position, be sure to secure it with jack stands placed underneath the frame rails. Never leave the weight of a car supported only by a hydraulic jack.

improved access to the engine compartment for cleaning, rust repair, and refinishing.

Bolt-on body panels may also be removed at this stage, particularly if they will be replaced, or have multiple coats of paint or surface rust that need to be removed by media blasting. Once the doors, windshield, and rear window glass are removed it is advisable to also remove the seats and interior panels so these parts can be stored in a safe, clean area. If the dash or other interior parts will not be removed, protect them from dust, damage, and paint overspray by covering them with towels, blankets, or a large plastic drop cloth.

Chrome-plated parts, the bumpers in particular, should be removed early on if they will be sent out for plating. Many chrome shops require six months or even longer to turn around a set of bumpers, so don't delay or you'll end up waiting for the bumpers on an otherwise completed car.

The front suspension and rear axle should be among the last components to be removed. Without them the car body is more difficult to move or transport. However, a stripped body shell is fairly light, and with the rear axle still in place the shell may still be rolled around your shop with the help of a 4x4 beam and floor jack. Temporary roller wheels may also be used to move around a bare body shell. These typically incorporate light-duty (think wheelbarrow) wheels with brackets attached to existing mounting points underneath the car's body. Useful during body repair and painting, they are not designed to support more weight than just the body shell.

I cannot state strongly enough that you should *never* rush the disassembly process, or toss all of the bolts and hardware into a coffee can intending to sort them later. Do not allow friends to help with the disassembly if they are not willing to follow through with labeling and bagging all of the hardware and fasteners as they are removed.

Be sure not to overlook any important details that may be found during disassembly, as these will need to be duplicated later. Always take plenty of photos during the process. These photos, along with any notes, sketches, or diagrams will be invaluable months later when it's time for reassembly.

Door Data Tag Removal

You may prefer to leave an original door data tag with its unique rosette rivets in place, essentially restoring the rest of the car around it. If the driver-side door has to be replaced, media blasted, or if you wish to repaint underneath the tag, care must be taken to prevent permanently damaging the thin aluminum tag during removal.

Simply drilling out the rivet heads causes them to spin, quickly boring a hole through the tag that is larger than the rivet head. Once this happens, original-style rivets cannot be used for reattachment.

Here is the proper way to remove a door tag without causing damage.

1) AMC door data tags are made of soft aluminum and can easily be damaged during removal. Star-shaped "rosette" rivets were used originally to secure the tag to the trailing edge of the driver's door.

2) Before drilling to remove the rivets, securely clamp the backside of the rivet inside the door with a small pair of locking pliers. Prior removal of the latch assembly makes the rivets easier to reach.

3) The rivet heads can now be drilled without spinning. A spinning rivet quickly cuts a large hole through the door tag making it impossible to reinstall it with original-style rivets.

4) Careful removal of the door tag maintains the small original mounting holes. Store the tag in a safe place where it will not be lost or damaged. The special rosette rivets used to reinstall the door tag after painting the car can generally be sourced online from private sellers, because they have not been reproduced.

Storing the Parts

Once disassembled, the space required to house your project car and all of the parts removed will grow considerably. Any parts or components not sent out for service or repair must be safely stored, preferably in a dry, dust-free area. Designate a section of your storage area for parts that need to be rebuilt or repainted so this can be done as time allows. As smaller parts are cleaned or refinished they can be wrapped in paper or bubble wrap for protection, then boxed with other similar items. Be sure to label all of the boxes with their contents or location on the car to save time later.

Avoid leaving parts where they will be in the way, become lost, or get damaged. Wooden pallets, sturdy shelves, or an overhead storage loft are ideal for stowing many of the

CHAPTER 3

bulky parts removed from the car, as well as new parts purchased for installation later on. Items as large as seats, fenders, or a complete dash panel can be safely stored in an overhead loft. Large plastic storage totes are useful for keeping smaller parts organized, clean, and dry.

If you happen to be working on more than one project car at a time be especially diligent about keeping everything separate! Label every box or hardware bag with a short description of the car the parts belong to, such as "Red 68" or "70 Jav."

Replacement Parts Sources

During the disassembly process keep track of any broken parts that are unrepairable, or worn items in need of upgrading. Add these pieces to the list of missing parts from your initial inspection. Keep this "AMC hot list" with you when attending swap meets, visiting fellow AMC owners, or attending car club meetings, and when looking for parts online.

Check eBay Motors, online auto classifieds sites, and the AMC forums daily to see what original parts turn up for sale. Network with local AMC car club members to find good used parts nearby. Many NOS parts are still available, but most are becoming pricey.

Unlike GM, Ford, and Chrysler owners, AMC muscle car restorers have a relatively limited selection of reproduction parts from which to choose. Although more and more reproduction parts are developed each year, especially for AMX and Javelin models, availability will never match that of most other makes. Some reproduction parts are also manufactured in limited runs and may become unavailable once they're gone. For this reason, purchase reproduction AMC parts as you find them; there is no guarantee they will be available later when it's time for reassembly.

With your AMC project car now largely disassembled, some components being serviced, and missing or damaged parts being sourced, it's time to move to the next important step of the project: body repair.

Use otherwise wasted space in your shop with an overhead parts storage loft. This is a great way to safely store bulky items such as seats and fenders to keep them out of your way until needed. If you are working on multiple project cars, build a storage loft for each one.

Supplies of NOS parts are dwindling, but many uncommon parts can still be found at larger AMC shows and swap meets. Websites such as eBay are another good source for hard-to-find original parts. Buy them when you can because when they are gone they will most likely never be reproduced.

Plastic storage totes provide an efficient way to organize new parts along with original parts as they are cleaned and painted. They will stay clean and dry in the tote until you are ready to use them. Each tote can be labeled with its contents, such as "engine compartment," "brakes," or "interior" to save time when retrieving parts for installation.

CHAPTER 4

BODY REPAIR

Body repair is one of the most important, and visible, parts of the restoration process. When done correctly it will last forever.

Evaluating Condition

With your project car's body shell stripped of its drivetrain, bumpers, trim, bolt-on body panels, carpet, and interior parts you can now better assess its condition with fewer items in the way to conceal rust or other flaws. Inspect the body closely for structural rust damage in the rocker panels or frame rails. Inspect the inner rocker panels from both inside and underneath the car, as well as the condition of the floorpans. Inspect for rust perforation of the front fender gussets (also known as "troughs" in AMC lingo because of their resemblance to a feeding trough) and anywhere else where rust may have been hidden previously.

If the car has a vinyl top that will be replaced, remove it completely to check for rust damage on the roof and upper quarter panels. Remove any body filler in rust-prone areas if there is any indication that the repair has failed. This includes even a tiny bubble or crack, or the slightly raised outline of a patch showing through the filler. Any patches secured by rivets need to be removed and replaced with new patches properly welded in place.

A thorough inspection of the body shell prevents any unpleasant surprises later. If you are lucky there is no structural damage present, and little if any outer body rust (a leaking rear window or trunk seal can cause lower quarter panel and trunk floor rust in any climate). If the car has had previous collision repairs check for obvious misalignment of the frame rails or substructure where the front fenders mount, and, if questionable, have these areas checked by a qualified body repair facility.

Front fender gussets may be rusted so badly that they are missing. But because they are integral to the strength of the front end, the gussets should be repaired if rusted or replaced as required.

CHAPTER 4

Assuming that you find no serious issues, the next step is to perform any required repairs, including bodywork for the body shell and all of the bolt-on panels that will be used.

Paint Removal

A car still wearing its factory-original paint in reasonably good condition has a pretty good base for refinishing, and may not need to be completely stripped. However, a body that has been painted multiple times or one with peeling or weather-checked paint, surface rust spots bleeding through the finish, or any questionable body repairs must be stripped to bare metal before refinishing. The choices include removing the paint by hand using a dual-action sander, chemical stripping, or media blasting.

Hand Sanding

Hand sanding using 80- to 120-grit discs is very time consuming and dirty but fairly inexpensive, especially if you have several good friends willing to help for nothing more than pizza and liquid refreshments. However, when using this method it's easy to permanently damage window glass or stainless trim pieces such as the drip rail moldings if they are not removed first, or well protected by several layers of duct tape. A body grinder is fine for removing a thick coat of body filler but should *never* be used to remove paint, because it will permanently damage the surface of the panel.

Chemical Stripping

Chemical paint strippers do much of the hard work, but may come back to haunt you later if any of the residue remains trapped in a body seam, or anywhere else underneath the new paint. Several months or even a year later an area of small bubbles may appear, indicating contamination of the surface underneath your new paint job. Care must also be taken because chunks of paint lifted by the chemical stripper may fall into the cowl vent screen, and will not be easily accessible for removal, even with the windshield wiper motor removed.

As you remove the bolt-on body panels of your project car, watch for hidden rust or improperly repaired collision damage. Structural rust should be the first repair made to the rolling shell, as long as the damage is not so severe as to render the car not worth restoring.

Removing multiple layers of paint and body filler using a dual-action sander is safer than using a chemical paint stripper that can run into seams or the cowl vent, causing problems later. When sanding, be sure to protect any nearby glass or body trim with a couple layers of duct tape just in case. Never use a body grinder just to remove paint!

Finding surface rust underneath the paint is never a good sign; it indicates poor preparation. If multiple spots such as this are found while stripping the paint, consider media blasting instead to be sure that the entire body is free of surface rust, even the spots that may still be hidden from view.

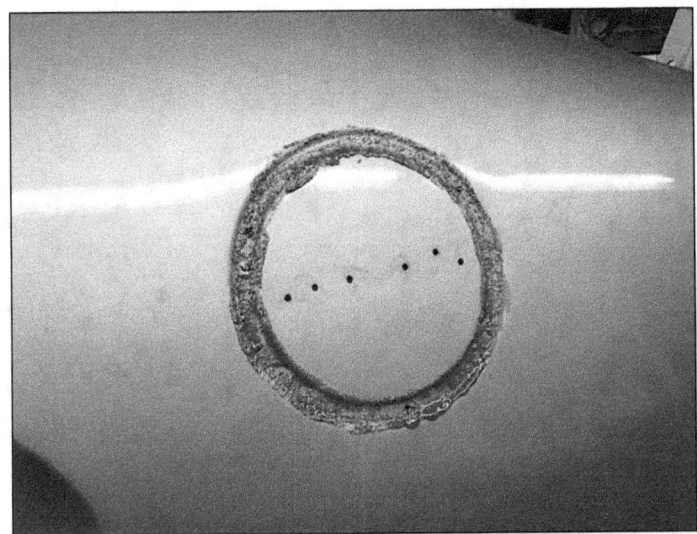

Chemical paint remover can eventually destroy a new paint job if any residue remains when the primer is applied. However, in some instances, chemical stripper is preferable, such as when sanding multiple coats of paint from this AMX quarter-circle recess. Sanding here could, potentially, remove enough metal to alter its appearance.

Following chemical paint removal and a thorough washing, this circular emblem recess remains clearly defined. The remaining paint on the outer surface of the panel can be removed easily with a dual-action sander. A qualified media blasting shop can also remove all traces of paint without damage to the sheet-metal substrate.

Media Blasting

Professional media blasting is more expensive, and generally requires transporting the car's body and panels to a different location, but almost always ensures a higher-quality end result. Media blasting completely removes the paint, as well as any body filler and rust that is present. This process may even expose pinhole rust perforation, which would otherwise be overlooked.

Expect to pay between $800 and $1,300 to have a bare body shell stripped inside and out, or $1,500 to $2,500 for stripping a car along with all of its bolt-on panels. When deciding whether to have your car stripped by media blasting, keep in mind that many shops may require it to be mounted on a rotisserie, and have any undercoating removed before delivery to the shop. Otherwise, undercoat removal adds considerably to the final cost.

Media blasting an entire car both inside and out uses a variety of methods and different abrasives depending on the particular car and its condition. The shop may start with a gentle plastic media that removes only paint and primer. Because the plastic media does not generate heat, it does not warp sheet metal so it is used as much as possible when stripping a car body. The plastic media is then followed with a more aggressive sand-like material used for removing areas of rust. Lower air pressure may be used at this stage to help prevent metal distortion, but warping is still a danger because of the heat generated.

Soda blasting, or using sodium bicarbonate as a blasting media, has the advantage of not damaging glass or other parts left on the car. However, if the media is recycled it may become mixed with like-size particles of paint and other impurities that can damage glass and trim parts. The soda residue must also be neutralized and washed off before the body shell or parts can be coated in primer, and this invites the growth of surface rust.

You may find a paint-stripping specialist that offers an epoxy primer coat as an optional service following the paint removal process. If they do not, never allow the stripped body shell or parts to get wet; completely coat all bare metal parts as soon as possible, because even the humidity in the air can cause surface rust to appear within 24 hours.

If you have decided to have the body shell or panels stripped by media blasting, be certain that the person doing the work is experienced with working on sheet-metal parts. Saving money by taking your project to a general sandblasting shop can lead to disaster because using the wrong media or air pressure, or even just operator inexperience, can destroy an entire car body. Always ask for references before sending out your valuable car body or parts for stripping.

CHAPTER 4

Slight differences can be found on most Javelin and AMX bolt-on body panels. This double set of bolt holes on a lower fender is for a brace that was used beginning early in the 1968 model run. The single hole is for the brace used on even earlier cars; it was discontinued because of tire clearance issues with the E70-14 tires.

Bolt-On Panels

Rusted fenders or badly damaged doors, hood, trunk lid, or rear valance panel can be replaced if better quality parts can be sourced. These body panels, with the exception of the rear valance, have not been reproduced in steel for AMC cars, and likely never will be, so NOS or better-quality used parts are generally the only options. Good-quality front fenders and hoods, in particular, are becoming difficult to find (and expensive when you do) because of their tendency to rust, as well as their vulnerable position on the car.

Although there is a great deal of interchange between AMX and Javelin body parts, minor differences are found on every bolt-on panel depending on build date or, sometimes, the model. And while many of these similar parts fit and function just fine, the subtle differences, if incorrect for your particular car, could make reassembly difficult, or cost points in stock class car show judging. Naturally, it is preferable to have matching doors, fenders, and fender extensions whenever possible because the minor differences that do exist can be seen by a knowledgeable AMC car show judge.

For Javelin and AMX models, the entire front clip can be swapped as a unit between model years or even

A later-style Javelin or AMX fender extension above has a notch to clear the edge of the headlight-mounting panel without having to peen it over. The earlier-style extension has a small groove running along the back edge because some were sealed to the fender with a bead of white caulk.

This strengthening rib runs along the front and sides of later AMX and Javelin hoods, in particular 1969 and newer models. This upgrade was added after the underside bracing of some early hoods was found to flex and crack. Most AMC car show judges know to look for this detail when inspecting stock class cars!

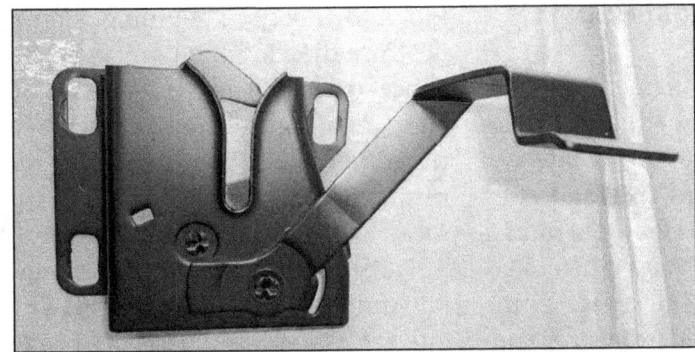
The hood latch is designed differently for AMX and Javelin models, as it has to clear the front grilles, which are also styled differently. A trained eye can see the difference in the length of the drop for the handle. This latch is from an early-model AMX.

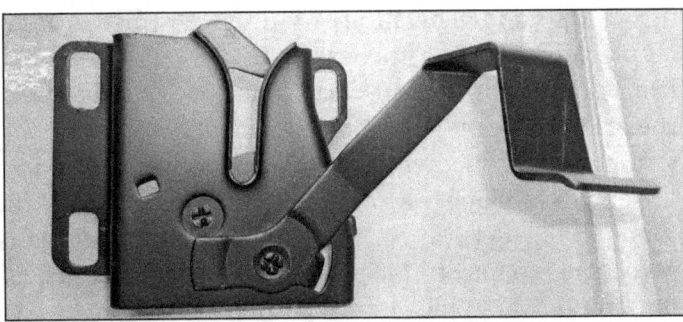
This latch has a longer drop, making it correct for an early-model Javelin. Although both types of latches interchange and function, only one type is correct for a particular model. For 1968, the hood latch was added after the body was painted; on 1969 and newer cars, it was installed and painted along with the body.

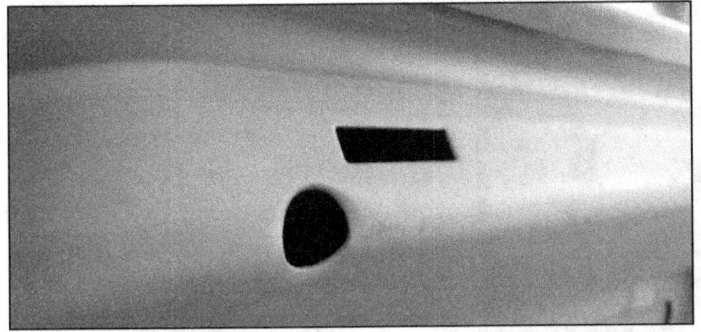
Javelin and AMX trunk lids also changed. The slot shown here was added for 1971 for the installation of a rubber bumper due to the extra weight of the Javelin AMX fiberglass spoiler. Trunk lids installed on 1968–1970 models had only the round drain holes (shown).

Just like the panels they attach, bolt head markings differ from year to year. Label and bag all of the attaching hardware as it is removed so it can be reused in the same position. If assembling a car that was purchased disassembled, be sure that any visible fasteners are the same type with uniform markings.

Two production versions of the 1968–1970 AMX and Javelin rear valance panel were available (early on top). A subtle difference on the later version (bottom) involved the threaded inserts used for mounting the rear license plate bracket. A third type of valance (not shown) appeared for 1971 when the fuel filler opening was relocated slightly. This panel has a wider cutout so it can be retrofitted to earlier cars as well. It is currently the only style of valance to be reproduced.

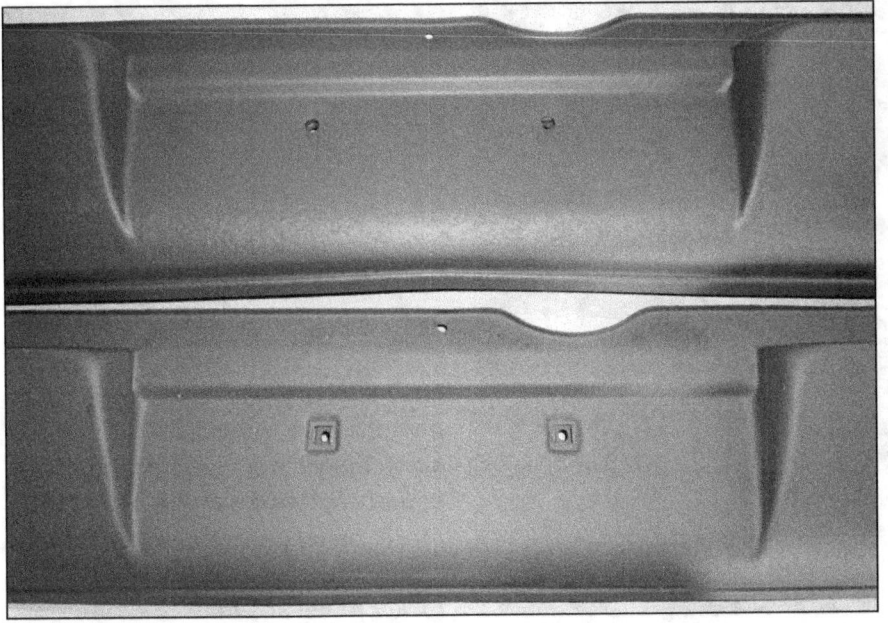

CHAPTER 4

Structural Rust Repair

first- and second-generation cars. Just be prepared for all of the comments from people who will speculate that the car in question was involved in a serious wreck, whether or not it was!

Subtle differences can also be found on fenders, doors, and other body panels of most AMC models, so it's always a good idea to make sure, whenever possible, that any replacement panels are from the same year and model as the car that you are working on.

Rocker panels, frame rails, and floorpans are all key structural components for an AMC unit-body car, and should be the first areas addressed if rust damage is present. For minor frame repairs, use heavy-gauge steel that matches the thickness of the original. AMC rocker panels are constructed of three (or sometimes four) separate panels spot-welded together for strength. If the outer rocker or the innermost section running underneath and inside the car shows evidence of rust damage, you can be fairly certain that the middle section is rusted as well. Not repairing all of the rust compromises the strength of the rocker panel and ultimately the car.

A badly rusted or damaged frame rail can be replaced as a unit with one salvaged from a parts donor car, but this is not a job for a beginner because the body structure *must* be braced and supported until the repair

This AMX rocker didn't look as though it was badly rusted; opening it up revealed extensive rust damage and debris trapped inside. The center panel, characterized by large round holes, received little if any rust protection. Center panels are generally in worse condition than the inner or outer portions.

This AMX required almost complete removal of both rocker panels due to advanced rust damage. Only the rear portions were retained. AMC–issued scissor jacks work well to support the underbody when the strength of the rocker panel assembly is temporarily removed. Remove or repair only one rocker panel at a time.

BODY REPAIR

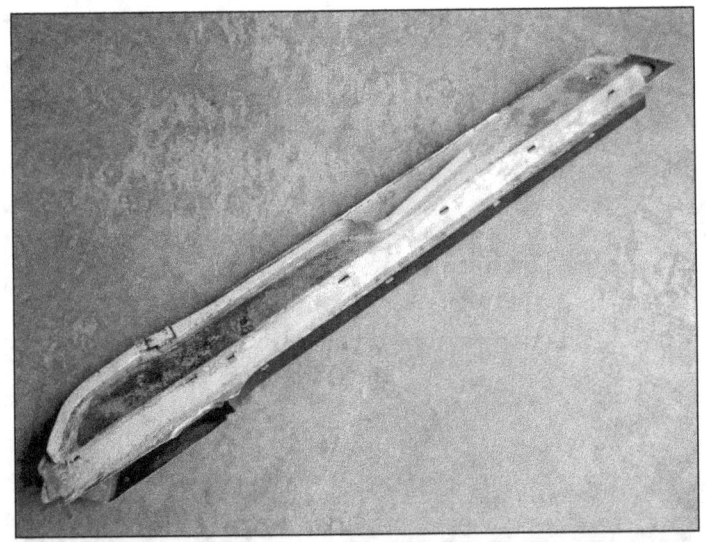

A complete rocker panel assembly salvaged from a parts donor is an efficient way to repair a badly rusted car. This one even has a portion of the original floorpan remaining, which makes attaching the existing floorpan sections easy. After trimming, the center panel was left longer than the rest, allowing it to extend inside the existing rear portion of the rocker panel that was left in place.

Another common area for rust damage is the rear portion of the rocker panel, inside the wheel well. This replacement was fabricated to include the access hole (that was originally sealed with a rubber or plastic plug). Recreating details such as these ensures an original appearance. Once undercoated, nobody will ever know that a repair has been performed here.

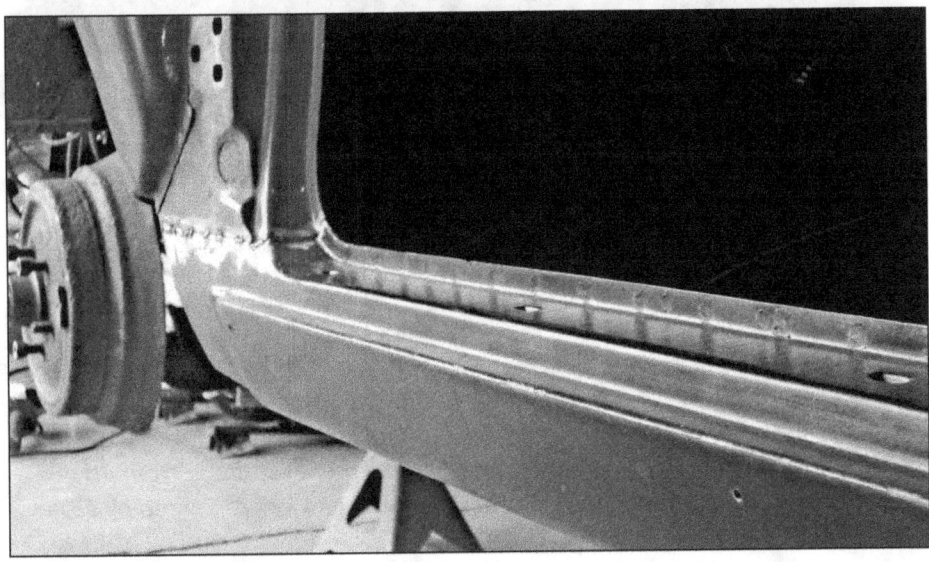

Careful measurement is required when replacing a complete rocker panel assembly to have neat butt-welds with no large gaps or overlap. A good reference point for measuring is the small hole for the doorjamb light switch, which is present on every car. After tacking in the rocker panel, measure again and check for straightness before solidly welding the panel in place.

A small access hole must be used to attach the replacement inner panel to the original portion. Once the center is attached, the outer panel can be welded closed. With proper installation, including attachment of the floorpans and supports, a replacement rocker panel is just as strong as the original.

With the rocker panel replacement complete, a coat of POR-15 paint protects the inside against future rust damage. The portion of the inner rocker underneath the car can also be protected with POR-15 for maximum protection. A quality rust inhibitor can also be sprayed inside the rocker through the lower drains or sill plate screw holes.

is complete. Similarly, a complete rocker panel can be salvaged from a rust-free car and replaced as a unit or grafted to the undamaged portion of the original if temporary access is allowed in order to connect the center panel. Afterward, the access hole may be patched and smoothed before refinishing.

Floorpan repair or replacement is straightforward, as long as the frame and rocker panels are in good condition, or repaired beforehand. Small rust holes can be repaired by cutting out all the problem areas and then welding in patches made from steel of the same gauge. More serious rust can be eliminated by installing complete reproduction front or rear floorpans, which are available for 1968–1974 AMX and Javelin models. Do not repair a rusted floor with fiberglass, or use pop rivets or screws to attach new floorpans, as the original strength and much of the support will be lost.

Serious structural repair requires bracing the unit body shell against flexing. Temporary supports can be welded in place, and then removed once the repairs are finished. Complete frame rail replacement can be performed this way; it restores the original strength and integrity of a car damaged by severe rust or collision damage.

BODY REPAIR

A common area to find structural rust perforation on an AMC muscle car is the lower part of the driver-side front frame rail. If the rust is not bad enough to warrant replacement of the complete rail, the rusted area can be cut out and replaced with steel of the same gauge.

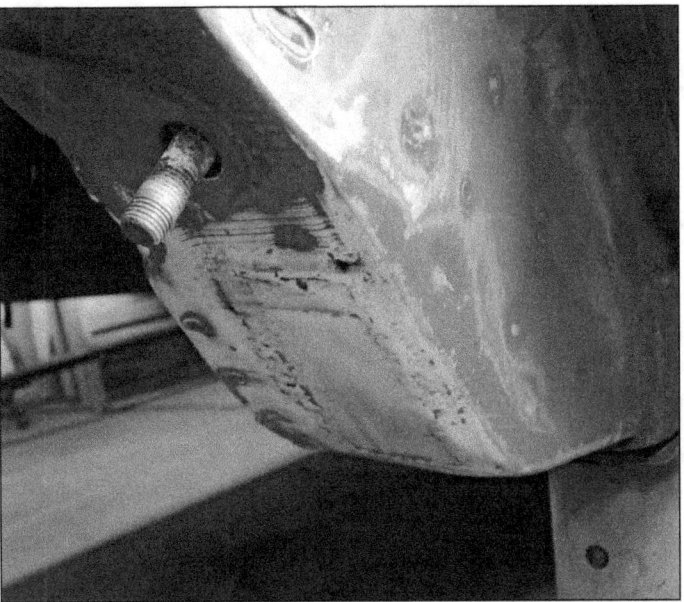

After welding in the replacement section, followed by grinding and finishing the welds, this frame rail is as good as new. The frame rails, along with the rocker panels, provide the main support for an AMC unit body. However, a small area of rust such as this is no reason to pass on a potential project car.

Floorpan rust is fairly common, especially at the seam in 1968–1970 AMX floors, but excellent-quality reproduction floorpans are available. The complete pan can be replaced, or the new sections can be trimmed to replace only what is needed. Although not shown, front floorpans are available as well.

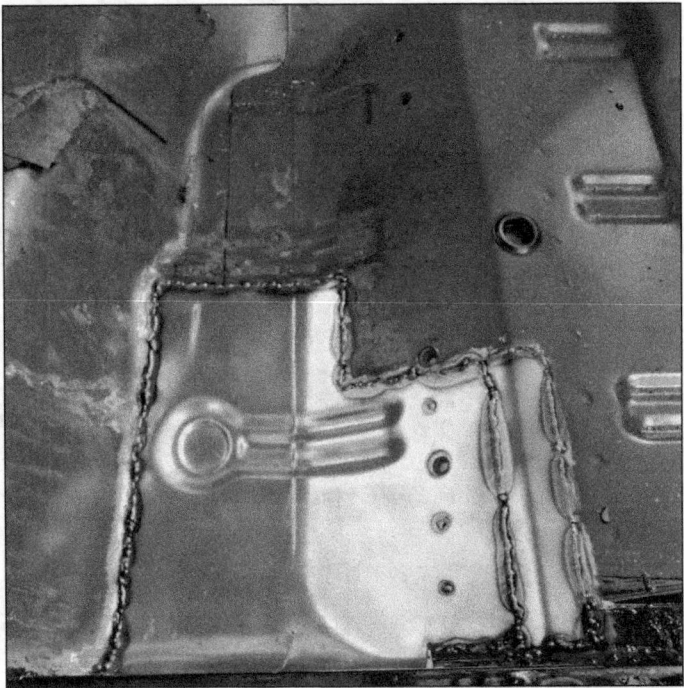

Welding is the only method that should be used for floorpan replacement. Here, the new section did not extend far enough forward to completely replace the rust damage, so a small patch was welded in. The new floorpan was then attached to the patch.

CHAPTER 4

With some paint applied and the original AMX underlayment replaced it's hard to tell that this car ever had floor rust. When repairing the floorpans, a good way to store the original underlayment is layered between sheets of wax paper. This method keeps the underlayment clean and doesn't allow it to stick together.

These are replacement gussets removed from a parts donor car. Media blasting is recommended if heavy undercoat or surface rust is present. Gussets such as these from a 1971–1974 Javelin are different from the earlier models, but can be made to work without too much trouble.

By leaving the upper sill in place and sectioning in the rest, there is no chance of fender misalignment. This method also allows a completely invisible repair. The AMX pictured also required rust repair to the cowl and fender baffle panels before the new gussets could be installed.

BODY REPAIR

The final step of gusset repair is a couple generous coats of POR-15 paint inside and underneath. Be sure to coat the upper part of the cowl covered by the fender because it was not painted originally and is often rusted. Using POR-15 allows the satisfaction of knowing that rust will never return to these parts.

Front fender gussets (or troughs) are also structural components designed to strengthen the front end of the car in the event of a collision. Because of their position underneath the fenders, the gussets are prone to rust damage after gradually filling with dirt and water thrown by the front wheels. Mice often find their way inside as well, with their nests adding to the problem. In time, the fender tops tend to rust through because of all of the moisture trapped underneath. If not badly rusted, the gussets can be patched and then coated with POR-15 paint. In extreme cases, the gussets should be completely replaced with rust-free parts salvaged from a donor car.

Gussets from a 1968 Javelin or AMX, which often incorporate a separate triangular brace at the cowl, are wider at the back than those from a 1969–1974 car. The later gussets were revised to fit along the vertical cowl flange rather than being notched to straddle it. However, fender gussets salvaged from later-model Javelins or AMXs can be used to repair a 1968 model with only slight modifications; you basically notch the back end and then use a little persuasion before tacking the gussets in place.

The outer edge of the gussets, along with the top of the radiator extension panels, were sealed to the underside of the front fender using rubber flaps that were attached with staples. In theory, this was to prevent dirt and water from filling the gussets, but these seals were only moderately effective, although certainly better than nothing at all. Reproduction seal kits are available and generally include replacement staples.

To reuse the existing staple holes, apply a piece of masking tape over all of the holes, mark them on the tape, and then use the tape to transfer the position of the holes to the replacement seal. After punching or drilling staple holes in the new flap, install and crimp the new staples using pliers.

Another method to attach the seals is to use a generous bead of weatherstrip adhesive and clamp the flaps in place until dry. Once the fender is installed be sure that the flaps make a positive seal and that they are not half in and half out of the gusset.

Every Javelin, 1968–1974 AMXs, and Rebel Machine models have the structural gussets underneath the front fenders. Curiously, the Hurst SC/Rambler, Hornet SC/360, and Gremlin X models do not; they have only a flat upper sill where the fenders are attached. Unfortunately fender-top rust-through is still a problem with these models, even without the gussets trapping dirt and moisture underneath.

Outer Body Rust

Less critical, but more visible, is outer body rust damage. Areas prone to rusting on AMC cars include the lower rear quarter panels, the bottom corners of the doors, the lower lip of the trunk lid, and (as mentioned) the front fender tops. Good-quality, heavy-gauge patch panels are available for the lower quarters of Javelin and AMX models. For other cars, and for repairing doors and fenders that cannot be replaced, the preferred method of repair is to cut out the rusted section and then butt-weld a replacement steel patch.

When removing rust be sure to cut out a large enough area to ensure that *all* of the rust is removed. Always check the backside of the removed piece; if rust extends to the edge, cut out a larger piece until the edge is free of any visible rust. Once all of it is removed, form a patch made of clean steel of the same gauge, and then carefully trim the patch as needed to fit neatly inside the cut-out area. Position the patch flush with the surrounding metal using welding clamps, locking pliers, or alignment magnets until it can be tack-welded in place. Unless it is required for alignment purposes, the patch or replacement panel should not overlap the original metal because it could invite a recurrence of rust if water becomes trapped between the layers. The use of weld-through primer around the repair and on the backside of the patch helps to fight corrosion.

Precise alignment of patches and repair panels is crucial to a quality repair so minimal body filler is required to finish the repaired sections. Take your time lining up a patch or panel before tacking it in place. Check the fitment again before continuing because the tack-welds can easily be ground off if the panel has shifted and has to be repositioned. Once everything is lined up as closely as possible, go back and fill in along the seam, welding 1 to 2 inches at a time. Move around as you fill in between the tack-welds to avoid overheating one area, which can warp the surrounding sheet metal and create additional work. *Do not* place a wet towel near the weld area to control heat because of the risk of electrocution.

Once the panel or patch is completely welded in place, use a light source held behind the repair (wherever possible) to check for small gaps or pinholes. If any are present, weld them closed. Once a solid butt-weld is complete, the next step is to grind the welds smooth. Again, avoid excess heat and warping by keeping the body grinder moving, especially if any hot spots appear. If your weld bead has good penetration you will be able to grind it nearly flat without seeing the original seam appear.

After grinding, check again for any pinholes that may not have been visible earlier. If everything looks good apply a coat of POR Patch sealer to both sides (if possible) of the weld to keep moisture from getting behind the repair.

Body Rust Repair

1 Quarter panel and outer wheelhouse rust repair is a multi-step process that begins with removal of the affected metal. Be sure to cut back until neither side of the pieces removed has any rust showing at the edges. Use an air-powered cut-off tool rather than shears; it does not distort the panel surrounding the cut. When finished, be sure to file the edges to remove burrs.

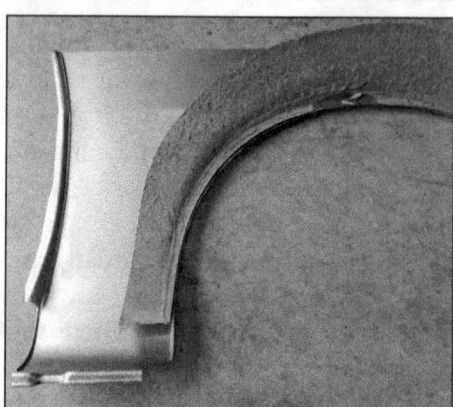

2 The wheel lip from a rusted out 1968–1970 Javelin or AMX front fender can be salvaged to repair the rusted edge of an outer wheelhouse. Here, a front fender lip fits nicely when placed inside the replacement outer rear quarter panel section. Careful alignment is crucial, because these panels will eventually be welded together around the wheel opening, just like the original.

BODY REPAIR

3 As with the quarter panel, trim the outer wheelhouse back until clean metal is reached. The reproduction outer quarters are made in two sections (front and rear); complete one half of the job at a time. Keeping half of the original quarter in place temporarily allows for perfect alignment of the replacement panel.

4 Slot or notch the replacement wheelhouse edge as needed for it to conform to the original contour. Measure, test fit, and clamp the new edge in place. Be sure it does not extend out too far or the outer quarter panel will never fit correctly.

5 After welding in the new edge made from a front fender lip, the front half of the outer wheelhouse is complete again. Coat this area generously with POR-15 paint for permanent protection against rust (except for the lower edge where it will be welded).

CHAPTER 4

6 With the front half of the outer wheelhouse repaired, fit and tack the outer quarter panel in place. Note how the body's lines and reflections prove that the new panel is perfectly aligned. If you don't have access to a spot welder, first drill a series of small holes for plug welds around the wheel opening.

7 Following the replacement of the front half of the quarter panel, repeat the process for the rear half. Take as much time as needed to align the replacement panels perfectly. Misaligned quarter panels will never look right, regardless of how nice the paint job is.

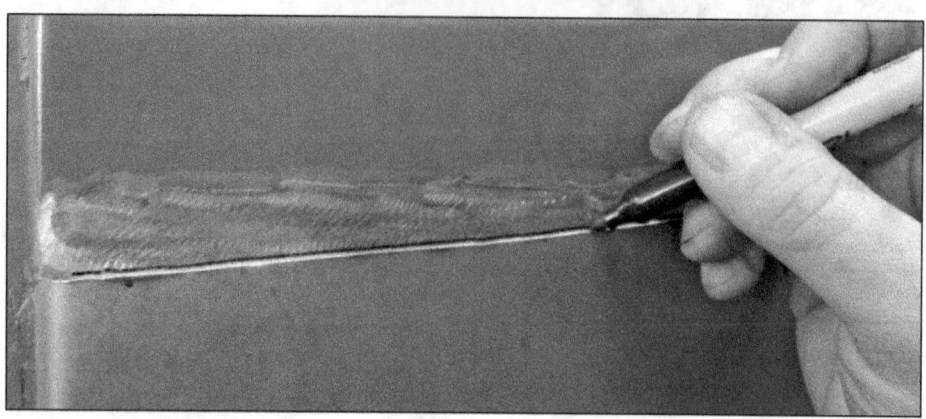

8 After repairing the outer wheelhouse, align and clamp the replacement quarter panel in place. Mark along the edge so you can trim the existing metal for a perfect fit. With no overlap, a perfect butt-weld can be used to secure the replacement quarter sections.

BODY REPAIR

9 After trimming the existing quarter panel, tack it in place. Inspect the alignment one more time before welding the seam solidly. The lighting and reflections show excellent alignment of the new panel relative to the old panel.

10 When replacing lower rear quarter panels, always test fit the rear valance before completing the welding. There is no way to hide the defect if the lower edge of the quarter panel ends up too high or too low. The rear valance here is perfectly aligned with the quarter panel.

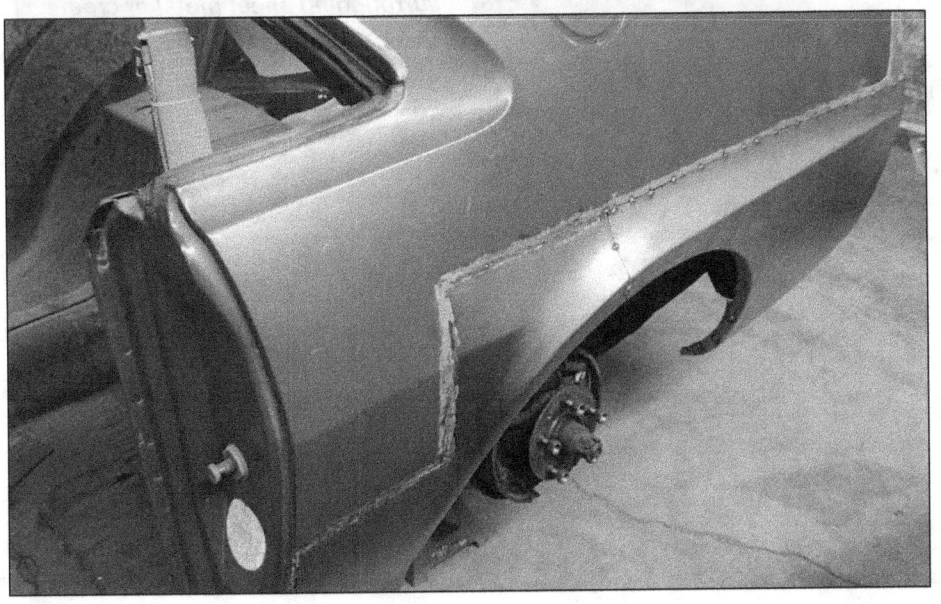

11 With the replacement panel tacked in place, double-check the alignment from every angle. If the panel has somehow shifted, it's a lot easier to reposition it now than to hide the problem later with body filler. Here, everything looks great; all of the bodylines match up perfectly.

CHAPTER 4

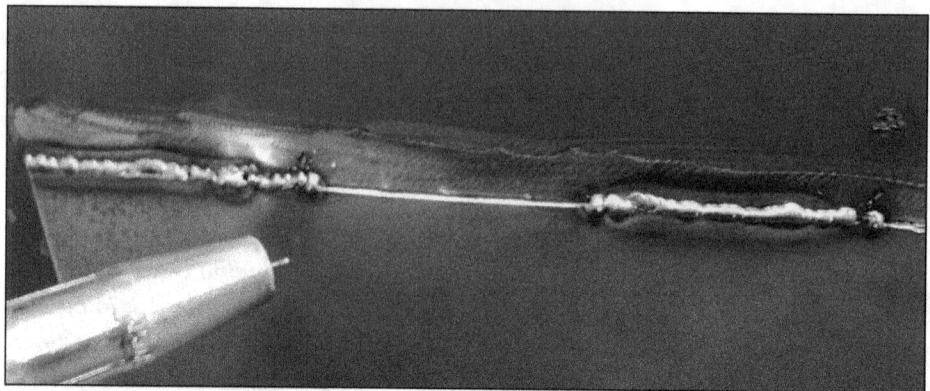

12 After fitting and tacking the panel in place, begin filling in the weld. To control the heat and avoid warping the surrounding sheet metal, weld only 1 to 2 inches at a time, moving around and then doubling back to an area once it has cooled. Keep the edge of the panel flush with the existing metal by tapping with a body hammer as needed.

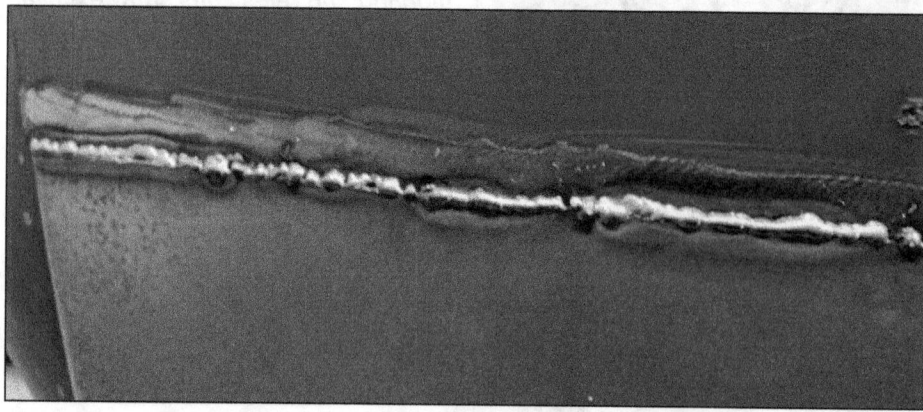

13 Once you have a continuous, even butt-weld, place a light source behind the repair whenever possible to check for tiny holes or missed spots. Weld these trouble spots closed to achieve a solid, continuous bead. Once again avoid a concentrated buildup of heat so you don't create more work for later.

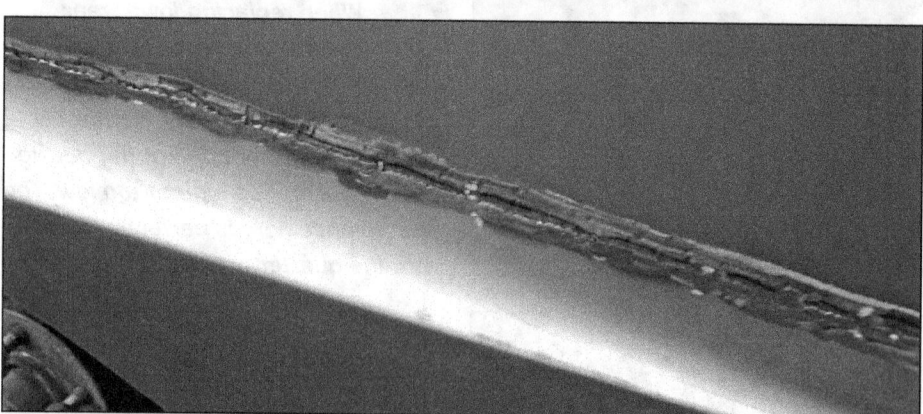

14 With precise panel alignment and good weld penetration you should be able to grind the weld nearly flush without compromising its strength. Use caution with the body grinder so you don't damage the surrounding sheet metal or create excess heat. Keep the grinder moving, especially if you notice discolored hot spots forming as you grind.

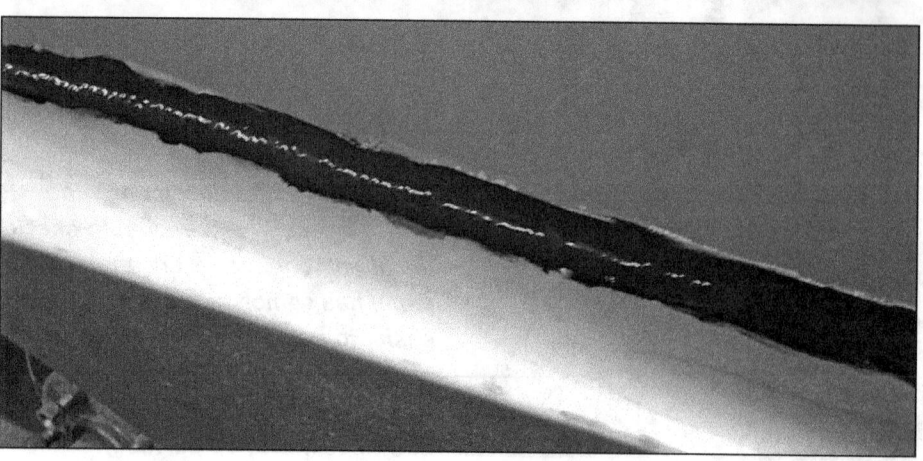

15 The final step for panel attachment is to seal the weld, preferably on both sides, with POR Patch. This permanent, waterproof sealer keeps moisture from getting behind the repair, as well as sealing any pinholes that remain after welding. Although much is sanded off during the final bodywork and prep, the important areas remain coated.

Surface Rust

Any car with outer body rust is almost certain to have some areas of surface rust as well. Vulnerable areas of the body shell include the lower corners of the rear window, underneath the battery tray inside the engine compartment, and on the trunk floor if water has collected underneath the mat. Although professional media blasting followed by coating with epoxy primer is ideal, surface rust can also be dealt with at home by using POR-15 paint directly over the rusted area.

Prepare the affected spots first by using a degreaser or surface cleaner, followed by scraping or lightly sanding to remove any loose paint or rust scale. Clean the surface again and then apply two coats of POR-15; allow 24 hours for the second coat to dry completely. Next, rough up the surface, being careful not to sand through the protective POR-15 base coat. Smooth with a skim coat of body filler, apply primer, sand, and finish with the topcoat.

This method works especially well to protect vulnerable areas that may be exposed to moisture in the future. Deeper rust pits can be filled with POR Patch, a solid version of POR-15, and then finished as described above. Light, superficial surface rust may need nothing more than sanding to bare steel, followed by a primer coat and topcoat.

One thing to keep in mind is that a muscle car, once refinished, will likely never be subjected to the same harsh conditions that caused the body to rust originally. Most restored cars are treated as valued collectibles, kept out of rain and bad weather, and certainly not exposed to road salt in the winter. For this reason even

An isolated area of surface rust, such as underneath a battery tray, can either be removed with media blasting, or sealed with two heavy coats of POR-15 paint. Scrape or wire brush first to remove any scale or loose paint. Deeper rust pits can be filled with POR Patch applied with a cardboard spreader.

Although difficult, POR-15 paint can be sanded with 220-grit wet or dry paper. However, if you sand through to the rusted surface you must apply another coat, wait 24 hours, and sand again. Complete coverage is essential to permanently seal the surface.

CHAPTER 4

After sanding and etching the primer, this inner fender is ready for final prep and paint. The area underneath the battery tray was shielded from paint originally, so painting the engine compartment without the tray installed is recommended to prevent a recurrence of surface rust.

serious body rust, once repaired properly, is unlikely to return.

Collision Damage

A powerful vehicle being driven by a youthful owner is a sure recipe for disaster, and for this reason many surviving muscle cars have a collision or two in their history. This is not necessarily something to shy away from when considering a muscle car purchase or restoration. However, rebuilding a wrecked car, or one with evidence of previous collision damage, requires careful inspection to ensure that the body structure is in alignment. Frame specifications can be found in the factory-issued TSM for your car's model year. Provide this information to a qualified body shop that can determine if the frame and rockers are within specifications, and then make any necessary adjustments.

Even a minor front-end collision can result in damage to the upper or lower core support as well as the radiator baffle panels, which are located behind the headlights. If badly damaged, these parts can be replaced; if only lightly damaged, they can be repaired and refinished in the same manner as any other body part. Minor dents and creases may be worked out using a hammer and dolly, and then smoothed using a minimal amount of body filler. If there is no access behind a damaged area, such as with the boxed upper core support, a slide hammer–type puller may be used to remove a dent. A small washer can be temporarily welded to the surface and then used to pull out the dent, after which the washer can be removed. If screw holes remain from using a slide hammer, be sure to weld them closed when you are finished. Likewise, unneeded emblem and molding holes also should be welded closed rather than merely covered with body filler.

Door Hinges

Sagging doors, caused by worn door hinge pins and bushings, is a common problem with AMC cars, and requires lifting and slamming the doors to close them. Over time, this damages the door latch and striker, and can even twist the entire door assembly. Rebuild or replace the hinges if any play can be felt when lifting the end of an open door. Afterward, keep the hinges well lubricated to slow the eventual wear of the replacement parts.

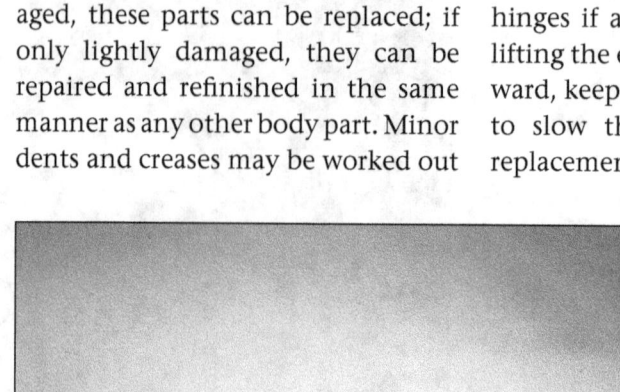

Unused emblem or body trim holes should be welded shut, along with any holes left from the use of a slide hammer–type dent puller. Simply covering holes with plastic body filler is not a permanent repair, and will likely fail.

BODY REPAIR

If not badly worn, door hinge pins can be driven out using a hammer and punch. Be sure to grind the end of the pin flush with the hinge, and then drill a small hole in the end to prevent the punch from walking. In some cases where hinges are badly worn, this method of disassembly may not work; they may have to be cut apart.

AMC door hinges are notorious for premature wear resulting in doors that are difficult to close. Hinges that aren't badly worn can be rebuilt right on the car after door removal. Oversize hinge pins and bushings are commonly available for other makes and can be used to rebuild worn hinges.

Door hinges were originally installed prior to paint. Hinges rebuilt on the workbench, or exchanged for rebuilt units, can be reinstalled using the shadow from the original. This way, only minor adjustment is necessary when reinstalling the doors.

Rebuild or replace the door hinges before painting the doorjambs, because they were originally body color. When painting the door edges, start the mounting bolts in their holes so the bolt heads are also painted. After painting, keep the door hinges well lubricated to prolong their life.

With the door removed, the hinges can be rebuilt right on the car. To drive out the old hinge pin, grind the protruding end of the pin flush with the hinge, and then drill a small hole into the end of the pin to keep a drift punch from slipping. The pin may now be driven out. Oversize hinge pins are available for other makes; these can be cut to length and then used to repair worn AMC hinges. However, if the hinge has worn all the way through the bushing and into the pin, it may be difficult or impossible to drive out the pin by normal means.

In this case, carefully sawing between the hinge halves allows the worn pin to be removed in pieces. However, sawing through the hinge is a last resort that may require shimming the hinge halves with flat washers when it is reassembled.

Before possibly destroying the hinge, consider replacing it instead with a rebuilt unit available from AMC parts vendors such as American Parts Depot.

Panel Adjustment

A common misconception persists that 45-year-old body panels should fit just as they do on a contemporary car, with narrow, even gaps and perfect alignment. The reality is that panel fitment standards were very different in the 1960s and 1970s. Back then, cars were not assembled to the exacting standards that consumers expect today. The bolt-on body panels of the 1960s and 1970s only fit so well even when the cars were new. They do not fit any better now without modifying the car, the panel, or both. For

After decades in place, door strikers are frequently very difficult to adjust or remove. The correct socket works much better than a crescent wrench, which is prone to slipping and rounding off the corners. A thin plastic gasket installed behind the striker protects the paint in this area.

After aligning the hood for even gaps at the cowl and fenders, adjust the two stops mounted to the upper core support to set the height in front. To adjust the height, loosen the lock nut and turn the head of the stop with a Phillips screwdriver.

Don't strip the Phillips head of a seized hood stop. If a new screwdriver does not adjust a rusted bumper, remove the stop from the car, soak it in penetrating oil overnight, and then secure a wrench in a bench vise horizontally for additional leverage. Once the screw breaks loose, glass-bead blast both pieces of the stop and then prime before reinstalling.

BODY REPAIR

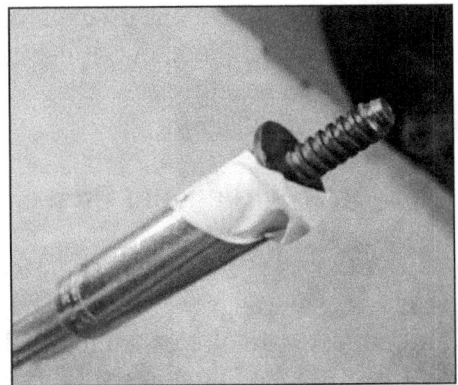

One front-fender mounting bolt is located between the upper and lower door hinges, and is installed from inside the car. It can be difficult to start, so tape it into the socket to avoid having it fall into the rocker panel where it will be lost forever.

With the front-end sheet metal perfectly aligned there should be even gaps and no differences in height between adjoining panels. Take your time to optimize the panel fitment now because you do not want to make adjustments after the car and engine compartment are painted.

The shadow knows, so use light to your advantage when assessing body repairs. This lower quarter panel repair section is not shaped exactly the same as the original panel to which it is welded; it needs to have the edge sharpened slightly with body filler to look perfect.

an authentic restoration, the doors, fenders, hood, and trunk lid must line up and fit as closely as possible, and operate without rubbing, chipping the paint, or otherwise interfering.

When reassembling the body expect to spend some time making adjustments. This includes aligning the hood to the cowl and the fenders to the hood, adjusting the trunk lid and latch, and possibly twisting the doors (especially on the driver's side) so that the lower rear corners don't stick out excessively. All of the bolt-on body panels can be adjusted. For example, the hood hinges can be adjusted up and down at the inner fender, while the hood itself can be adjusted fore and aft at the hinges.

With the engine out, have a helper crouch inside the engine compartment. Then, with the hood in the closed position, the helper can tighten the mounting hardware once the desired alignment is achieved. The front end of the doors can be adjusted in or out, and up or down at the hinges; the other end is adjusted with

CHAPTER 4

A skilled body man can easily feel high spots and other imperfections not visible to the naked eye. Another method of finding high or low spots is to spray a very light guide coat in a contrasting color, which, when sanded, highlights any minor defects found on the panel.

Any high spots found on the panel during repairs must be tapped down with a body hammer rather than using body filler to build up the surrounding surface. A very light coat of filler may be required afterward to perfectly smooth the affected area.

the striker. AMC seldom used shims in the body assemblies, but, if necessary, they can be added as needed for improved panel alignment.

Block Sanding and Prep

With the complete body reassembled, panel alignment optimized, and any repaired areas smoothed and sealed, the final step in the body repair process is priming and block sanding. With this step, any remaining minor imperfections are eliminated by applying one or more coats of filler primer, and then block sanding until the surface is perfectly straight and smooth. This is where touch becomes the primary sense; slight imperfections can be felt by an experienced hand even when they are invisible to the eye. A very thin guide coat of paint, which is actually little more than overspray applied over the primer, also helps to highlight any slight imperfections.

If you have never attempted final body prep consider hiring a professional shop or someone with years of bodywork experience, preferably the same person who will later apply the outer body paint. This final step of the body repair process is the most critical because it determines the quality of the finished product. No paint job ever looks right without adequate prep, regardless of how well it is applied. Especially a dark color such as black.

With the bodywork completely finished, it's extremely important to protect your work if the car will not be painted right away. Even contact with an air hose can inflict minor scratches that, if not sanded out, will show through the new paint and spoil the overall appearance of your restoration.

BODY REPAIR

Block sanding is a crucial step in achieving a perfect body repair. Flexible sanding blocks are used to smooth contoured areas of the body. Without the use of a block, uneven pressure on the sandpaper causes waves in the finish that cannot be removed by color sanding after paint is applied. This lower quarter panel has been completely repaired and blended into the original upper portion. After final prep and paint, this repair will be imperceptible.

Even if you are not planning to over-restore the underside of your project car, using a rotisserie is beneficial in that it allows the perfect height and angle to do major body repairs. A rotisserie also makes underbody repairs and seam sealing much easier; you don't have to do these tasks while lying on your back.

Completing another major step of the restoration process provides a great deal of satisfaction! Following many hours of welding, panel replacement and alignment, followed by smoothing and sanding multiple coats of primer, the bodywork is finished and your AMC project car is now ready for the next important step: paint.

CHAPTER 5

Painting Your Car

With the body repairs complete, all of the bolt-on panels aligned, and everything blocked and perfectly straight, the next step is to begin the painting process. But first you must decide how involved you will be in this phase of the project, and how much of it will be done by others. If you have used a paint gun successfully in the past there is no reason not to do some of this work yourself to save a sizable part of your restoration budget.

However, unless you are fortunate enough to have an extremely clean, spacious, well-lit, and ventilated work area (such as an actual paint booth) you may not want to tackle the outer body paint yourself, regardless of your level of experience. Dirt, insects, or not having adequate room to move around the car can quickly ruin a paint job, and the materials required to redo it are very expensive. Even if you plan to have the outer body painted at a body shop, almost anyone can set up a temporary painting area to spray the engine compartment, doorjambs, inside floor, or trunk area. These areas of the car were never painted with a show-quality finish. Be sure to check local regulations first before painting in a residential area.

Interior Body Paint

AMC workers originally sprayed the assembled body as a unit, first inside (engine compartment, trunk area, and door openings) and then with everything in the closed position for application of the exterior paint. The finish applied to the engine compartment can be described as functional at best. Coverage was the object here rather than high quality, so it is common with original cars to see some paint runs as well as thin spots.

Fresh from the booth, the finish on this Turbo Silver 1968 AMX looks factory new again. Proper use of a paint booth eliminates the element of luck otherwise needed when refinishing a complete car. With a consistent temperature, ample light, and good ventilation, as well as little danger of contamination from dust or insects, a paint booth provides an ideal environment for painting a car.

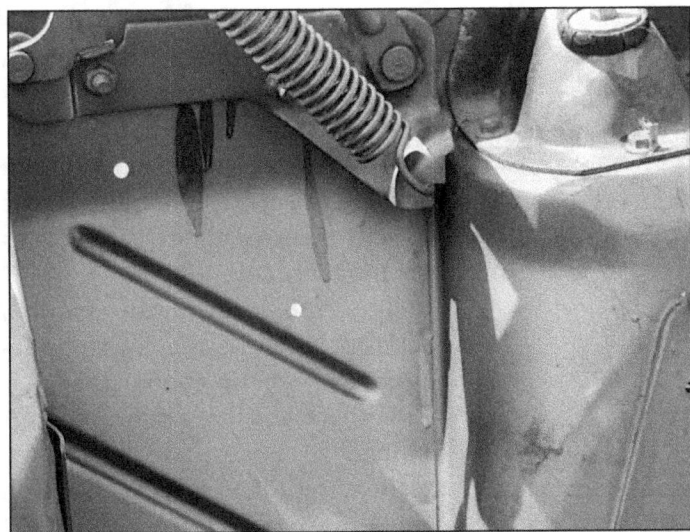

Because AMC engine compartments were originally painted from the front with the hood in place, it is common to find thin spots in the finish, especially on the backside of the spring towers. Paint runs are also seen resulting from the painter's efforts to ensure the hood hinges were adequately coated.

Significant runs on this Javelin inner fender offer proof that engine compartment paint was not originally applied to high standards. Metallic pigment in the paint makes the runs even more noticeable. Because an engine bay is fairly difficult to paint, ending up with a run or two can be considered an authentic detail when restoring an AMC muscle car!

Engine Compartment

Refinishing the engine compartment is best achieved with the engine and transmission removed, along with the wiper and fan motors, steering and suspension components, wiring harness, and brake lines. In fact, anything not originally painted in the body color should be removed. With everything out of the way, degrease the engine compartment so its condition can be assessed. If there is significant surface rust or multiple coats of paint, consider having the engine bay media blasted back to bare steel. However, good original paint can be left in place as a base coat.

One area that is commonly rusted is underneath the battery tray. The tray being originally installed between the application of primer and the body-color paint caused the rust. Rainwater combined with leaking acid from a faulty battery or charging system often didn't help either. After the battery tray is removed, you will see that this area is most likely rusted completely through. In this case, the inner fender can be patched by using a MIG welder or replaced with a rust-free panel removed from a donor car. Because the battery was positioned on the opposite side in 6-cylinder cars, they are an excellent source for replacement sheet metal. After repairs, this area can then be prepped and refinished along with the rest of the engine compartment.

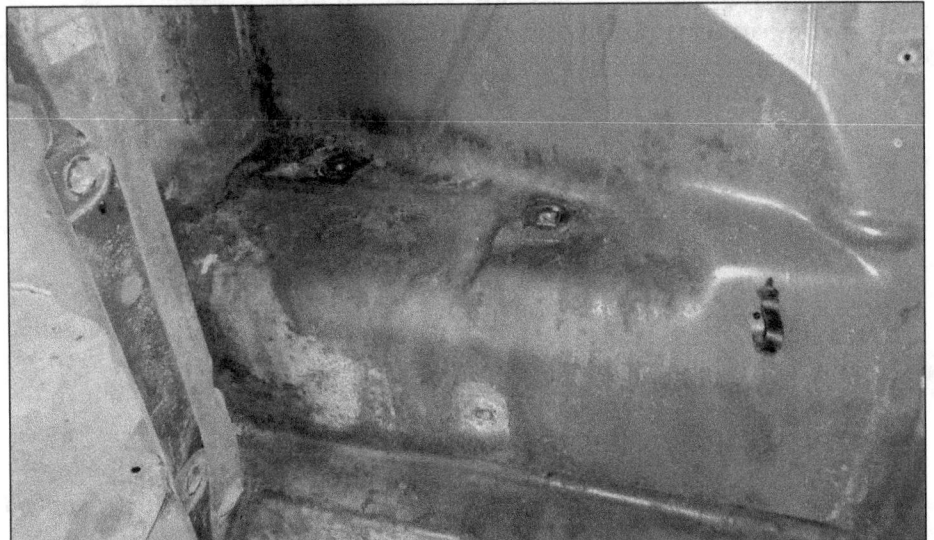

Never completely painted originally, the section of the inner fender located underneath the battery tray is vulnerable to rust perforation, especially if the car has had a leaking battery. If you're lucky, only surface rust is found here, which can easily be repaired before the engine compartment is refinished.

CHAPTER 5

This battery tray did not survive the ravages of time, moisture, and exposure to battery acid. Excellent-quality replacements are available, however, and should be painted top and bottom before installation. This prevents a return of corrosion to this area that is frequently seen on unrestored cars.

Any underhood parts not removed must be masked before painting the engine compartment. Even the threaded part of any screws protruding into the engine bay should be taped off. Larger parts not removed, such as the steering column, can be protected with tape and masking paper, or even aluminum foil. Any openings into the car's passenger compartment must be sealed before applying paint. Small pieces of cardboard work well for this and can be taped from the inside or wedged in place underneath the dash as necessary.

Once the engine compartment is prepared for paint, apply enough thin coats for complete coverage, following the paint manufacturer's instructions regarding temperature and flash time between coats.

Every AMC muscle car had the upper core support painted in the body color except for the 1970 AMX models with the Shadow Mask paint option, in which case it was painted low-gloss black. Because of its prominent position and visibility right up front with the hood open, make sure this part is perfectly prepared and refinished with a high-quality coat of paint.

On 1968–1969 Javelin models, the front edge of the lower grille-support panel, or "boomerang," is visible between the grille and front bumper, so be sure it is finished nicely as well. This panel, however, is completely hidden by the 1968–1969 AMX grille.

The underside of the hood may be painted in place or separate from the car. The hood hinges, however, should be installed and properly adjusted before they are painted, along with the engine compartment. Because the engine bay was originally sprayed from the front with the hood installed, some areas did not receive complete coverage. This is especially noticeable on the back portion of the spring towers, the back of the radiator baffle panels, etc. When painting an engine compartment stripped to the bare body shell, it is possible to actually crawl up inside to do a better job than was originally possible at the factory.

In addition to thin spots, the factory-original underhood finish often included excess paint in some places. Engine compartment painting was done more for preservation than beauty, so often large runs and sags were the result of achieving adequate coverage.

A common place to find runs is underneath the hood hinges; on some cars it almost appears that paint was poured over the hinges rather than being sprayed on. For your engine compartment restoration you

Small squares of cloth tape were used to prevent the black sound deadener from entering the engine compartment through unused holes, such as those used for installation of the 6-cylinder battery tray. The tape was apparently applied during the painting process so body color paint is found on both sides of the tape, as well as underneath it.

PAINTING YOUR CAR

Stainless steel 1968 VIN plates were applied to the passenger-side spring tower before the paint process, so they were hastily masked with a similar-size piece of tape. It is common to see evidence of misalignment around the tag of original cars. Any paint that hit the tag quickly flaked off from the polished surface.

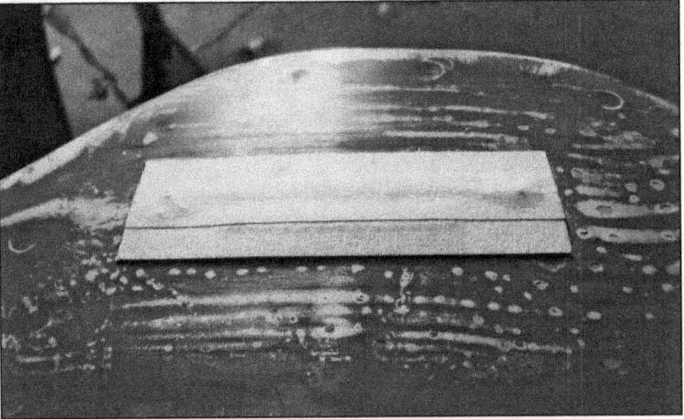

When restoring a 1968 or earlier AMC model, a little more care may be taken to neatly mask the spring tower VIN plate. Not only will the tag and spring tower have a cleaner appearance, it will save having to explain repeatedly why the tag wasn't neatly taped before paint.

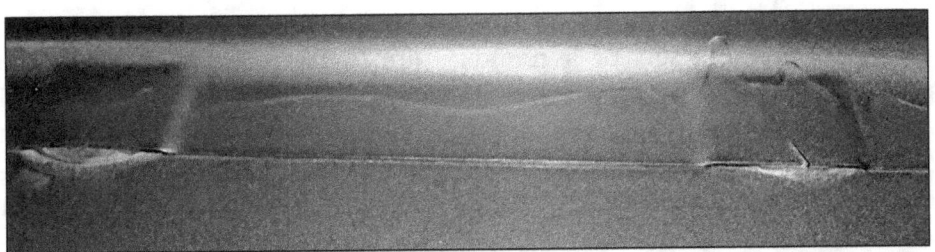

As with the engine compartment, AMC trunk areas were painted quickly; the goal was adequate coverage only. After paint, the trunk lid was closed to spray the exterior of the car. Any resulting paint runs on the underside of the trunk lid now appear to run uphill when the lid is in the open position.

Body-color paint found inside the body shell is merely the result of overspray from painting the rest of the car. This applies to the underbody as well. Cars with heavy, glossy paint on either side of the floorpan are actually over-restored, a look that is preferred by many owners.

may duplicate the factory-original painting method, or apply the finish as carefully as you would like. Keep in mind that even if you are being careful, a paint run or two cannot be considered a defect since nearly every car had some originally.

Trunk

The trunk area was originally painted in a similar fashion, but because it was a smaller area that was easier to reach, the trunk paint generally turned out nicer. Still, it is possible to find original cars with paint runs on the underside of the trunk lid. When spraying the exterior of the car, the trunk was closed while the paint was still wet, so with the lid open these paint drips appear to run uphill!

Overspray

Body-color paint originally found on the underbody or in the passenger compartment of the car was merely overspray deposited while painting the rest of the car. Here again, you have a choice depending on the type of restoration you have planned. A popular practice today is to actually over-restore a car by inverting the body shell on a rotisserie and painting the underside of the car as nicely as the top. Some also prefer to completely spray the body shell without any bolt-on parts installed, covering areas that originally received only a primer coat or no coverage at all.

Miscellaneous Details

Whenever possible, the front section of the driver-side frame rail should not be disturbed because this section contains the car's hidden partial VIN. This important number is often lightly stamped, sometimes not much deeper than the paint itself, and it can be obliterated with even moderate sanding. If this area is not rusted, simply degrease and then lightly scuff the surface with a Scotch-Brite pad before repainting. This will maintain the number's legibility as much as possible.

One detail often overlooked on 1968–1969 AMX and Javelin models is the small inspection sticker "shadow" found on the front part of the driver-side spring tower. This occurred as the result of a round sticker being applied to the spring tower before paint. The sticker then peeled off, leaving a small, round spot of primer that can often be seen on original cars. To include this original detail on your restoration, apply a small sticker (such as a garage sale price label) over black primer before painting the engine compartment. Following paint, the sticker can be removed, or left as is underneath the paint for a factory-fresh appearance.

Some 1970 model year AMX and Javelin cars had this painted-over sticker applied to the driver's side of the upper core support, but because not every car had one this detail is neither correct nor incorrect for 1970 cars unless documented as original.

On 1968–1970 AMX and Javelin models, the front fender and rear quarter panel extensions were also installed prior to paint. For 1970 AMX and Javelin models, the rear quarter extensions were made of plastic rather than metal, and these were loosely fitted, allowing some paint to get behind them. It should be noted that the rear quarter panel extensions differ between Javelin and AMX models, and that these extensions were eliminated with the 1971 redesign. Other AMC models, however, such as the 1970 Rebel Machine and 1971 Hornet SC/360, use rear extensions only.

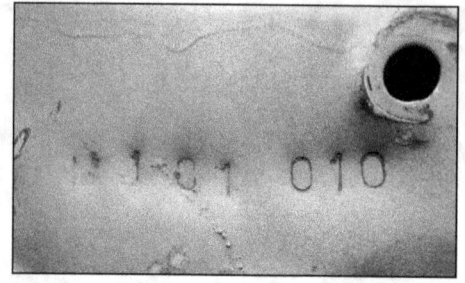

This frame rail VIN is heavily stamped. Most are stamped much lighter, in some cases barely through the paint. Even sanding lightly easily obliterates lightly stamped numbers, so that should be avoided. Instead, thoroughly clean and then scuff this area with a fine Scotch-Brite pad before refinishing.

This rust spot is the result of an inspection sticker applied to the front of the driver-side spring tower before paint. The 1968–1969 AMX and Javelin models had a circular dot of primer that soon appeared, then began to rust on cars used or stored in damp climates. Don't overlook this original detail when preparing your engine compartment for paint.

Before the original paint was applied, some 1970 Javelin and AMX models had an inspection sticker applied to the driver's side of the upper core support, resulting in a primer spot when the adhesive failed. After photo documenting it, duplicate this detail, if found, on your restoration project.

PAINTING YOUR CAR

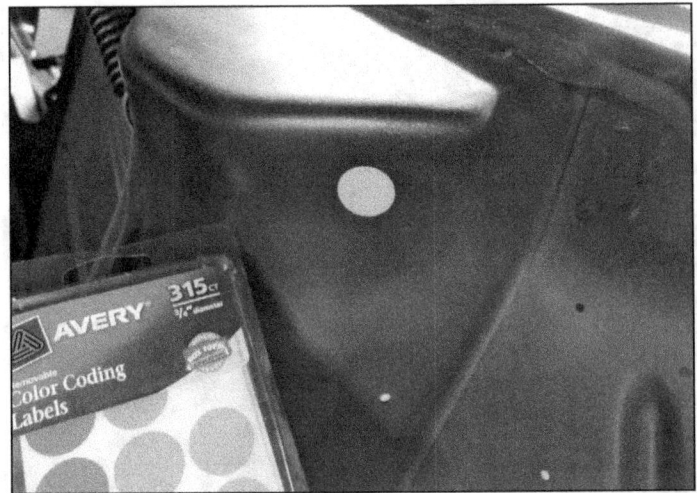

Inexpensive color-coded labels, or even garage sale price labels work well to duplicate the factory inspection label. Simply apply one over dark gray or black primer before repainting the engine compartment.

After applying paint, you have the choice of leaving the label in place or removing it to expose the primer coat underneath. Although this is a minor detail, it is one that will place your restoration above others, especially in stock class judging. Finished cars seen with an "OK" sticker applied over the paint are incorrect.

Front fender and rear quarter panel extensions were installed before the car was originally painted. An exception is the plastic rear extensions used on the 1970 AMX and Javelin. Because they were only loosely fitted, some body-color paint did get behind them. They were tightly secured after the paint process.

The hood latch for 1968 was installed after the car was painted, including the front-end blackout paint on light- to medium-colored cars. For this reason, the latch support should be painted as these are. However, the latch itself should be zinc coated rather than blacked out or painted to match the body color. The correct mounting bolts have a captive washer and phosphate coating.

A typical AMC car body was almost fully assembled before paint, including the hood, front fenders, doors, trunk lid, and rear valance panel, plus all of the required hardware and hinges. Other parts originally installed before paint were the lower fender braces (beginning mid-1968), hood latch support, grille support panel, front hood stops (minus the rubber bumpers), battery tray, cowl seal retainer band (secured by two screws), and steering column support rods located behind the dash, plus the trunk latch and striker.

The hood latch was installed after paint on most 1968 models, but was painted along with the rest of the body beginning in 1969. The hood and door strikers were installed after paint and should not be painted in the body color. On 1969 and newer 4-speed models, the clutch pedal was

CHAPTER 5

Bare steel showing on this 1969 AMX latch support reveals that the hood latch was installed before the car was originally painted. Beginning with the 1969 model year, the blackout paint added to the area behind the grille on light-colored cars also included the hood latch. Notice the paint runs on this original part.

With everything removed, and any surface rust or other defects repaired, this engine compartment is ready for primer and then body-color paint. Note that the 1968 VIN plate, located on the passenger-side spring tower, is carefully taped. These plates were actually installed before paint, and then masked before the car was first sprayed.

installed prior to paint, so the stud and nut in the engine compartment should be body color, and the pedal itself may have some overspray.

Cutting in the Color

If you have decided to apply at least some of the body color, single-stage acrylic enamel paint is great for cutting in the doorjamb areas as well as refinishing the engine compartment and trunk area.

Masking

After the prep work is complete, carefully mask off any areas that could be oversprayed with paint, including the outer body, windows, and any interior furnishings such as the dash, seats, or carpet that remains inside the car. I cannot say enough about careful and precise masking. Use a fresh plastic drop cloth to protect large areas, and as much tape as necessary to do the job right. The hours invested in a top-quality masking job is time well spent. In most cases, it takes a lot longer to mask than to paint.

Although actual masking paper is ideal, clean newspaper may be used for most masking jobs with adequate results. Just don't cut corners on the tape! Use only high-quality, automotive masking tape such as 3M green tape, which stays in place while painting, and then comes off cleanly even after several days. Aluminum foil is also effective for masking the front suspension, steering column, and other oddly shaped parts that remain on the car. Because it can be squeezed tightly against the part being masked, it does not block the surrounding areas from being painted. However, for the best results, remove everything from the engine compartment that should not be painted in the body color.

I recommend deviating a little from the original build sequence by painting the battery tray and cowl seal retainer band separately. That way, these items can be completely covered, even on the backside; if they are installed later, they will not prevent parts of the engine compartment from being coated. With only primer applied here originally, finding surface rust is fairly common in these vulnerable areas. By removing the front suspension and steering systems you can elevate the front of the body, and actually climb up inside to paint the engine compartment, ensuring better results than originally came from the factory. With care and patience, the underhood area can be

PAINTING YOUR CAR

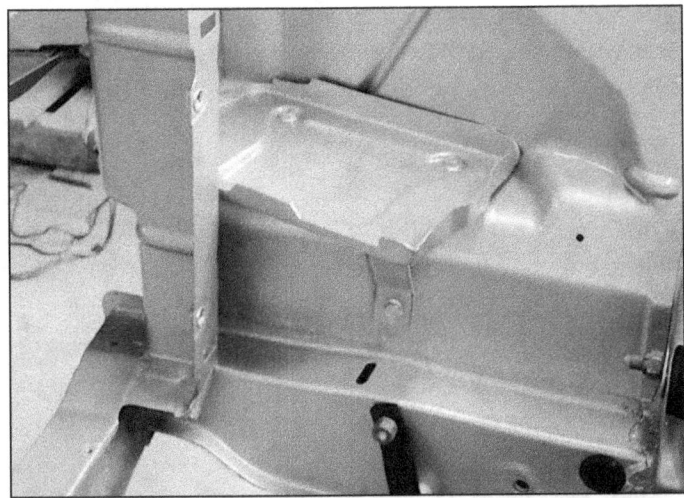

Although not done originally, painting the battery tray separately from the car allows adequate paint coverage underneath, as well as to the underside of the tray itself. Just be sure to paint the mounting bolts to match, and use great care not to chip them during installation.

Removing even thick areas of factory-applied sound deadener is easy once it is heated. Scraping off most of the undercoat with a dull putty knife leaves few gouges in the sheet metal; in fact it barely affects the original paint, making less prep work necessary before refinishing.

repainted with the body shell on its wheels.

Likewise, the area underneath the front fenders, as well as inside the rear wheel wells, can be stripped and refinished as necessary. The best time to paint underneath the front fenders is when spraying the engine compartment, which should prevent overspray and dry spots on either side of the inner fender.

Sound Deadener

If the factory-original sound deadener is still in good condition it can be scrubbed with a mild detergent and brush, and then freshened with a coat of semi-gloss black paint. Allow ample time for it to dry before refinishing. If the undercoat is chipping off, has become oil soaked, or shows signs of rust underneath, it must be removed.

The best way to strip the original sound deadener is to warm a small area using a heat gun, and then scrape it off using a dull putty knife; this does not scratch the surface underneath,

This brake hose bracket has become partially separated from the frame rail due to rust. It needs to be welded in place securely before this area of the wheel well is refinished. Check the brackets on both sides of the car to be sure nothing needs to be welded later.

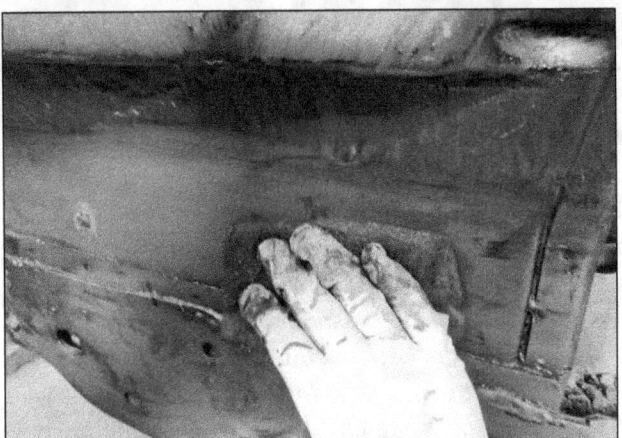

After time to cool, any sound deadener that cannot be scraped off is washed away easily with solvent and a Scotch-Brite pad. Follow up with paper towels and more solvent to finish. Once cool, the chunks of sound deadener scraped off earlier can be swept up easily.

AMC JAVELIN, AMX & MUSCLE CAR RESTORATION 1968–1974

CHAPTER 5

which would create additional prep work. As the chunks of discarded sound deadener fall to the ground and cool they become solid again, making it easy to sweep them up.

With the factory undercoat removed, you may notice that paint coverage underneath the fenders was minimal, covering little more than inside the spring tower where sound deadener would not be applied.

Coverage

When cutting in the paint be sure coverage is consistent with the surface of the outer body. This ensures a complete refinishing job, and allows easy masking of the areas previously painted when it's time to prep and paint the outer body. To achieve better coverage, the doorjambs and edges are frequently painted separately with the doors removed from the body. Although

With all of the sound deadener removed, the original paint pattern emerges underneath this front fender. Body-color paint was quickly applied, covering only the frame rail and parts of the inner fender that could be easily seen. When refinishing this area apply the paint in this fashion for a more authentic appearance, or increase the coverage if you prefer.

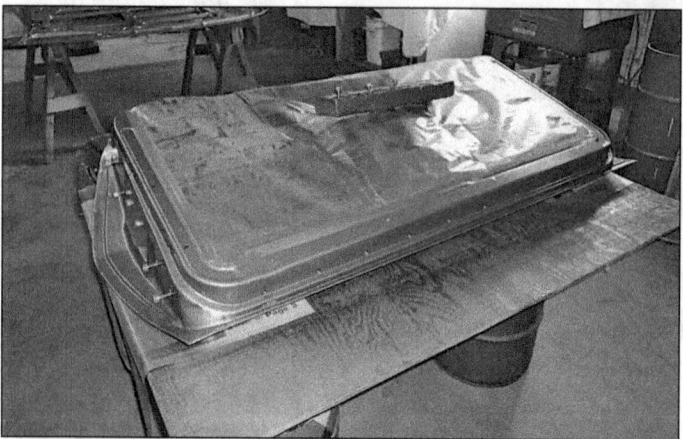

Refinishing the door edges separate from the car ensures even coverage. Unless you are painting a gutted door shell, cover any openings so the window regulator and door latch mechanisms are not oversprayed. Be sure to paint far enough onto the inside of the door so that the paint line is hidden by the interior door panel. Include the door mounting bolts so they are painted to match.

Although not following the factory-original assembly sequence, painting the doorjambs with the doors removed allows the hinges and the trailing edge of the front fenders to be well coated. Later, when installing the doors, protect the doorsills with towels or blankets to avoid scratching or chipping the new paint.

PAINTING YOUR CAR

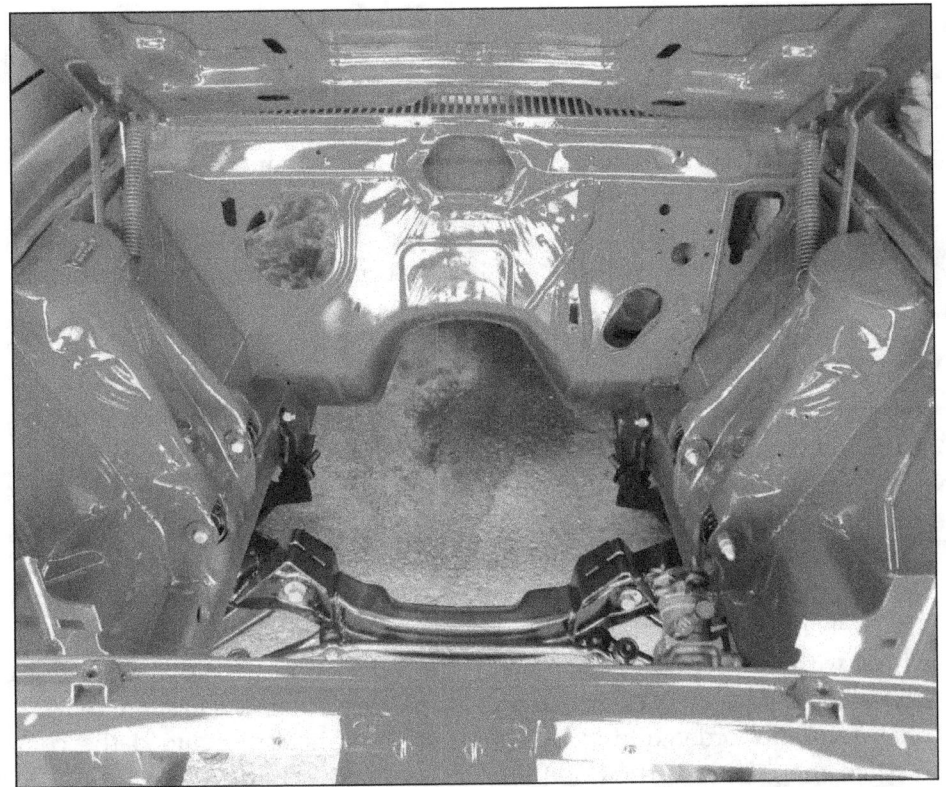

A gleaming engine compartment is the perfect place to install a hot AMC V-8. Even though all of this hard work will fade into the background somewhat once the engine is installed, a nicely painted engine bay looks terrific, and is easier to keep clean.

Oops, small parts such as these 1968 lower door hinge stops may be forgotten until after the car is painted. To refinish them later, mix a small amount of leftover body-color paint and then apply with a Preval paint sprayer setup. This is also a convenient way to touch up a small area, such as inside the engine compartment, if it becomes scratched.

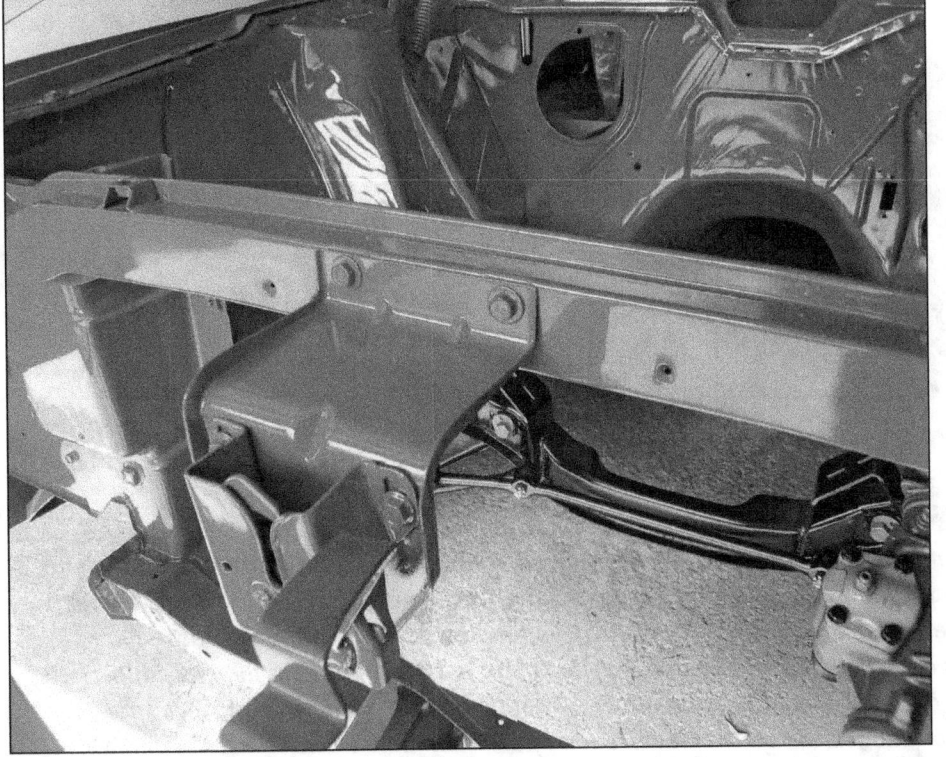

Because the upper core support is prominently located right up front, take extra care to prepare and paint it just as nicely as the outer body. Because of its boxed construction, small dents can be filled, and minor damage to the upper flange caused by careless engine removal can be straightened with a body hammer and dolly.

they were not done this way originally, better results can be expected using this method, especially around the hinges. Be sure to start the door mounting bolts into their holes in the leading edge of the door so they will also be painted.

Some additional parts may need to be painted separately, such as the aforementioned battery tray, cowl seal retainer band, and even the lower hinge door stops used on 1968 models. A good time to spray these parts is when painting the edge of the doors. For painting, small, three-dimensional parts can be hung from a bent wire coat hanger and smaller parts such as bolt heads can be inserted through a piece of cardboard and then placed on the masked center portion of the inner doors.

If you forget to paint something or need to do some minor touch-up, a Preval paint sprayer can be used to apply custom mixed paint with excellent results. Simply follow the recommended mixing ratio of color, reducer, and hardener as if using a paint gun. Because the spray pattern is very small, like that of an aerosol can, a Preval sprayer is only recommended for painting smaller parts. Also available are matching ready-to-use aerosol paints custom mixed by APS Tower Paint or Milwaukee Paint.

Exterior Body Paint

Most AMC muscle cars were painted in a conventional manner using a single color, but there were some exceptions. Trans Am Javelin models were sprayed white first, followed by the red front and blue rear sections that were painted later. Code 25A Rebel Machines were painted white, with the center of the hood, hood scoop, and lower body painted blue. Machines ordered in other colors had the center of the hood and scoop blacked out.

Hurst SC/Ramblers with the "A" paint scheme (characterized by red side panels) were painted a couple of different ways. Some cars were painted white first, then masked for application of the bright red sides. Other cars had the sides painted red first, which was then masked before the entire car was sprayed in white. This process can only be determined when stripping your car for paint, so be sure to document the original paint process when restoring an original SC/Rambler.

Just like the SC/Rambler, Javelin AMX models from 1971 to 1974 had the tail panel painted in low-gloss black if the car was equipped with the performance Go Package. This was done even on Go Package cars ordered in Classic Black paint. Of course, 1970 AMX models with the Shadow Mask two-tone option featured low-gloss black paint on the hood and fender tops that extended around the side windows; it also included the complete engine compartment.

Prep Work

If you will not be painting the exterior surface of your project car, follow your body shop's recommendations concerning any prep work

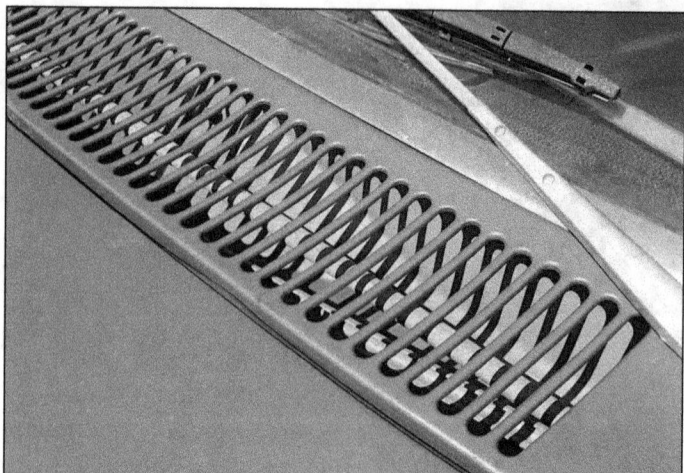

The windshield wiper transmission or linkage located within the cowl is commonly oversprayed in the body color during repaints. However, it should be removed before paint and detailed separately. The arms of the linkage were originally a light olive green. This is one item commonly checked by knowledgeable AMC car show judges.

Once removed, the windshield wiper transmission can be detailed after being stripped by glass-bead blasting. This one was refinished while completely assembled by carefully masking and then painting the individual parts in stages. Attending to details such as this will set your restoration apart from the others.

PAINTING YOUR CAR

Black paint requires extra care and close inspection of the surface before application, because this color accentuates any tiny ding or ripple that may have been missed during body repair. Here, the surface preparation was more than adequate, as the black paint applied to this AMX looks perfect.

The Shadow Mask paint option was only offered on the 1970 AMX, and is included on the door tag paint code. Low-gloss black was applied to the hood, fender tops, and around the side glass, as well as covering the complete engine compartment. A 1/4-inch-wide silver tape stripe divided the two colors.

or materials used so you don't create additional work for the painter. If you will be painting your car avoid mixing materials of different brands, or using outdated products left over from other projects. It's not worth the risk just to save some money; you have undoubtedly heard your share of painting horror stories!

If the front or rear window channels show signs of surface rust, excess paint build-up, or have become clogged with old sealer, remove the glass so you can properly clean and paint the channels. With the glass out, the channels can be sprayed along with the rest of the body. However, if all or part of the interior is still in place you may want to reinstall the glass before painting the car; window glass is much better than paper at keeping paint mist away from the dash and seats. Consult with your paint shop for their recommendation before deciding.

Also be sure to carefully mask any areas of the body that are already painted, or do not need to be refinished. This includes your rebuilt suspension and the rest of the underbody. It works well to mask from the backside of the lower rocker panel flange right to the floor below. If you are not the one masking and painting the exterior of your car, be very specific with your instructions about which areas need to be protected from overspray, or the car may come back with body-colored springs, gas tank, etc. It's always better to speak up and avoid a lot of unnecessary disassembly and detailing.

The bumpers, grille, exterior door handles, and most of the outer body trim must be removed before your project car is painted. A possible exception is the bright drip-rail moldings (also called rain gutters) found on many AMC muscle cars. Although these stainless steel moldings are easily removed by tapping along the bottom edge with a hammer and small block of wood, reinstalling the moldings is much more difficult, and often results in damage. A thicker coat of paint than originally applied to the drip rails may prevent the moldings from going on at all. For this reason, it is a common practice with AMC cars to leave these moldings in place, using great care to protect them when grinding, sanding, or painting nearby.

Paint Types

Body prep and paintwork is fairly straightforward: tedious hours spent block sanding primer and sealer until everything is perfect, then applying multiple coats of paint. Spraying metallic colors requires even more skill to achieve a uniform distribution of the metallic pigment.

As noted earlier, if you don't have a suitable area and painting experience, the outer body paintwork is best left to professionals. If you are determined to paint the car yourself, be sure to pick up a book on automotive painting. Because of the high cost of materials this is one area not to rely on beginner's luck! Professional bodywork and paint are expensive due in part to the high amount of labor involved, but it's worth it to ensure a successful outcome for what is likely the most visible part of your AMC muscle car restoration.

Even if you have used single-stage paint for the engine compartment or other areas, your body shop may recommend, or even insist on, using basecoat/clearcoat (BC/CC) paint for the exterior of the car. This may be the only type of paint they are experienced with, especially when spraying

Color sanding involves using extra-fine 1,500- and 2,000-grit sandpaper with a sanding block and lots of fresh water to remove any unwanted "orange peel," small specks of dirt, or other raised imperfections in the new finish. After wet sanding, the surface is polished with a high-speed orbital buffer until a very high gloss is achieved.

If your goal is an authentic appearance you may be satisfied with the finish right out of the paint booth, or with minimal color sanding. Notice here that the front fender extensions were installed before paint, just as original. Completing the exterior paint is a giant step in the restoration process!

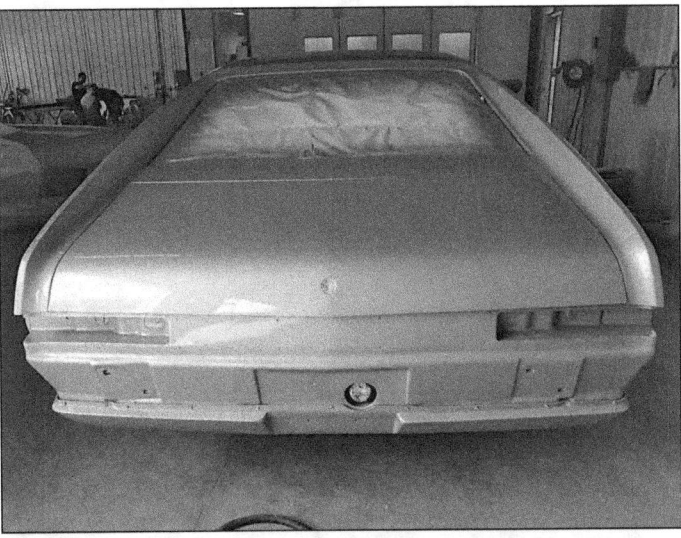
Before painting, be sure to seal off every opening to the trunk or passenger compartment, especially if interior parts are still in place or if the trunk area has already been refinished. This includes the openings in the firewall from the steering column, heater fan motor, throttle linkage or cable, etc.

metallic colors. However, when applied correctly, the difference in appearance is negligible and the color should be identical. Nevertheless, for a particularly authentic restoration of an AMC muscle car only single-stage acrylic enamel paint should be used for every area of the car.

Finishing

Once the exterior of your car is painted you have to decide how smooth you want the finish to appear. Most factory paint jobs, even on contemporary cars, have some "orange peel," which is a slight texturing of the finish resulting from paint that has not flowed out smoothly. Most painters strive for a perfectly smooth "wet look" by color sanding the paint with 1,500- then 2,000-grit sandpaper, followed by skilled buffing and hand polishing. If you want to maintain a more authentic, factory-type finish you may not need to color sand and buff the car at all. Otherwise, urge your paint shop to leave a slight amount of orange peel

Following a complete paint job, no emblems, moldings, or sidemarker lights should be installed until all of the buffing and polishing is complete, the paint has had adequate time to cure, and the body has received its first coat of wax. It's tempting to start installing these parts right away, but don't get ahead of yourself as it only makes more work for you later.

Caring for Paint

Even a catalyzed finish (paint mixed with hardener) needs time to cure. Do not cover a fresh paint job with blankets, a car cover, or even a fender cover until the paint is fully cured. Wait at least 30 days before applying tape stripes, graphics, or a vinyl top over fresh paint. This is also a safe time frame before using any type of wax or sealer.

If you need to roll the body shell outdoors temporarily, don't allow bird droppings, tree sap, or fresh grass clippings to come in contact with a new paint job (or any paint job, for that matter) because these caustic substances can inflict permanent damage. If you find any of these substances on the body, immediately move the car to a shaded area and gently wash off any of the residue without scrubbing, using only cool, clean water.

Common sense dictates not setting anything on or against a newly painted car. Do not allow tree branches or anything hanging nearby to contact the paint in case the wind suddenly picks up. The primary goal for a successful restoration is for the entire car to look brand new when it is completely assembled; the overall appearance of the paint job is a big part of this. Take any precautions necessary to ensure this outcome.

CHAPTER 6

ENGINE AND TRANSMISSION

If your AMC restoration project happens to be a car that you have been driving, even infrequently, you are in a good position because you already know the car in a mechanical sense. This means that you know how it runs and drives, and if there are any leaks or other concerns including low oil pressure, a slipping clutch, or tired automatic transmission to be concerned with. However, if your project car is newly acquired, particularly if it was purchased not running, you have to assume the worst but hope for the best.

Inspection

With a newly purchased car, especially one that has not been driven in a while, begin with a thorough visual inspection of the running gear. Note any leaks, missing or damaged components, or other potential faults. You may want to pull one or both valve covers to check for sludge buildup on the cylinder heads and to make sure that all of the rocker arms are in their proper position and not excessively loose.

If everything looks good, replace the valve covers and check all of the fluids. Look for the milky appearance of coolant in the oil, contaminated or brown-colored automatic transmission fluid, or any other problems. Make sure that the radiator is topped off and that the coolant is not brown with rust. Don't forget the automatic transmission, as well as the power steering and brake master cylinder reservoirs.

If the oil level and all of the other fluids check out okay, the next step is to prime the oil system. Do this by removing the distributor, and then use a powerful drill to rotate the oil pump shaft with a priming tool. A priming tool can be purchased or

A more secure way to park an engine and transmission is with a sturdy crate underneath the transmission mount, and the engine mounts resting on jack stands. The engine or transmission can actually be serviced this way because the oil or automatic transmission pans may still be removed.

made from the shaft removed from an old distributor. Simply clamp a short section of rubber fuel hose flush with the end of the blade to keep the tool positioned on the oil pump shaft. Afterward, reinstall the distributor in its original position. Remove the spark plugs, and try to turn over the engine with a 1/2-inch-drive breaker bar and socket on the crankshaft bolt. If it rotates freely, clean and reinstall the spark plugs.

If the engine has been dormant for more than six months, disconnect the fuel supply line where it enters the fuel pump and install a temporary source of fresh gasoline. You may also wish to change the carburetor and fuel pump with ones known to be good, since a faulty pump can leak gas into the oil pan, which thins the oil and can potentially cause damage to the engine. Install a trusted mechanical oil pressure gauge, even if it is only temporarily held in place by the windshield wiper so it can be seen from inside the car.

Unlike other makes, AMC V-8 engines don't produce or require a lot of oil pressure, so expect about 60 to 70 psi of oil pressure from a cold engine. At hot idle, 20 psi is adequate. Oil pressure significantly lower than this indicates a potential problem that needs to be addressed right away.

Check all electrical connections as well as the complete wiring harness; look for cut or bare wires, evidence of anything modified, or wiring that had become too hot at some point. With good wiring, a fresh battery installed, and a helper with a fire extinguisher standing nearby, try cranking the engine. Cars that have sat unused for an extended period may not start using the key. If this is the case, double-check all of the electrical connections, then if everything looks good replace the starter solenoid switch mounted on the inner fender, or use a jumper wire to bypass it with the key in the "run" position.

As soon as the engine fires, check the oil pressure gauge and listen for any unusual noises such as knocking or ticking. If the oil pressure is low, or if you hear *anything* that you don't recognize, shut it down immediately and consult a qualified specialist. But, if everything sounds good, check now for any new leaks or for smoke coming from the oil filler tube, which can indicate worn piston rings or cylinder wear. Initial smoke at startup coming from the exhaust should clear momentarily. Within a few minutes the engine should settle into a nice smooth idle.

With the engine running well, now is the time to assess the condition of the transmission. If your car has good brakes it can be "yard driven." If not, secure the car with sturdy jack stands on a level concrete floor, and run the transmission

Bringing a long-dormant engine back to life requires a specific procedure. This includes installing a good battery and a temporary source of fresh gasoline. An empty plastic jug from windshield washer fluid along with a section of 5/16-inch fuel hose works well; it can be tied to the inner fender or core support so you can yard-drive the car.

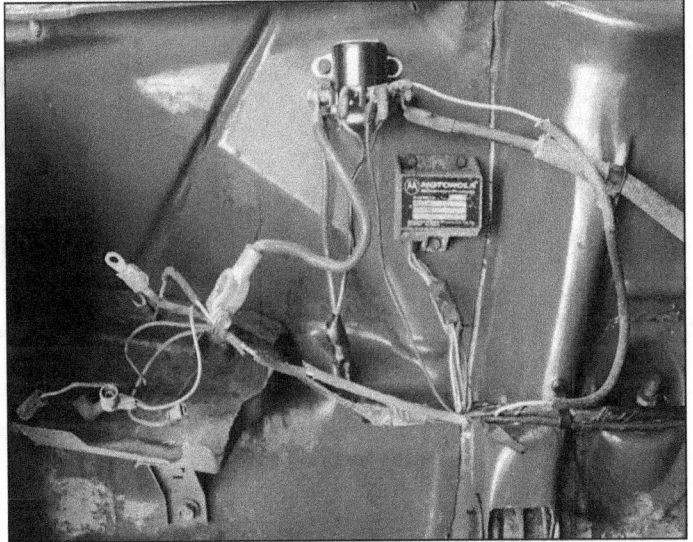

If the engine does not start with the key after long-term storage, the problem could be the starter solenoid. Test it with a jumper wire connecting the large terminals. If the engine now cranks, replace the solenoid with a new one. The original positive battery cable from this car was apparently discarded along with a dead battery.

through the gears, including reverse. Check the operation of the speedometer and other gauges now. Make note of any instruments that do not work so they can be attended to later.

After running the engine and driving the car, or at least simulating some driving, you now have a much better idea of how to proceed with the engine and transmission service. If everything turns out to be in excellent condition, which frequently *does* happen, you may opt to simply replace some gaskets, and then clean and refinish the drivetrain before putting it back in the car. However, if fluid leaks, blue smoke, or any strange noises have presented themselves during your inspection, a more thorough repair, or possibly a complete rebuild, may be in order.

Removal

Before attempting to remove the engine, make a checklist to be sure that *everything* is disconnected. This includes the exhaust system, heater and coolant hoses, automatic transmission cooling lines, all of the electrical connections as well as the starter cable, the fuel line, throttle linkage or cable, any vacuum hoses, both engine mounts, and the ground cable located on the passenger's side of the engine crossmember. Don't forget to disconnect the speedometer cable and shifter or clutch linkage if the transmission remains with the engine.

The engine and transmission can be removed as a unit, and if necessary, separated later. The engine and transmission can be removed from the top or from the bottom. If the front suspension and steering systems are being removed for rebuilding or detailing, it is fairly easy to raise the car body off the engine and transmission, which remain below on a rolling cart. This method reverses the factory original build sequence, and reduces the possibility of damage caused by removing the engine from the top. With enough overhead clearance you do not even need to remove the hood using this method.

More common, though, is to extract the engine, with or without transmission, from the top. Of course, this requires removal of the hood as well as exercising great care to prevent damage to the firewall and upper core support. Always remove and safely store the grille before beginning to prevent damaging it. Wrap the upper core support with towels and tape them in place to protect it.

Proper placement and adjustment of the chain used for lifting the engine is crucial to achieve the optimum angle for removal. An engine tilter, used in place of a single chain, allows the angle of the engine to be adjusted during the removal process, and may prove to be helpful. Be sure to use Grade-8 bolts to attach the chain because lower-graded or ungraded bolts can break when you least expect it, causing serious injury or damage.

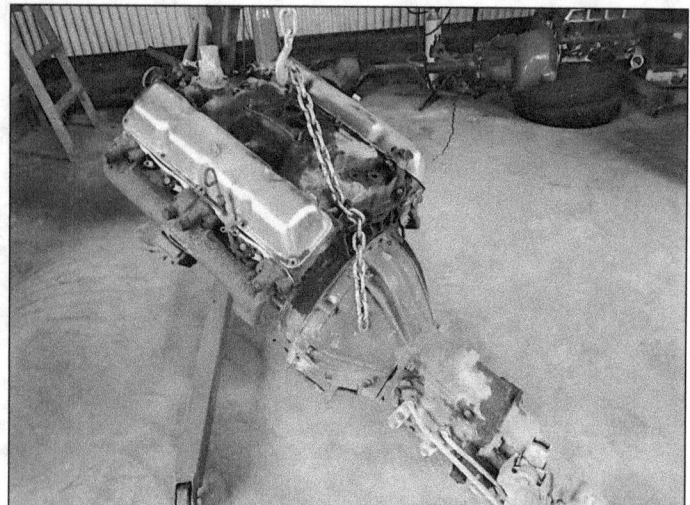

After testing the mechanical condition of the drivetrain, the engine and transmission can be removed from the car as a unit. If the engine will be rebuilt, separate the transmission and bellhousing and deliver it to a qualified machine shop for inspection. Otherwise, set it aside for future detailing and reinstallation.

A traditional method for storing an engine and transmission is to set the complete assembly on an old, unmounted tire. Just be sure that the oil pan does not contact the ground because it could be damaged. Also be sure that the engine does not list to one side once the chain is removed!

ENGINE AND TRANSMISSION

As the engine and transmission are slowly hoisted from the engine compartment, maintain adequate clearance front and rear, as well as at the sides. Once the engine is free of its mounts it may want to rotate it, so have a helper ready to guide it. Prior removal of the crankshaft pulley as well as any accessories and brackets reduces the mass and makes the engine much easier to remove from the top.

If the transmission has not been drained beforehand, the driveshaft can remain inserted in the transmission (when separated from the rear axle) to contain the fluid, until the engine is nearly out. Of course, a better solution is to use a specialized transmission plug, or an extra yoke that will take the place of the driveshaft and that can be left in the tailshaft the entire time.

With the engine about halfway out, and the transmission entering into the engine compartment, clearance underneath the car is now less important than the oil pan clearing the upper core support. At this stage, you may lower the core support liftover height a few precious inches by temporarily deflating both front tires.

A heavy-duty wheeled cart is the best choice for an engine and transmission that must be moved often. An engine cart is also required for removing an engine from the bottom; it can be used to scoot the engine out from underneath the car as soon as the body is lifted high enough for clearance.

With the engine and transmission fully removed from the car, set them aside, supported by jack stands or resting on an unmounted tire. Be

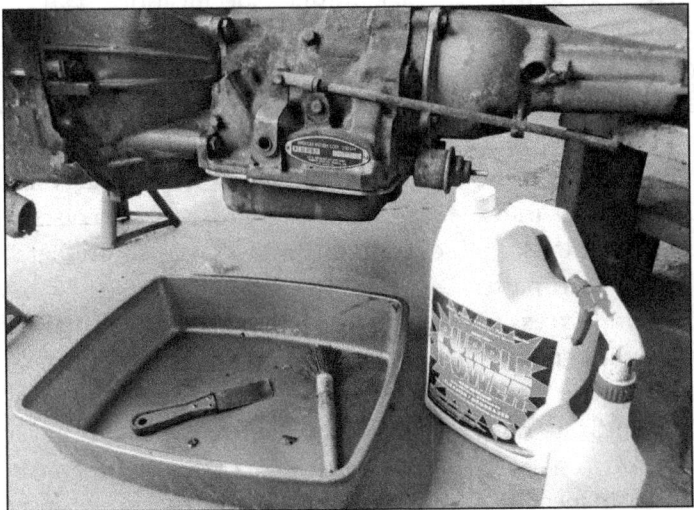

Careful hand washing with a strong solvent and parts cleaning brush is the preferred method of degreasing an original engine and transmission. A large pan used underneath the section you are working on can contain a lot of the mess. Use a dull putty knife first to remove the heaviest deposits of oil and gunk.

Hand washing your engine may reveal important original details that could be lost by steam cleaning or pressure washing. This orange paint daub marks the passenger's side of a 1968 BorgWarner M11-A automatic transmission bellhousing. Record these details so they can be duplicated as the finishing touch to your restoration.

CHAPTER 6

The original application of AMC engine paint was spotty. Although some engines received inadequate coverage and began rusting almost immediately, others received so much paint that runs appeared before it had a chance to dry. The exhaust manifolds and spark plug heat shields were originally painted along with the engine.

The AMC V-8 starter motor was also installed before the engine was originally painted. The nut that secures the starter cable was painted as well. Notice that the starter housing was black originally, and remains black on the side that faces the engine.

especially careful that the engine doesn't tip, and be sure not to damage the oil pan or transmission parts. There will likely be a puddle of engine coolant or automatic transmission fluid left on the floor. Have some oil absorbent ready so that no one slips and is hurt.

If you suspect that your engine needs to be rebuilt, deliver it to a qualified automotive machine shop so the block, cylinder heads, and crankshaft can be checked and machined as required. Consult your favorite speed shop for manufacturer's specifications to select a new camshaft and lifter set designed for your car's intended use.

If the engine will not be leaving, it can be degreased in preparation for internal inspection, disassembly, or repainting before it is reinstalled. Be sure to seal any openings before washing or degreasing the engine. Careful, deliberate cleaning may reveal original inspection markings, so take your time and have your digital camera ready. If the engine will be sitting for a while, cover it to keep out dust, insects, and other foreign matter.

Disassembly

If your engine has average miles or an unknown history, partial disassembly is required for a complete internal inspection. With the transmission and bellhousing removed, secure the engine to a sturdy four-leg engine stand, which allows rotation for ease of service.

Before beginning the disassembly be very careful to keep track of all hardware and every part that was removed. When inspecting the internals be sure to number the crankshaft bearing caps with a punch so they can be reinstalled in the same position. Keep the rocker arms, pushrods, and lifters in order for the same reason. Rearranging parts such as these without completely rebuilding the engine almost certainly results in shorter engine life and eventual component failure. If you plan to disassemble multiple engines you may want to locate or build a specialized tray to index your internal engine components.

Start by removing the "tin" parts: valve covers and oil pan. Excessive sludge buildup on the cylinder heads or in the lifter valley with the intake manifold removed can indicate high miles or infrequent oil changes. In this case, be sure to inspect the crankshaft bearings for wear. Further inspection may require removal of the cylinder heads to examine the pistons and cylinder walls.

Even if everything else checks out fine, replacement of the timing chain set and water pump is recommended for every engine. Always change the valvestem seals and rear main oil seal as well. Also inspect the oil pump gears and thrust plate for wear. If the oil pump gears are worn and have razor-sharp edges, replace them! Be sure the oil pickup screen is free of debris.

The reassembly sequence and exact torque specifications can be found in your TSM. Follow these instructions to the letter and you will have no leaks or mechanical malfunctions to deal with later. Use only top-quality, name-brand gaskets and seals such as Fel-Pro; this is no place to cut corners just to save a few dollars!

Painting and Detailing

With the engine reassembled and completely degreased, it's time to apply a good coat of high-temperature engine enamel in the color used originally. Early 1968 cars used Caravelle Blue metallic, while late-1968 through 1973 engines wore AMC Blue metallic (which is a bit greener). Engines installed in 1974 and later used a similar but nonmetallic AMC

ENGINE AND TRANSMISSION

After removing the engine, a variety of small parts can be stripped by glass-bead blasting, and then refinished separately or painted along with the engine if appropriate. Be sure to completely disassemble the oil pump for inspection before stripping the timing chain cover. Original water pump housings are becoming scarce, but your pump can be rebuilt if necessary.

Unless recently rebuilt, any engine benefits from the installation of a new timing chain. If the engine is partially disassembled be sure to seal any openings before scraping, sanding, or preparing for paint. Leave an old set of spark plugs in place when degreasing and painting an engine.

Blue. An exception to the blue AMC engines was found in cars shipped to California in 1972. These cars were required by law to have red-painted engines indicating their emissions compliance. If your car has a red California engine be sure to document the original color with photos before refinishing the engine.

Despite being fully assembled, AMC V-8s were not painted well originally, so in many cases chipping and surface rust quickly appeared. Other engines received so much paint that it looks as if it were poured on instead of being sprayed with a gun. Taking a bit more care in painting your engine ensures that it will look great for years to come with little or no touch-up required.

Surprisingly, the chrome-finish valve covers used for the AMX 390-ci V-8 were installed before painting the engine. Instead of masking them with paper and tape, which would have been much too time consuming, rectangular covers were set over them to shield the chrome finish from paint spray. For this reason, it is common to see original 390 valve covers with blue engine paint showing on the lower edges. This small detail can be duplicated for an extremely authentic 390 restoration.

Other parts installed before the engine was originally painted were the alternator bracket (except for the upper Z-shaped brace), timing cover, water pump, harmonic balancer, oil filler tube and cap (except for the chrome-plated cap on the AMX 390 engine), oil dipstick handle and tube, exhaust manifolds with heat shields, emissions control air tube assemblies on manual-transmission cars, vertical air cleaner heat duct, and starter motor. Naturally, all of the related attaching hardware would have been painted with the engine as well,

Intended to identify emissions compliance, some 1972 engines were required by law to be painted red if the vehicle in which it was installed would be sold as a new car in California. An original red engine should be well documented before beginning the restoration process as proof that the color is indeed correct.

Despite the fact that American Motors painted every engine with the valve covers installed, most restorers prefer to install the chrome-plated 390-ci V-8 valve covers following the paint process. Carefully mask the tops of the cylinder heads as shown, as well as the intake manifold valley if an unpainted aluminum intake is planned for the engine.

including the crankshaft bolt and washer (that were then removed to install the crank pulley).

AMC engines were also painted with the transmission bellhousing bolted up, so this part generally received at least some engine paint as well. Many automatic transmission bellhousings were completely covered, while 4-speed bellhousings generally received only overspray covering the front 3 to 4 inches. Engine paint application was done quickly and varies from car to car, so pay close attention to your engine's original spray patterns and coverage during your teardown if you wish to faithfully duplicate its original appearance.

Some parts not painted along with the engine include the mounts and brackets, all pulleys, and the alternator bracket support. These were all finished in semi-gloss black paint. Also installed after the engine was painted was the thermostat housing, as well as the power steering and emissions equipment mounting brackets. (I discuss detailing of the engine accessories as well as the rest of the engine compartment in Chapter 7.)

Transmission

Transmissions used in performance models were originally left unpainted. The BorgWarner T-10 4-speed used a cast-iron case that can be protected after cleaning by using clear engine enamel or cast-iron-finish paint. The 3-speed manual transmissions can be similarly refinished. BorgWarner model M11 and M12 automatic transmissions used through the 1971 model year included a cast-iron case combined with an aluminum tail shaft and bellhousing. After cleaning or media blasting, the aluminum tail shaft can be clearcoated while the bellhousing is finished in the engine color.

Chrysler-sourced automatic transmissions found in 1972 and later cars used an aluminum case that can also be clearcoated after careful cleaning and prep.

Although the exhaust manifolds were originally painted in enamel along with the engine, the paint quickly burned off, leaving them bare cast iron. Many restorers prefer to coat the manifolds with a high-temperature coating that is durable enough to remain in place and prevent surface rust.

Take whatever precautions are necessary to avoid scratches or damage to the car or engine when reinstalling the drivetrain. Here, a blanket protects the engine crossmember while foam sheeting covers the intake manifold where the lifting chain makes contact. Previously, the upper core support was wrapped with another blanket for protection.

ENGINE AND TRANSMISSION

The cast-iron case of a BorgWarner automatic transmission is mated to a fully painted bellhousing. This transmission was removed from a one-owner 1968 AMX and had not been out of the car since being installed on the Kenosha assembly line. Original cars are the best source of definitive restoration details.

This is a BorgWarner M12 transmission that has been refinished with cast-iron paint on the main case and clear engine enamel on the aluminum tail shaft. The bellhousing still needs to be painted in AMC Blue along with the engine. Although it won't be entirely visible, there is satisfaction in knowing that your transmission is protected from the elements while having an authentic appearance.

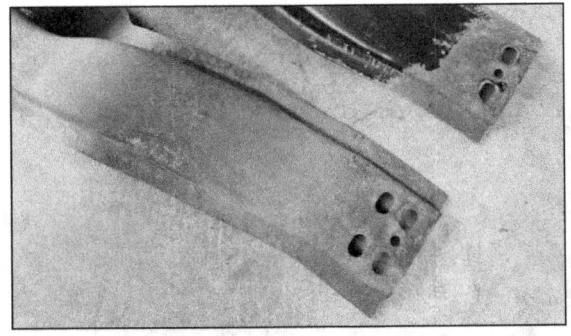

The transmission crossmember used for 1968 models was painted semi-gloss black, while 1969 and newer ones (with additional bolt holes) were left natural. After glass-bead blasting, preserve the appearance of the bare-steel crossmember with a coat of clear engine enamel.

Exhaust-manifold heat shields were designed to protect spark plug wires. As with manifolds, these were originally installed and then painted with the engine. Although all four shields appear to be interchangeable, the passenger-side front shield (right) is a modified two-piece design that is used in conjunction with the air cleaner heat duct. These shields are often rusted away, or missing completely from cars that had exhaust headers. Fortunately, good replacements are generally available.

CHAPTER 7

ENGINE COMPARTMENT

Your car's underhood area represents a detailing opportunity that can elevate your car above all others at a judged show or other automotive competition. As you know, a car's hood is generally left open while on display at most car shows and even at casual cruise-ins. This illustrates the importance of careful engine compartment detailing and presentation. The engine is a muscle car's primary focal point so don't rush this aspect of the restoration; it is just as important as the outside of the car.

Unlike Ford and General Motors muscle cars, which commonly had black-painted engine compartments, AMC vehicles were painted in the body color under the hood, which looks great and photographs better when the subject is a brightly colored car. The trade-off is additional upkeep, as lighter-colored engine compartments need to be cleaned more often to maintain their factory-fresh appearance.

Before disassembling your project car be sure that you have a complete set of clear, well-lit photos showing the engine compartment from every angle. Include shots of the wiring harness routing, the arrangement of the windshield washer system, any vacuum hoses, and the position of every clamp or retainer found under the hood. Take detailed photos of the wiring, hoses, or cables that pass through the firewall just behind the driver-side hood hinge. If necessary, make a diagram as there are differences depending on model year and equipment. Unused holes in this plate were sealed with plastic body plugs.

Also document everything in the vicinity of the windshield wiper motor because a wiring harness retainer or windshield washer hose tee may be included with the wiper-motor mounting hardware. It may seem very simple, but after weeks

Begin your engine compartment restoration by taking a complete set of photos after degreasing, but before beginning the disassembly. Include overall shots and detailed photos documenting every underhood detail. These pictures will come in handy when it's time to reassemble everything.

ENGINE COMPARTMENT

An original lower radiator hose removed from a 1968 AMX displays the part number and early-style "AM" logo in white. Lower radiator hoses commonly contain a spring to prevent collapsing. As with the top hose, it was secured with Wittek tower-style hose clamps at either end.

The hood striker and mounting bolts were installed after the body was painted, so they retain their original plated finish. Directly behind this is a formed rubber seal that fits against the upper core support on factory air-conditioned cars. Also included with air conditioning were thin rubber flaps clipped to the lower core support and stapled to the top radiator filler panel.

or even months pass you may not remember how things were originally installed or routed, and your "before" photos will save you a lot of unnecessary research.

Refinishing Small Parts

Many underhood parts were originally painted by dipping a rack of identical parts through a layer of black paint suspended on a large vat of water, then hanging them until dry. The evidence of this coating method is the runs found on many brackets and other small parts. It was simply more efficient to paint a large quantity of parts this way rather than spraying them individually.

Most restorers, however, are unwilling to go to this much trouble just to refinish individual parts, regardless of how authentic the restoration, preferring to spray them instead. For small parts that were originally painted, many specialized spray paints are available that duplicate a variety of factory-type finishes. Don't buy into the dreaded stigma of "rattle can" restorations! Every restoration shop uses some spray paint, and aerosol paints manufactured by Seymour, SEM, Eastwood, and others do an excellent job for refinishing interior, underhood, and chassis parts.

Cast-iron finish paint is great for preserving steel parts originally left bare by the factory. Clear engine enamel also works well for steel parts that have been glass-bead blasted first. Other paints simulate a variety of original plated coatings such as gold-cadmium or galvanized. Aluminum and stainless finish paints can be used on a variety of parts as well. Experiment with test panels to find the exact finish that you have to duplicate. You will soon have a few "go to" colors that you use again and again.

After being stripped or blasted and then washed with solvent, three-dimensional parts can be suspended from straightened wire coat hangers with a hook formed at the end. This allows the part to be completely painted all at once, then left to air dry without sticking to newspaper or anything else. Make at least a half-dozen parts hangers so multiple pieces can be painted together.

When restoring an original, unmodified car, close-up, detailed photos of the windshield wiper motor and surrounding area record important original details including the wiring harness routing and the position of the small plastic tee used for the windshield washer system. These items vary by year and equipment installed. Duplicate these details exactly for a high-quality restoration.

For the highest-quality, most authentic restorations, bolts and other hardware that are rusted or discolored may be replaced with new pieces, or stripped and replated in the original finish. In many cases, a fastener's original coating can still be seen on the threads or underneath the head where it was protected. Having hardware replated can be expensive and time consuming.

For most projects, simply refinishing bolts and other hardware with paint is preferable. Bolt heads can be painted by inserting the threaded portion of the fastener into holes drilled in a board, or even holes punched through thick cardboard. Great care must be taken when installing painted bolts since wrenches or sockets may chip the paint on the head, quickly causing it to rust. Protect painted bolt heads from chipping with a layer of plastic bag while installing them. You can use the small snack bag that held the bolts. Once carefully installed, properly refinished hardware will look great indefinitely.

Cowl and Firewall

An AMC windshield wiper motor is located at the center of the cowl. Optional electric wiper motors originally had a gold-cadmium–plated finish, while the standard vacuum-operated motor was plated with a silver-colored finish. It is common to upgrade to electric windshield wipers when restoring a car, but before spending good money for the parts required for this upgrade (motor, linkage, switch, etc.) consider how often the wipers will actually be used on a show car, or even one driven only on weekends. For the rare instances when you may be caught in rain, a coat of Rain-X on the windshield is generally all that you need. Vacuum-operated wipers also have variable speed adjustments not found on the early electric setups. After giving it some thought you may elect to stay with vacuum-operated windshield wipers.

Windshield Wiper Motor Installation

Great care must be taken to install the windshield wiper motor without damaging the painted surface of the cowl. Follow these steps to prevent unneeded damage to your newly refinished engine compartment.

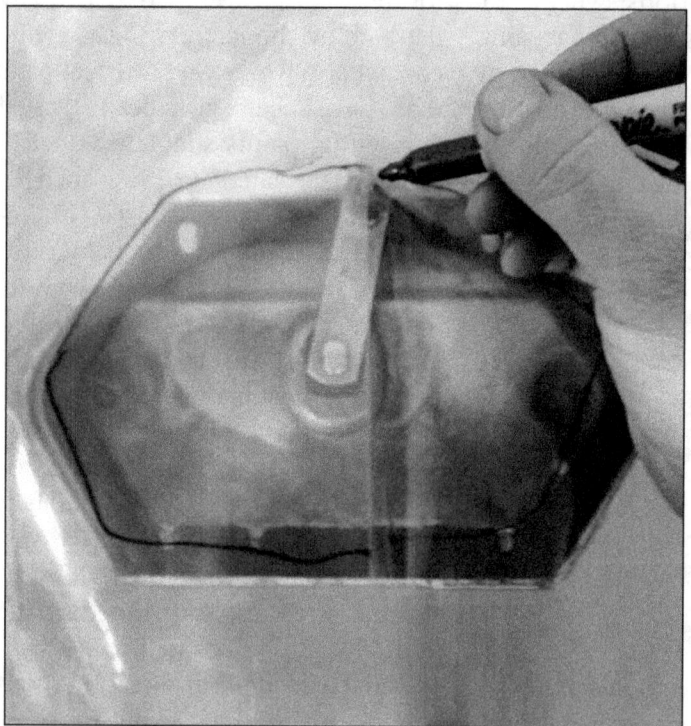

1 Begin by locating some heavy plastic or protective foam sheeting. Trace a rough outline of the wiper motor mounting plate, then cut an access hole.

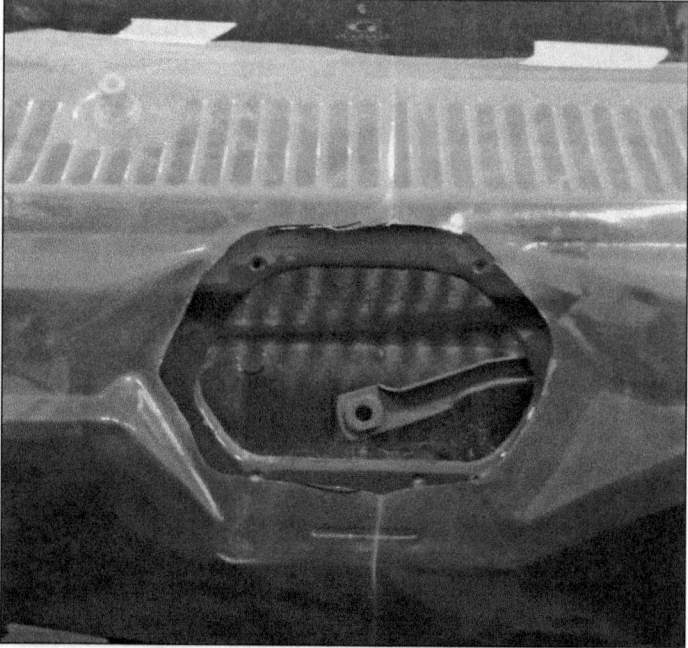

2 After installation of the wiper transmission linkage, securely tape the protective sheet in place. Leaving the nuts on the wiper mounting posts slightly loose allows the linkage to be rotated a bit, which makes connecting the wiper motor easier.

ENGINE COMPARTMENT

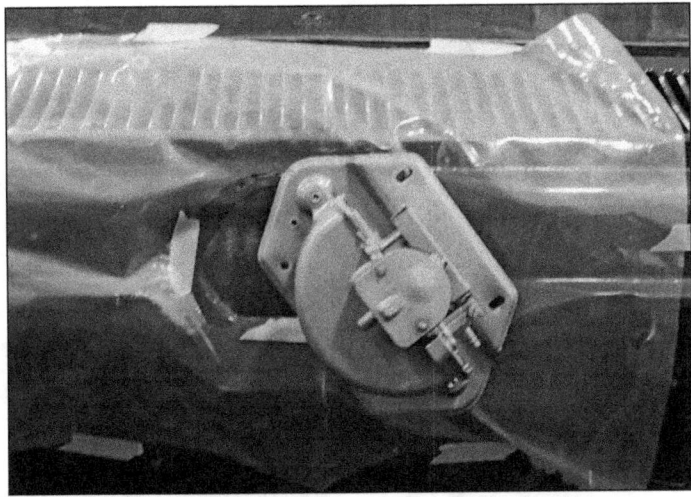

3 Rotate the wiper motor until the transmission linkage can be fully engaged and secured to the motor with the locking clip. This is where protective sheeting can save your paint job.

4 Once the wiper motor is in position, remove the protective sheeting and secure the motor to the cowl with Phillips screws. Tighten the mounting post nuts to complete the installation.

Early reassembly of the engine compartment includes the brake lines, heater fan motor, and windshield wiper motor. Here, the rubber cowl seal above the wiper motor is also installed, secured by a formed steel band painted in the body color.

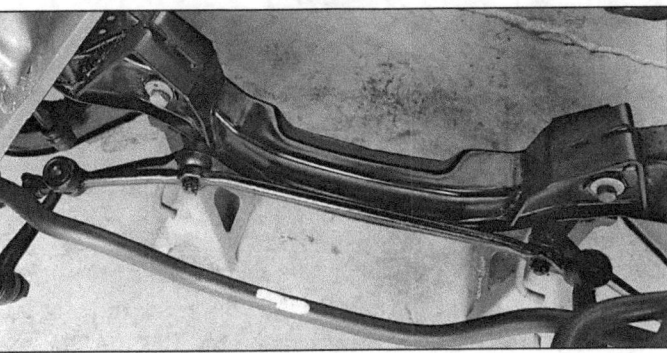

As with many chassis parts, 1968 cars have a black-painted engine crossmember. This component needs to be removed from the car to properly refinish it. Parts from newer cars that were never originally painted must be protected from surface rust. Using cast-iron paint or even clear engine enamel works well for this purpose.

The windshield wiper motor, whether vacuum or electric, is attached with a small clip to the wiper linkage, which is positioned inside the cowl. Because the linkage must be installed first, protect the painted cowl area, and then insert the linkage and wiper motor gasket before attaching the linkage to the motor. Once attached, remove the protective covering and secure the wiper motor mounting plate with original-type Phillips screws.

If the engine will be reinstalled from the top, and the engine mounting crossmember has been removed, replacing it early in the process is beneficial because it provides a lifting point to help stabilize the car. Engine crossmembers were painted black in 1968; they were left bare for 1969 and later model years.

When protected with a towel or blanket, the crossmember also provides a place to sit when installing the brake distribution block and formed steel brake lines, which run across the firewall. The brake lines should be installed before the wiring

CHAPTER 7

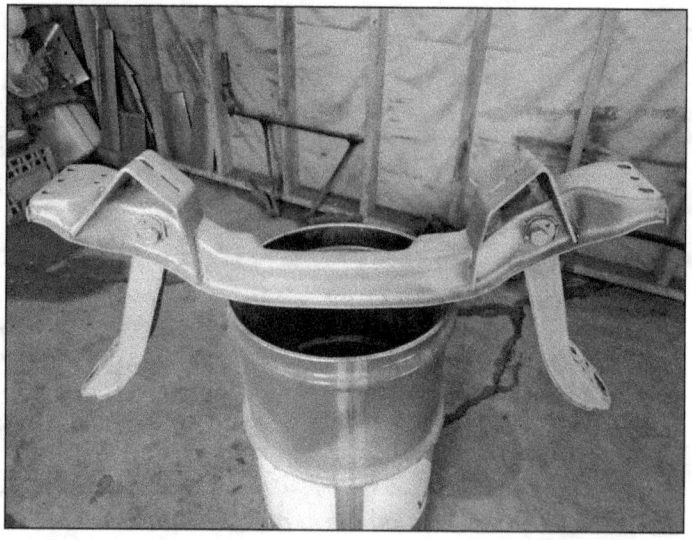

After replacing the lower control arm bushings, the engine crossmember can be media blasted as an assembly. The 1968 cars had this part painted semi-gloss black. The crossmember and suspension components on 1969 and newer models were left bare, and must be protected from the formation of surface rust.

After stripping, a 1968 crossmember can be refinished while assembled by first coating the hardware with clear engine enamel. After it dries, carefully mask the bolts and eccentrics and then paint the complete assembly black. Originally left unpainted, 1969 and newer crossmembers can be protected after media blasting with a complete coat of clear paint.

harness because the steel lines are attached directly to the firewall and inner fenders and then the wiring passes over them.

Early 1968 Javelin and AMX models used a firewall-mounted heater valve that was attached with three screws. When the position of the V-8 heater valve was changed to the passenger-side rear part of the intake manifold during the 1968 model year, the three holes left from the earlier-style heater valve were covered by small plugs of sealer applied after the car was painted.

Because 6-cylinder Javelin models still used the firewall-mounted valve, the three holes remained, however. They were not plugged on later V-8–powered cars, although the top hole was repurposed to secure a wiring harness retainer.

Wiring Harness

AMC muscle cars use a common wiring harness for both the under-dash and engine bay wiring, so care must be taken when removing it. The triangular plate, used where the harness passes through the firewall, has a galvanized finish. If this plate has been painted or looks dark and corroded, it can often be restored by removing it from the harness, glass beading very lightly, and applying a thin coat of clear engine enamel to preserve its appearance.

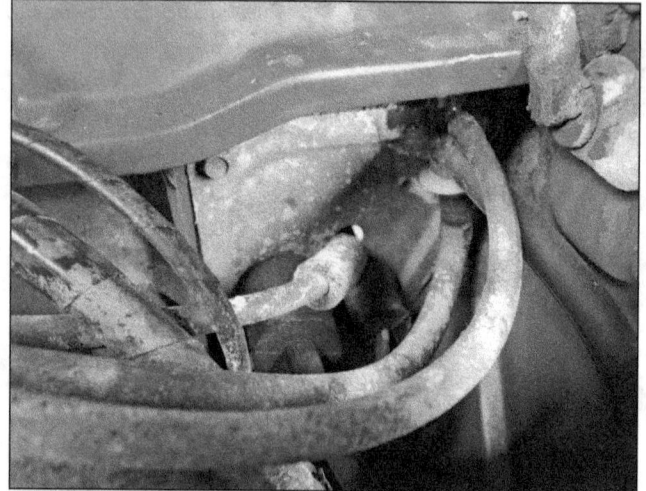

A galvanized plate on the driver's side of the cowl seals the firewall where the wiring harness, windshield washer hose, or heater control cable pass through. Unused holes are plugged. Be sure to make a diagram of your particular car's arrangement because this varies by year and equipment.

If a reproduction wiring harness is not available for your particular model, an original harness can be inspected and cleaned, or if necessary, rewrapped with new harness wrap available from a restoration parts supplier. Be sure that any fusible links are present and in good condition. Also check for missing and melted plugs or other signs of thermal damage or modifications to

ENGINE COMPARTMENT

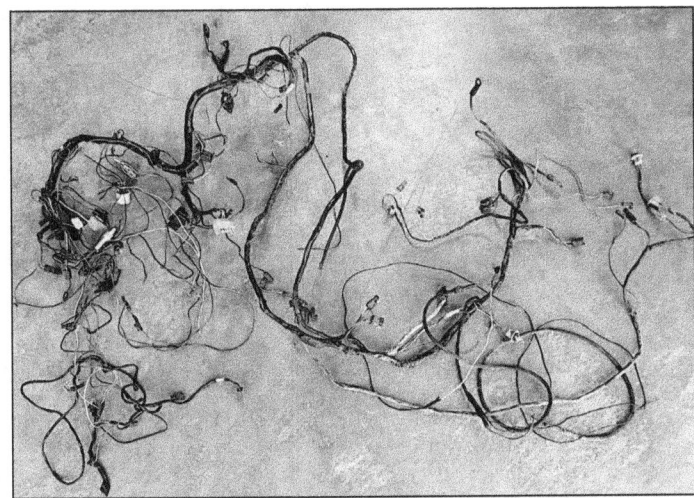

Straight from the car, the main wiring harness looks like a tangled mess. Before investing too much time, check the complete length of the harness for missing ends, splices, and burned spots. If you find more than a couple of damaged spots, consider discarding the harness in favor of a new reproduction or better-quality used harness.

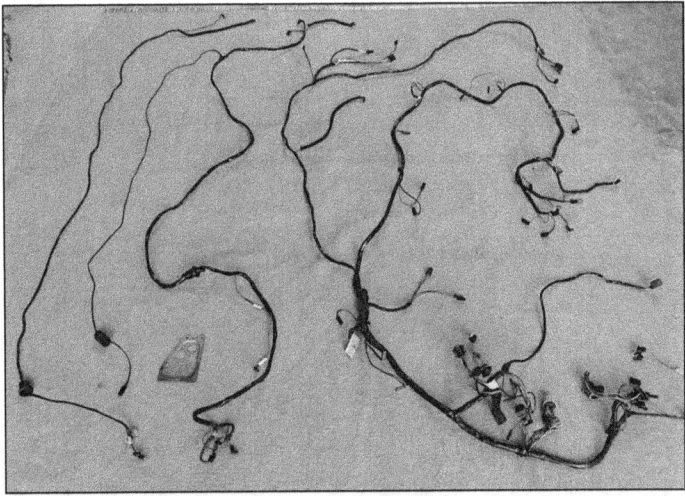

Once everything looks good, rewrapping or occasionally just cleaning the harness with Prep-Sol makes it look new again. Working on a blanket protects the harness against abrasion from the concrete floor. Use the wiring diagram in your TSM to be sure everything underneath the dash is connected properly.

the harness. Using common electrical tape to rewrap a harness may be easier but tape can deteriorate over time and become sticky. The original harness wrap contained no adhesive and was tied at the ends. If your wiring is brittle from age or damaged beyond repair, replace the harness with a new reproduction from M&H Electric Fabricators, or better-quality used harness.

Routing of the engine compartment wiring harness did change. The 1968 cars had the underhood harness attached to the upper cowl on both sides; for 1969 and later cars, the harness ran across the cowl and then dipped between the upper cowl and heater fan motor. This revised routing of the harness freed up space to install the emissions/tune-up specs sticker on the passenger-side upper cowl beginning early in the 1969 model year. Previously, this sticker had been applied to the top of the driver-side spring tower where it really wasn't a good fit. Some very early 1968 models have no emissions sticker.

The brake system distribution block acts as an intersection, and trips the warning-light switch if the front or rear brake system loses pressure. Early disc brake cars have a separate proportioning valve located near the rear axle. A cast-iron combination valve replaced both brass valves for 1971 and later disc brake cars. The brass distribution block can be disassembled for cleaning and detailing, or rebuilt if necessary.

Beginning in 1972, a bulkhead connector was used to split the main wiring harness at the firewall, resulting in separate engine and dash harnesses. Although this seems like a great improvement over previous one-piece harness, depending on the car's equipment there may be one or more individual wires separated from the main harnesses that are routed through the firewall using individual grommets. This wiring can generally be removed for engine bay restoration by carefully applying some heat to the grommet to soften it.

Engine Compartment

Reassemble your engine compartment beginning at the back with the windshield wiper setup, steel brake

The power brake master cylinder, lid, vacuum booster, and mounting bracket were assembled and then painted as a unit. To protect the painted master cylinder lid, the hold-down bale can often be installed onto the ends of the reservoir, right over the lid, rather than being rotated into position.

Power-brake vacuum boosters were numbered with three digits that varied by year and disc-versus-drum application. A rubber stamp can be created to reproduce these numbers after the booster is refinished. The numbering usually appeared at the top or side of the booster facing the inner fender.

lines, and wiring harness. Next is the brake master cylinder. The power brake vacuum booster, bracket, master cylinder, lid, and bale assembly were originally assembled and then painted semi-gloss black as a unit.

The vacuum booster was identified by a three-digit number stamped in paint. Non–power brake master cylinders were left natural, with a gold-cadmium–plated lid.

Once the master cylinder is in place, the brake lines can be connected, which lessens the possibility that they will be snagged or damaged during engine installation.

The heater fan motor is another underhood item often refinished incorrectly. The motor itself is semi-gloss black for 1968–1969 cars, but the mounting plate may be light gray or black depending on the car's build date. When in doubt, match the color of the mounting plate to the color of the steel portion of the underdash heater box where it is

Pre-bent brake lines manufactured by Fine Lines fit just like the originals and have correct fittings that don't require brass adapters. The steel brake lines are among the first things installed in the engine compartment because they attach directly to the firewall and inner fenders. No wiring or hoses pass behind the brake lines.

ENGINE COMPARTMENT

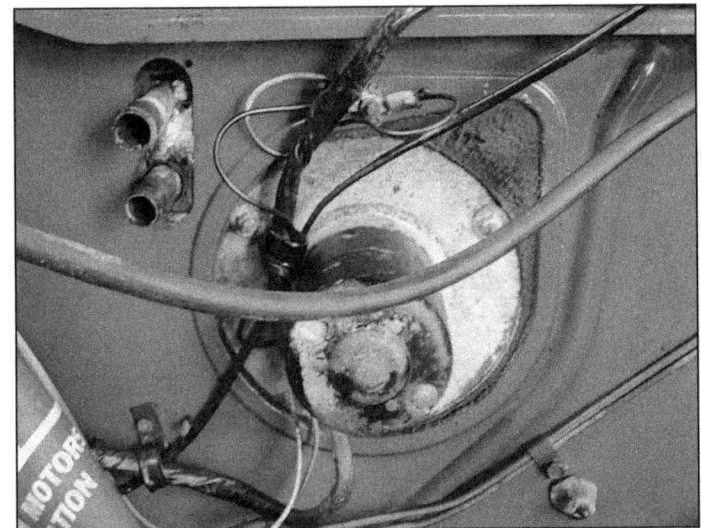

Heater fan motors used in 1968 and 1969 were painted black until plated motors were introduced in 1970. The round mounting plate was painted light gray before being changed to black. PAL nuts used to secure the heater motor mounting plate should be plated in a silver color. Note the lump of sealer surrounding the plastic carpet retainer protruding through the firewall.

This is a 1969 heater fan motor with the black mounting plate. Removing the squirrel cage allows separation of the motor from the mounting plate for refinishing. If the circular gasket located between them has deteriorated, a new one can be made from thin rubber. Fan motors from air-conditioned cars have a curved hose that allows cold air to reach the fan motor.

attached. This is visible through the firewall once the mounting plate is removed.

Air-conditioned cars have a curved cooling tube attached to the fan motor, and a resistor is installed nearby. The resistor may be detailed by light glass-bead blasting followed with a coat of clear engine enamel.

Engine Installation

As with removal, reinstallation of the engine with or without the transmission can be accomplished from the top or from the bottom. Lowering the body over the engine and transmission is generally safer, with less chance of damage to the upper core support or firewall. However, using care and patience, the drivetrain can be installed from the top without inflicting any damage on the car. As a precaution, always remove the grille and protect the upper core support and engine crossmember with thick towels. Use corrugated cardboard taped in place to protect the firewall.

It is always preferable to have at least one helper when installing

Just because the drivetrain is in place it doesn't mean that you're out of danger. Leaning on AMX and Javelin fender tops may cause minor denting even when installing the hood. Protect these vulnerable areas with folded blankets or other protective coverings to prevent any damage at this stage of the project.

an engine, even if only as a spotter, someone to adjust the jack underneath, or keep the engine from rotating as it settles into position. Be sure to warn any helpers not to lean on the fender tops because elbows can leave dents! Protect these vulnerable areas of pristine sheet metal by covering them with folded blankets.

With the engine and transmission back in position, both crossmembers securely bolted, and everything reconnected, go over your engine removal notes to be sure nothing is missed, such as the small ground cable on the crossmember.

Next up is installing any accessories that are attached to the engine, including the fuel and power steering pumps, alternator, and emissions control system found on 4-speed–transmission cars.

Engine Accessories

Even more visible (in most cases) than the engine itself are the various accessories bolted to it. Be sure to refinish and install these items carefully.

Carburetor

AMC muscle cars produced for the 1968 and 1969 model years used a Carter AFB 4-barrel carburetor. Beginning in 1970, Motorcraft carburetors were sourced from Ford. Carter carbs used a screw-in fuel filter at the inlet while Motorcraft carbs relied on an inline filter. The steel fuel line running between the fuel pump and carburetor changed between 1968 and 1969, and accordingly was completely different for 1970 and later cars.

Air Cleaner

Air cleaners changed as well, with 1968–1969 units having a smaller opening in the base than those from 1970 and newer. Air cleaner tubs and lids were painted gloss black, except for bright chrome-plated lids used on the 390-ci V-8. The air cleaner snorkel was a Ford design that was painted separately and attached with silver hex screws. A sticker affixed to the front of the air cleaner tub has square corners for 1968–1969 and rounded corners later.

The 390 air cleaner lid was finished in chrome plating that was much shinier than the valve covers or oil cap. For best results start with a rust-free painted air cleaner lid so original chrome plating does not have to be ground off then polished smooth. A 390 air cleaner sticker is easier to install correctly if the middle part of the sticker is lined up and applied first.

A 390-ci V-8 engine with 4-speed emissions controls from a 1970 Rebel Machine. Functional ram air induction, introduced the previous model year, necessitated a thick rubber seal that joined the air cleaner housing to the hood scoop. The small, chrome-plated air cleaner lid had no "390" identification, although the same lid used on a 360-equipped 1970 AMX or Javelin did have a "360" sticker.

Fuel Pump

Fuel pumps were very different depending on whether vacuum or electric windshield wipers were fitted. Cars with vacuum-operated wipers required a vacuum pump, which was combined with the fuel pump.

Cars with electric wipers used a basic mechanical fuel pump manufactured by Carter. Both fuel pumps used a natural aluminum housing, and have a right-angle brass hose barb at the inlet with a 5/16-inch-diameter hard steel line exiting the fuel pump.

Wiper Motor

Cars equipped with vacuum wipers also require one or two additional hard lines (depending on build date) and a section of vacuum hose connecting the combination pump to the wiper motor. A small 3/16-inch-diameter formed steel line was also used for the distributor vacuum advance; it was positioned just in front of the carburetor. In most cases, vacuum-operated windshield wipers were standard equipment on AMC vehicles through 1971, with electric wipers available as an option.

Upgrading to an electric setup requires changing not only the wiper motor, but also the transmission linkage inside the cowl, as well as the switch inside the car. Be careful, because the electric wiper motors' design changed between the 1972 and 1973 model years.

Distributor

Points-operated distributors and ignition coils used by American Motors during the muscle car years were Delco units sourced from General Motors. Distributors have a specific casting number on the base, and coils were embossed with model number 266 B-R on the can. The coil was installed with a slight counterclockwise rotation when viewed from the front of the car. The two-piece coil bracket has a galvanized finish and incorporates a single white plastic spark plug wire retainer, as do both rocker arm covers.

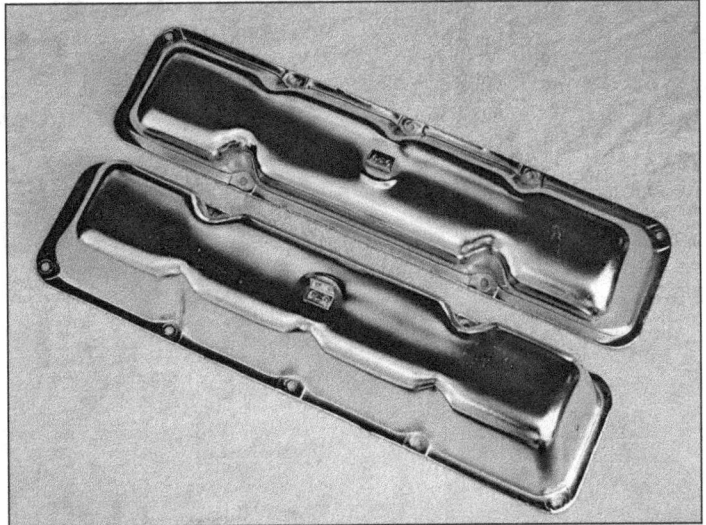

Original 390 valve covers had a unique dull finish because the covers were not polished before being plated. To duplicate this look, start with rust-free painted valve covers, clean and glass-bead blast the outside surface, then have your chrome shop plate them without any polishing or other prep. Chrome plating is only as shiny as the surface underneath.

With the air cleaner assembly removed, the proper routing of the heater hose is visible. The position and rotation of the Delco-Remy ignition coil is shown, along with the white spark plug wire retainer attached to the coil bracket. Although dirty, the valve cover engine identification tag is unpainted.

AMC V-8 valve covers were painted to match the engine except for the 390-ci engine, which had dull chrome finish covers. The aluminum engine identification tag, mounted to the front of the passenger-side valve cover, was not painted.

Alternator

Alternators were manufactured by Motorola, and were rated at 35 or 55 amps depending on options ordered (including air conditioning). Alternators used a cast-aluminum housing and typically had a dull-black fan and pulley. Original alternators were equipped with an oval-shaped Motorola identification tag riveted to the housing; it matched the rectangular tag affixed to the voltage regulator that was mounted to the passenger-side inner fender. In the late 1970s, AMC switched to Delco alternators; many older vehicles have been retrofitted.

Power Steering

Power steering was a popular option found on many AMC muscle cars. Early models used a pump manufactured by Eaton that is characterized by a round reservoir mounted fairly high on the engine. Use caution when servicing motor mounts, because the wing nut for the reservoir may damage the hood if the hood is closed during these repairs. The Eaton power-steering pump is cast iron with a semi-gloss black-painted steel reservoir, lid, and pulley. The bracket mounting the pump to the engine is natural aluminum.

Pumps found on 1968 and 1969 cars are stamped "1100 MAX" while 1970 pumps are stamped "1200 MAX" on the large steel hex located at the side of the pump. It is common to find yellow or green inspection paint daubs on original Eaton pumps.

By 1972, the Eaton power-steering pumps were replaced by Saginaw units purchased from General Motors. These are much more compact and have the pump built into the back of a bell-shaped reservoir. The complete unit, including the pulley, is painted semi-gloss black with a natural aluminum mounting bracket.

Emissions Control System

As a way to address growing concerns about air pollution, AMC's first vehicle emissions control

A yellow inspection mark on this 1970 Eaton power-steering pump only became visible after a careful cleaning. Many underhood parts that were coated with oil early on have details such as this well preserved even after 40 or more years in service. Be sure to document these daubs in photos so they can be duplicated later.

The Eaton power steering pump used on early AMC muscle cars consists of a cast-iron body with black-painted mounting bracket, reservoir, and lid. The top washer and wing nut should remain plated. Careful cleaning reveals both yellow and green inspection marks that can be photographed and duplicated after the pump is refinished or replaced.

Refinished and reinstalled, this Eaton power steering pump shows the subtle difference in color and texture between the cast-iron housing and the cast-aluminum mounting bracket. The steel bracket, pulley, reservoir, and lid are painted semi-gloss black as original.

ENGINE COMPARTMENT

A nicely prepared 343-ci V-8 with air-conditioning presents well at any car show. This 1969 AMX also has a 4-speed transmission with emissions controls in place. This particular engine bay is nicely detailed and authentic in appearance except for the air cleaner assembly, which could be a bit shinier.

The emissions control system installed on 4-speed cars consisted of an air pump that injected fresh air into the exhaust mixture through tubes attached to the exhaust manifolds. The air tubes were originally painted along with the engine and exhaust manifolds, although the manifold paint burned off quickly, allowing it to rust.

systems appeared on cars equipped with 4-speed-transmissions in the late 1960s. The system included a belt-driven air pump designed to more effectively burn exhaust gases by injecting air through steel tubes attached to the exhaust manifolds.

The pump was natural cast aluminum with a white fan and black pulley; the steel tubes attached to the exhaust manifolds were painted along with the engine. Engine paint quickly burned from the manifolds; however, it generally survived much longer on the air tubes. Air pump mounting brackets were generally plated in yellow zinc, along with the round diverter valve.

When these cars were new, many emissions systems were removed and discarded, making the air pump, hoses, and related parts hard to find today. Most components have not been reproduced, so assembling a complete emissions control system from scratch today takes patience and a bit of luck.

Air Conditioning

Air conditioning compressors used by AMC originally were either black or the more common silver color. Air-conditioned Javelin and AMX models differed from others with the installation of three additional underhood air seals located near the radiator. Rubber flaps were clipped to the lower core support and stapled to the upper filler panel; a formed seal was attached to the underside of the hood to seal tightly against the upper core support.

A resistor mounted near the heater fan motor was found only on air-conditioned cars. This resister changed in appearance and location between 1968 and 1969, moving from beneath the fan motor to above it. All

CHAPTER 7

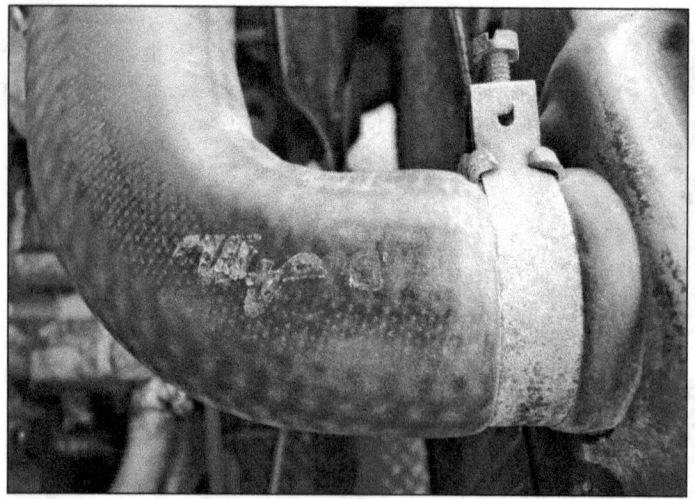

This is an original top radiator hose and Wittek clamp from a 1968 AMX. "RAD" indicates the radiator end of the hose. If an accurate replacement cannot be found, original-style markings can be duplicated on a parts store hose. Later hoses are numbered and include the AMC name and the newer logo printed in yellow.

Original 1968 heater hoses and clamps differed in size. The ring-type upper hose clamp is also used at the back of the water pump bypass hose and is painted red. Note the small ribs and yellow stripe running the length of the upper heater hose. Red heater hoses on an AMC muscle car are not correct.

fan motors installed on air-conditioned cars included a molded-rubber cooling tube, which was routed through the firewall to connect the fan motor and heater housing.

Radiator

American Motors sourced radiators for their muscle cars that were manufactured by Blackstone. Each upper tank contained an embossed part number that varied by application, as well as a larger two-digit date code representing the month and year of manufacture. For example, a radiator coded "E9" was made in May 1969.

Fan shrouds were generally steel for Go Package–equipped cars and fiberglass for cars with air conditioning. Original early-production radiator hoses were marked with a white "AM" script as well as "RAD" to indicate the radiator end. Heater hoses were black with a narrow yellow stripe. Newer OEM radiator hoses generally have yellow identification.

By the 1972 model year, the coolant-level caution sticker was relocated from the hood latch support to the end of the upper radiator filler panel. It later moved to the upper core support. Be sure to document the position of any original stickers before disassembling your restoration project.

A white coolant-level warning sticker was installed (often crookedly) on the hood latch support for 1968–1970, but on 1971–1974 Javelins the location of this sticker varied to include the latch support, radiator filler panel, and upper core support.

Clamps and Hold-Downs

Most hose clamps used on AMC muscle cars were tower-style clamps manufactured by Wittek. They can be released by unscrewing the hex head bolt, then gently tapping the extended tower portion with a hammer and deep-well socket that is slightly larger than the bolt head. Another type of clamp found on early cars was a red-painted Corbin round wire-pinch clamp that was used at the end of the bypass hose attached to the thermostat housing.

ENGINE COMPARTMENT

Original upper radiator filler panels illustrate the typical 1968 (top) positioning versus later (bottom) positioning of the battery warning sticker. Reproduction stickers are available from AMC parts suppliers. Staple holes found in this panel are from a rubber seal used on air-conditioned cars only. These staple holes can often be carefully reused when attaching a replacement seal.

the battery case instead of clamping it over the top.

A battery polarity warning sticker was applied to the radiator filler panel parallel to the inner fender, readable from the front of the car. Some 1968 models had this sticker positioned parallel to the core support.

Prestolite manufactured positive battery cables. The negative cables were flag terminal–style grounded to the engine block with the same bolt that secured the alternator's Z-brace.

Blackout Paint

An underhood detail found on many cars is the front-end blackout paint intended to prevent the hood latch and other body-color parts from showing through the grille of light- and medium-colored cars. The blackout was quickly applied to the hood latch support, radiator baffle panels, and lower core support after the body shell was painted, but before any further assembly. With no masking used, black overspray is commonly found on the upper core support and other nearby panels. Very early 1968 models did not have the blackout paint, but once started, the process was continued through 1974, even though it was unlikely that anything could be seen through the extended nose and dual-layer grille of a Javelin AMX.

Application of the blackout paint was fairly random, with some cars of one color receiving the blackout while others did not. Some cars also received minimal black paint while others received much more. For this reason the blackout paint can be applied as carefully or as randomly as you like, and as long as it is *not* carefully masked or applied to parts separate from the car, it cannot be considered incorrect.

Semi-gloss black paint was used to conceal the area behind the grille and front bumper of light- and medium-colored cars. Because it was low-quality paint, it faded over time to look like flat paint. The application of the blackout paint was fairly random because original cars painted in certain medium hues can be found with or without the blackout applied.

Because the two heater hoses were of different diameters, different types of hose clamps were used where the hoses attach to the heater core. Generally the lower clamp is a Wittek side-screw type and the upper hose is either a tower or Corbin wire clamp. Smaller clamps used on vacuum or fuel lines were commonly a flat spring-steel type and color-coded by size.

Battery hold-downs changed between 1968, 1969, and 1970 with the latest type securing the base of

Application of the blackout paint differed widely from car to car depending on who was doing it. Here, a 1968 Javelin has only minimal coverage. For this reason, apply the blackout paint as carefully as you wish. As long as it is not neatly masked, or applied to the hood latch support separately, it cannot be considered incorrect.

Although 1971–1974 Javelin and AMX models received a longer front end and redesigned grille, the application of front-end blackout paint continued on light- and medium-colored cars. Models built after the 1968 model year had the hood latch installed before application of the body color and blackout paint.

The blackout paint found behind the grille of light-colored cars varied greatly in coverage and appearance. During restoration, apply the black paint as neatly as desired because it is your car! The only way it can be considered incorrect is if masking is done beforehand, or if the hood latch support is painted black and then installed.

This original 1968 AMC fan belt is embossed with the early-style "AM" logo. Later belts have AMC identification printed instead, and included the newer-style A-mark logo. Original NOS belts and hoses are in short supply and command high prices when found.

Windshield washer fluid was stored in a canvas and rubber pouch through the 1970 model year, when the bag became a bit wider than the bag shown here, which was used in 1968–1969 models. Cars with optional electric wipers used a similar bag that incorporated a small pump near the bottom; the fluid hose did not pass through the cap. Try Go-Jo orange hand cleaner with pumice to clean up an original washer fluid bag.

Other Details

Some of the other underhood details included the red windshield washer fluid bag (later replaced by a clear plastic reservoir), and two diagonally mounted braces spanning the upper core support and fender sill. These bars were finished in semi-gloss black along with the upper shock mounts found on 1970 and newer cars. The 1972–1974 models received a square sticker on the passenger-side spring tower stating that the car's alignment specs were factory calibrated during assembly.

Rectangular rubber pads were placed where the fender sills kick up and nearly contact the underside of the hood. Small rubber hood bumpers were also installed on the fender side sills, with the higher side of the bumpers closer to the engine.

Passenger-side front frame rails have an access hole for a 6-cylinder fuel supply line to pass through the rail. These holes were closed off with black plastic body plugs on V-8 cars.

Every Hurst SC/Rambler and Rebel Machine, as well as Go Package Hornet SC/360 models, plus 1970 and later Javelin and AMX models equipped with optional ram air induction include ductwork and a vacuum-actuated flapper assembly on the underside of the hood. This

ENGINE COMPARTMENT

allowed fresh air to be directed to the open-top air cleaner under hard acceleration. Although some of these components have been reproduced in limited quantities, many are difficult to locate.

Cleaning Tip

Once your engine compartment is assembled and detailed, spend as much time as necessary to keep it clean and dust-free. Even washing your car with water may spot the inner fenders and other underhood parts. Whenever possible use only a car duster or detailing spray with lint-free microfiber towels to maintain the engine, accessories, and engine compartment.

As with other forced-air induction systems, the AMC Rebel Machine employed a spongy seal to join the air cleaner body to the underside of the hood and scoop. Ram air parts for all AMC models are in short supply because few have been reproduced, leading to high demand and equally high prices when they do appear for sale.

The 1971 Hornet SC/360 featured an optional forced-air induction system that was similar to those of other AMC performance models. Missing or worn-out parts are often expensive and difficult to locate, so you should factor this into the purchase price of your muscle car project. Most replacement parts must be sourced from cars parted out by private owners.

A well-dressed AMX 390-ci V-8 includes chrome-finish oil cap and air cleaner lid. Valve covers were also chrome plated on every 390, although this car has been upgraded with an Edelbrock aluminum intake manifold and finned aluminum valve covers.

CHAPTER 8

Undercar Components

Many car show entries, even those with terrific paint jobs and a lot of detail under the hood, come up a little short when the car show judges look underneath. For whatever reason, the underside of these cars are largely ignored, or freshened with nothing more than a quick application of undercoat, and maybe some black paint for the rear axle and springs. However, just as with the engine compartment, the underside of your AMC muscle car project will benefit from careful detailing. This includes the frame rails, floorpan, driveshaft, rear axle, steering and suspension systems, brakes, exhaust, wheels, and tires.

As noted previously, AMC car bodies were coated in primer, and then painted while assembled with all of the bolt-on parts in place. Except for the front and rear wheel wells, there wasn't a lot of effort spent painting the bottom of the car. Most of the body-color paint found on the underside of an original car was merely overspray deposited while painting the rocker panels. Heavily textured black undercoating was usually planned for the bottom of the car anyway. This was added to mute the sound of gravel and other objects kicked up by the tires, to isolate the passenger compartment from heat, and to protect the bottom of the car from chips and corrosion. Areas of the underbody that didn't receive paint or undercoat remained in primer.

Other than rare exceptions, such as the small run of Super Stock AMX race cars, almost every AMC received at least some undercoat inside the transmission tunnel and wheel wells, on the bottom of the trunk floor, and covering the bottom of the fuel tank. The areas underneath the front fenders were coated after installation of the splash shields, which were located directly behind the front tires. For early cars, these shields were made of galvanized steel stapled to rubber flaps, but were replaced by plastic shields in later years.

In most cases, coating the front suspension was avoided, although it was often hit with some undercoat

Early-style front coil springs also have a part number and other information cast into the end coil. These digits are usually not visible until the front suspension is disassembled and the spring is glass-bead blasted to remove the original paint, surface rust, and undercoat. When repainting a coil spring, be sure to spray from every direction to achieve complete coverage.

UNDERCAR COMPONENTS

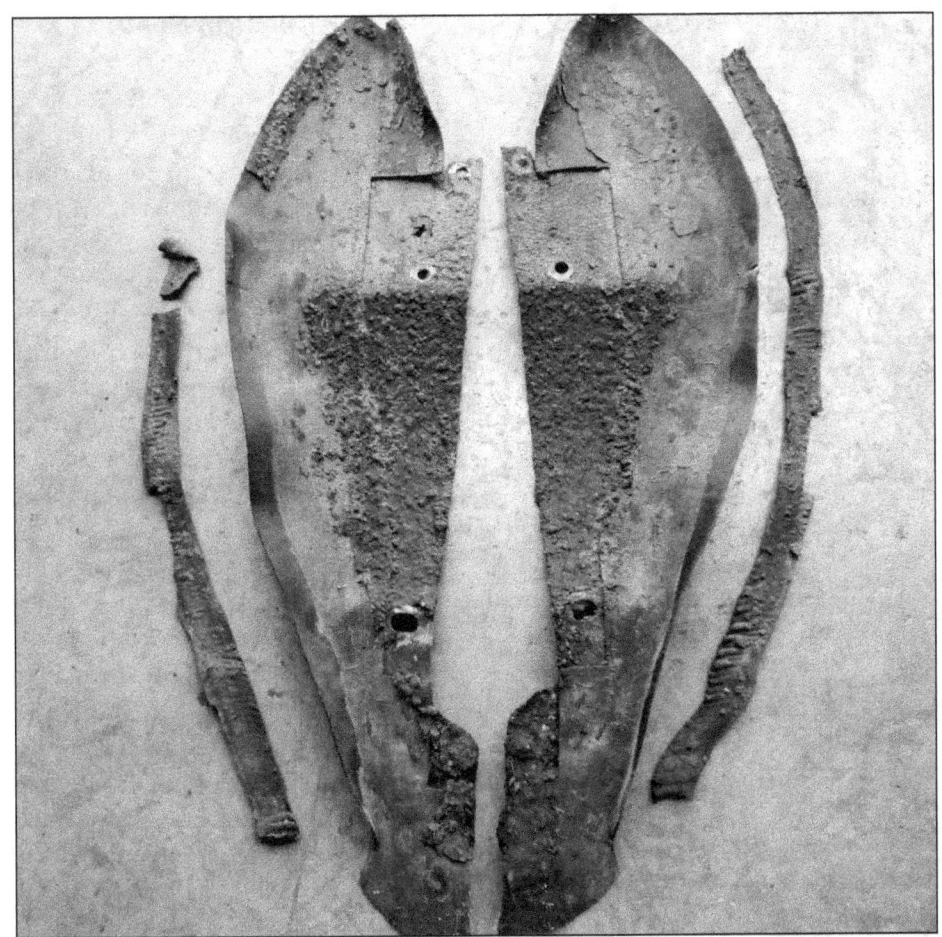

Installed after paint, but before undercoating, these splash shields sealed off the rear part of the front fenders from water and road debris. First-generation AMX and Javelin models used shields made of galvanized steel with rubber flaps stapled in place. These were actually sealed to the inside surface of the fenders with strips of tar-like material. Second-generation models used one-piece plastic shields that were wider to seal against the redesigned front fenders.

One method of replacing or just touching up the factory-applied undercoat is to use a truck bed coating such as this product from Dupli-Color. Unlike most spray-on undercoats, it comes in a true black color and dries to a hard, durable finish. Protect the rear axle, lower body, and other areas in danger of overspray with newspaper or masking paper taped in place.

as well. Because the car was almost completely assembled before application of the undercoat it is common to find some sprayed onto the backside of the front bumper, the bumper brackets, engine crossmember, rear axle, or springs. Generally, the main fuel supply line and front-to-rear brake line were also well coated. Because additional undercoat was an option, some cars received a lot more than others; it liberally covered almost the entire underbody.

Sound deadener was also applied to the car's interior, especially inside the doors and quarter panels, and to the front floorpans prior to paint. Not to be confused with undercoating, the interior sound deadener was pale yellow rather than black. This material was also sprayed on as seam sealer along the inner rocker panels, and inside the trunk of very early 1968 models.

Once the original undercoat is removed and the underside of the car is cleaned and prepared or repainted as desired, the textured undercoat can be replaced for a factory-fresh appearance. Fusor 805 sprayable wheel well coating from Lord approximates the look of the factory-original undercoat, but must be applied with specialized equipment.

An easier option is to use spray-on truck bedliner that can be purchased at auto body supply stores. Some bedliner kits include cans of material and a gun that uses compressed air to dispense the product. Bedliner can also be found in ready-to-use spray cans. The benefits of using truck bedliner as undercoating are its ease of application, its true black color, and that it dries completely into a durable

CHAPTER 8

Pre-1970 AMC cars utilized a trunnion-type front suspension with the shock absorber located outside the spring. The trunnion setup worked well for decades, and, once rebuilt, it outlasts many other components of the car. Replacement bushings and complete trunnions are readily available. The 1968–1969 coil springs were painted black with various colored stripes used as identification.

Model year 1970 saw the switch to an upper and lower ball joint suspension across the AMC line, with the front shock absorbers now positioned inside the spring (not shown). Along with many other front-end parts, the coil springs were now left unpainted and had paper tags attached for identification.

Suspension System

Beginning with the 1970 model year, American Motors updated the front suspension setup for all models to an upper and lower ball joint system. Earlier cars used a trunnion setup with lower ball joints only. The trunnion suspension has developed a bad reputation over the years, which is largely undeserved. It was a good design and was used for decades with no unusual problems. It is fairly easy to rebuild, and when maintained properly will last for the life of the car. The biggest drawback to the trunnion front suspension is possibly the unique service procedure required to remove or install the front coil springs.

The factory issued a service tool set used for removing the front springs on a trunnion suspension car; the tool is merely a pair of hooks that engage the tabs found on the upper and lower spring mounts. Each tool includes a semi-circular shield that prevents the spring from bowing or escaping from between the hooks. Jacking up the opposite rear corner of the car allows the front spring to compress enough to attach the tool.

Once the car is lowered and the weight is off the spring, it can easily be removed from the car and remains compressed. However, once the coil spring is removed it cannot be refinished while attached to the compressor tool.

Also, if the drivetrain has already been removed from the car, the body shell is not heavy enough to compress the spring far enough to attach the tool. For this reason, another method must be used for removing the trunnion-type front suspension during a complete teardown.

chemical-resistant finish. Most automotive undercoat sprays are actually dark brown, and remain soft because they are rubberized to act as a sound deadener.

If your project car is especially clean, you may be able to retain the factory-original undercoating that is already in place. Be sure that it is not flaking off, soaked with oil or power steering fluid, or hiding spots of surface rust. If usable as is, pressure wash the undercoat, or scrub it with detergent and a stiff bristle brush and then rinse with plenty of clean water. After allowing time for it to dry completely, the undercoat will likely still appear to be a dirty light brown color, but it can be refreshed with a coat of semi-gloss black paint or black bedliner spray.

Trunnion Suspension Disassembly

AMC cars with trunnion-type front suspensions require a special disassembly procedure when the engine and transmission have already been removed from the car. Without the extra weight of the drivetrain, the factory service tool cannot be used for spring removal.

Using the following method allows the trunnion suspension to be safely disassembled for rebuilding or refinishing.

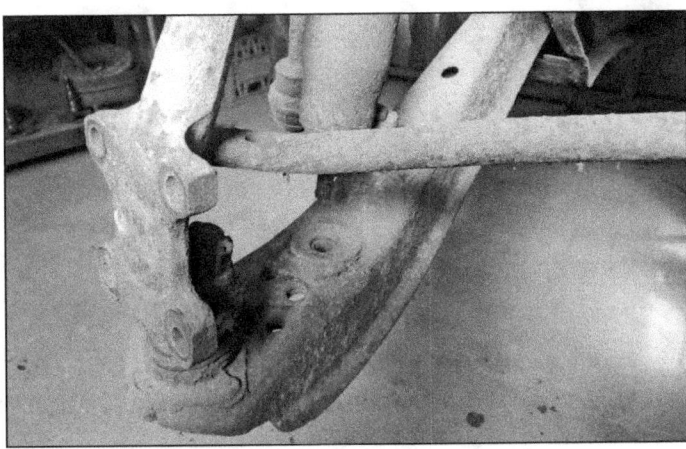

1 Removing the front suspension of a trunnion-equipped car requires a different procedure than outlined in the TSM, if the drivetrain has already been removed from the car. The factory service tool relies on the extra weight to compress the spring. Begin by removing the brake assembly, spindle, backing plate, and steering arm. Next, disconnect the shock absorber, strut rod, and sway bar mount from the lower control arm.

2 Allow the upper control arm to rest against the frame rail. Support the lower control arm with a floor jack, and securely wire the coil spring to the upper control arm for safety. Next, remove the bolt passing through the trunnion; you may need a punch to drive it out of the bushing.

3 Be very cautious because there will still be some tension on the coil spring, even with the suspension fully extended. Be sure no people or other vehicles are in the vicinity of the coil spring. With the trunnion bolt removed, stand in front of the car and slowly lower the jack to unseat the coil spring.

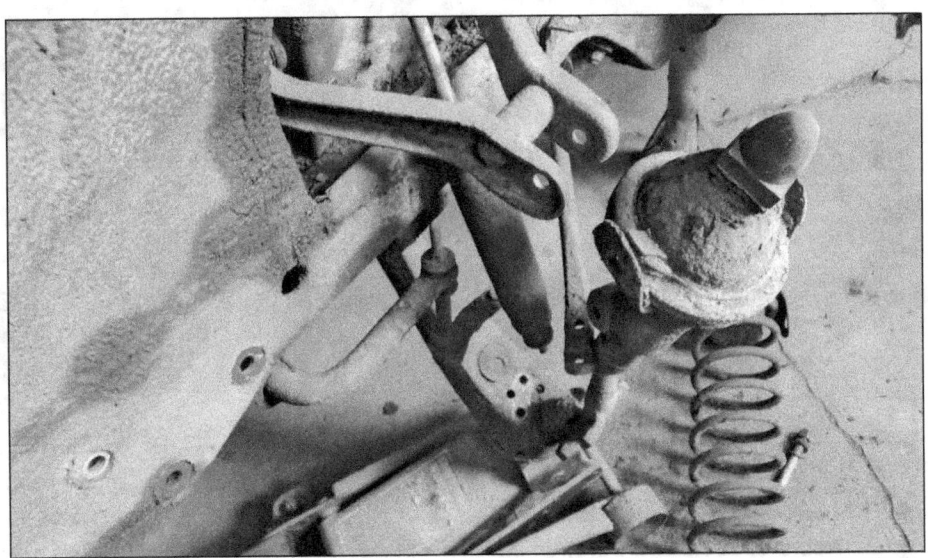

4 After repeating this procedure for both sides, the engine crossmember, lower control arms, steering knuckles, and trunnions can be removed from the car as an assembly. Now the upper control arms and strut rod brackets can be removed. Remove the sway bar mounts from the frame by hand using great care; the captive nuts inside the frame rail can break loose.

CHAPTER 8

5 Surprise! This strut rod appeared to be fine when it was in place, but road salt and water had collected inside the rubber bushing, causing rust to eat halfway through the rod. Fortunately, the steel mounting bracket remained undamaged.

Trunnion Suspension Reassembly

An alternate procedure is also required when reassembling the front suspension of a pre-1970 AMC car with the engine and transmission already removed. Do not risk personal injury or damage to your car by attempting to compress the coil springs using ratchet straps, turnbuckles, or other questionable methods.

Follow these guidelines for a safe, successful installation.

1 Reinstallation of a trunnion suspension begins at the bottom. Start by installing the engine crossmember and lower control arms. Add the lower ball joints, upper control arms, then the steering knuckle and trunnion assemblies. Bolt the trunnion to the upper control arm and then add the steering arm and spindle.

2 These refinished coil springs and mounting cups are a good 4 to 5 inches too long to simply insert without being compressed. The factory service tool keeps the spring compressed by hooking through the holes found on the tabs of the cups. But, without the weight of the engine and transmission, the tool cannot be removed once the spring is in place. For this reason, another method must be used.

UNDERCAR COMPONENTS

3 Three-piece external spring compressors do not fit inside the spring tower of a Javelin, AMX, or similar vehicle. However, a qualified spring repair shop can compress and band the coil springs to shorten them. The steel bands hold the spring securely under tension until it can be installed. The cost for this service is minimal compared to the danger of attempting to compress the springs by any other method.

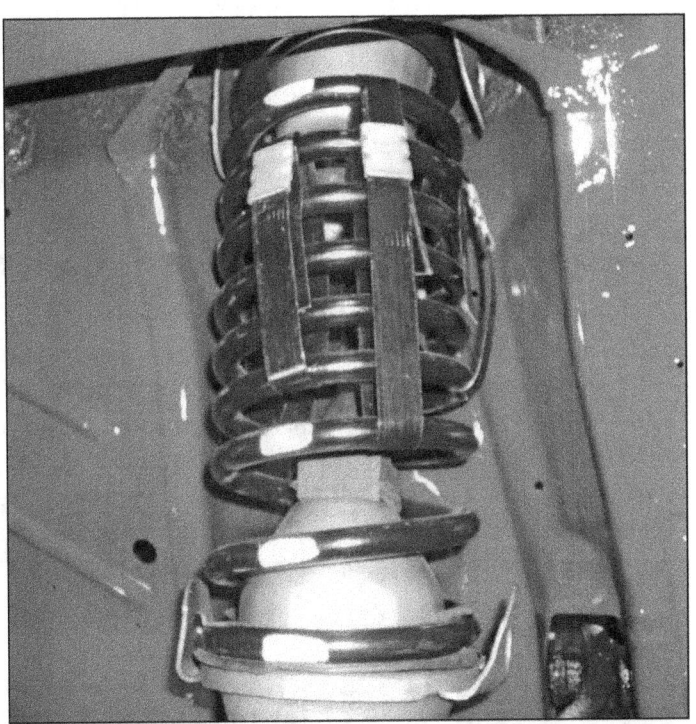

4 Assemble the compressed spring including the rubber isolators at both ends, and the tabs of the cups aligned as shown. Using a floor jack, raise the suspension to hold the spring tightly in place between the trunnion and the top of the spring tower. Double-check to be sure the spring is seated properly at both ends, and that the tabs of the mounting cups are still aligned.

5 With the weight of the car still supported by the floor jack, carefully cut the steel bands with tin snips. Once cut, the bands can be removed and the spring installation is complete. Rebuilt trunnions do not tilt. A trunnion that tilts and allows the coil spring to bow outward is a sure sign that repairs are needed.

CHAPTER 8

Following the 1970 redesign, servicing the front suspension became a bit easier. The open top of the spring towers allows a screw-type spring compressor to be used in conjunction with the upper and lower shock mounts. Essentially, the spring compressor replaces the shock absorber inside the spring, attaching to the lower shock mount to draw the coil spring upward. After the upper control arm is removed, tension on the spring is released and it can then be removed from the car.

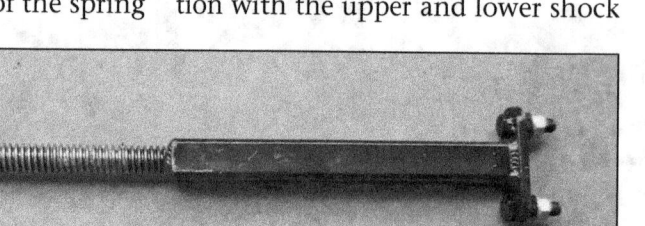

AMC models for 1970 featured a new upper and lower ball joint front suspension setup. With an open top spring tower now used for shock absorber mounting, the use of a screw-type coil spring compressor is now possible. Similar in construction to the factory service tool, this one basically replaces the shock absorber and draws the spring upward. The upper control arm can then be removed before releasing tension on the spring.

Front Suspension

AMC vehicles produced during the 1968 model year differ from those built in subsequent years in that many undercar components were originally painted black rather than left unpainted. After stripping and preparing these parts, refinish them with semi-gloss chassis black paint.

Beginning with the 1969 models, AMC discontinued painting many undercar parts to save money. Left unprotected from the elements, these bare-steel parts began to rust almost immediately. After replacing or glass-bead blasting these parts, protect their appearance with a generous coat of clear engine enamel or cast-iron-finish paint. Most argent silver– or aluminum-color paints are too bright for this purpose and do not look anything like bare steel.

Many three-dimensional parts that were originally painted black were dipped to expedite the process and ensure complete coverage. Paint runs are generally found when prepping these parts for refinishing. Pay attention to the direction of the runs if you want to duplicate them. Repaint undercar parts, such as this 1968 upper control arm assembly, by suspending them from the garage rafters using straightened wire coat hangers with hooks at the ends.

Front suspension parts painted black on 1968 cars, but left natural for 1969 and newer cars, include the engine crossmember and lower control arms, the upper control arms, plus the strut rods and brackets. Because the 1968–1969 trunnions were partially nickel plated, a distinct line can often be seen where the finish differs. Trunnion castings that are in good condition can be reused. Clean them by bead blasting lightly and then protect with a coat of clear engine enamel. Replacement bushings, thrust bearings, and O-ring seals are available to rebuild AMC trunnions.

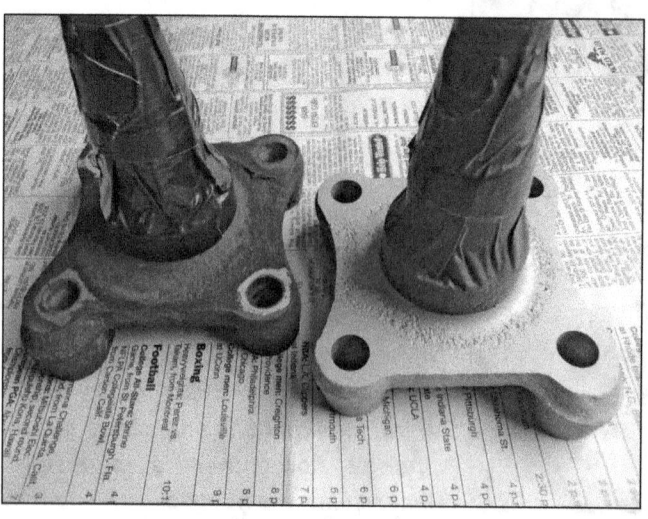

Glass-bead blasting removes every bit of rust from chassis parts such as spindles. Use a layer of duct tape to protect any polished parts from being roughed up by media blasting. The tape serves double duty because it can be left in place while painting the part also.

UNDERCAR COMPONENTS

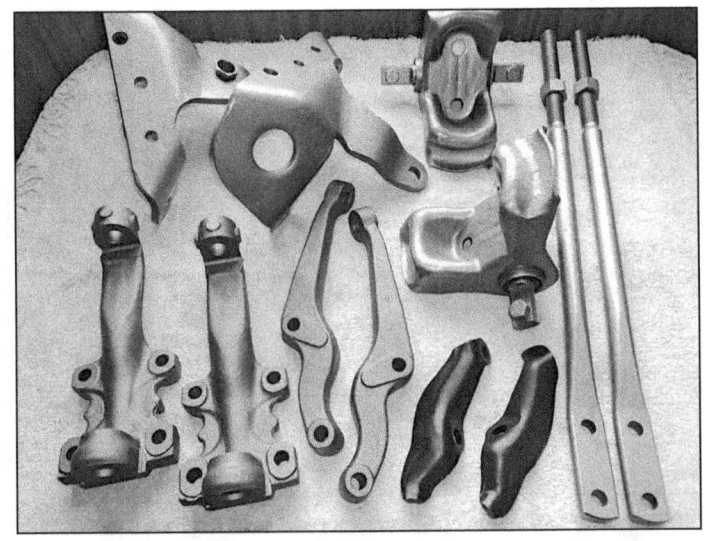

Beginning with the 1969 model year, many undercar parts were no longer painted black. Most were installed as received from the vendor, including the complete rear axle assembly and most of the steering and front suspension parts. Because bare steel and cast iron begin to rust almost immediately, these parts must be protected with clear or cast-iron paint to maintain their factory-new appearance.

Trunnion Rebuilding

Rebuilding AMC trunnions is not especially difficult, but be sure that you are starting with good-quality castings. If the inside bore is worn out of round, discard the casting and locate a better one. Be sure to replace the thrust bearings and O-rings as well as the bushings.

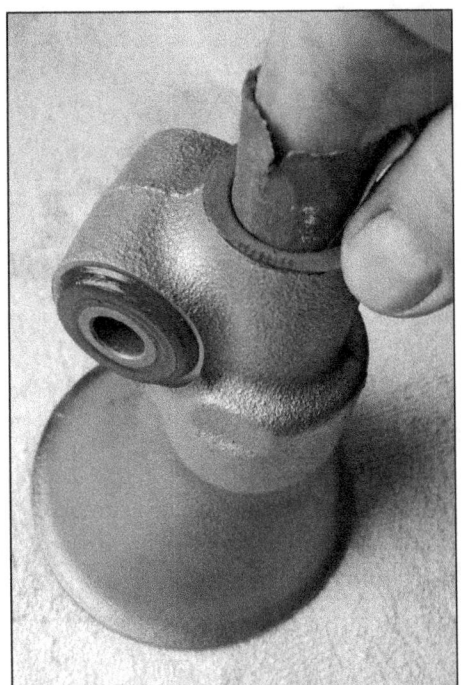

1 *Rebuilding a trunnion consists of inspecting and cleaning the casting, then replacing all of the original bushings. Be sure to polish the inside bore with extra-fine 1200-grit sandpaper before attempting to install the new bushing.*

2 *A 6-inch-long 1/2-inch-drive extension with a 1-inch socket installed backward makes a great tool for installing the inner trunnion bushing.*

3 *Gently press the new bushing into place. If the replacement bushing extends past the end of the trunnion casting, do not torque the retaining nut to spec. Instead, hand tighten it snugly and then secure the nut with blue Loctite.*

CHAPTER 8

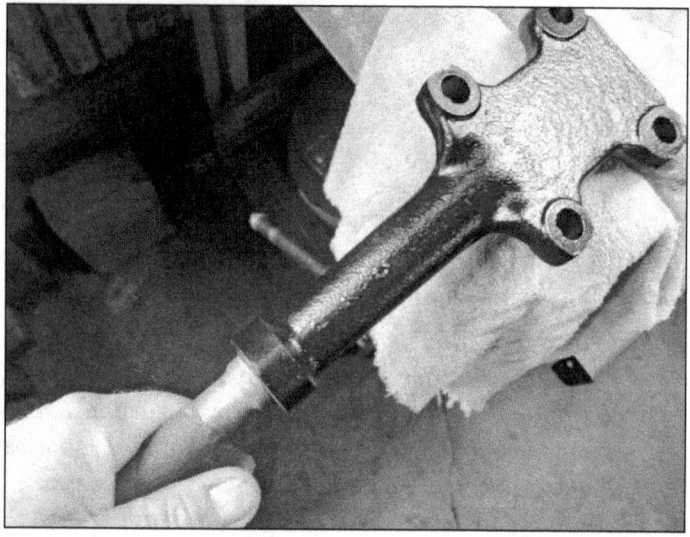

4 Polish the steering knuckle pin well or there will be too much resistance between the pin and bushing, even when using the lubricant provided with the bushing.

5 Assemble the O-rings, thrust bearing, and plastic washer in the order specified in the TSM for your model year. Then slide the polished knuckle pin into the bushing and attach.

Rebuilt and refinished with new bushings and bearings installed, these AMC trunnion assemblies are ready for years of trouble-free service.

Directly above the trunnions were the lower coil spring cups or retainers. Both these and the uppers were left natural, with the lower cup incorporating a cone-shaped rubber bumper within the spring. All front coil springs were painted black in 1968 and 1969, and identified with a contrasting paint stripe. For 1970, the coil springs were left bare and identified with paper number tags wrapped around one of the coils. With the revised suspension setup introduced for 1970, the lower coil spring perch and suspension bottoming bumper bracket (now bolted to the frame rail) were bare steel.

Sway bars were made of a treated metal that had a dark appearance similar to gunmetal gray. Only 1968 sway bars had a yellow paint inspection mark. Replacement sway bar bushings and end links are commonly available. The sway bar mounting brackets bolted below the front frame rails had a galvanized finish.

UNDERCAR COMPONENTS

Coil springs used with the trunnion front suspension are flattened at both ends to seat positively against the trunnion and upper spring seat. Colored stripes painted on the coils at both ends of the spring indicate standard or heavy-duty applications, such as for a car with air conditioning.

Springs used with the newer upper and lower ball joint front suspension are not flattened at the ends. Paper tags contain part numbers that indicate standard or heavy-duty application. Because 1970 and newer springs were no longer painted black, they began to rust almost immediately, often before the car was even delivered.

When restoring a 1968 model AMX or Javelin, the engine and transmission crossmembers are painted black, and the front sway bar includes a yellow paint daub. For 1969, however, both crossmembers are left bare, and the sway bar has no yellow marking.

Rear Suspension

Small-body AMC cars including all Gremlin, Hornet, Javelin, and AMX models used banded multi-leaf rear springs with the individual leaves isolated by rubber pads. The springs were bolted directly to the welded rear axle spring perches using inverted U-bolts. The bolts could be either fine- or coarse-thread depending on vehicle build date, with fine-thread U-bolts found on earlier production cars.

High-horsepower, short-wheelbase models also used torque links, which were basically traction bars running above the spring between the axle and rear frame rail on each side of the car. The torque links work well on short-wheelbase cars to reduce axle windup during hard acceleration, which prevents excessive wheel hop.

Models with factory-installed torque links included every 1968–1970 AMX, the 1969 Hurst SC/Rambler, and Gremlin models optioned with the 304-ci V-8. A torque link kit was available through AMC to retrofit other models. Cars with torque links used only one U-bolt per side; straight bolts also running through the shock mounts were used to secure the rear torque link brackets to the axle tube.

AMC leaf springs were originally painted chassis black before installation. Like many other undercar components they remained unpainted in

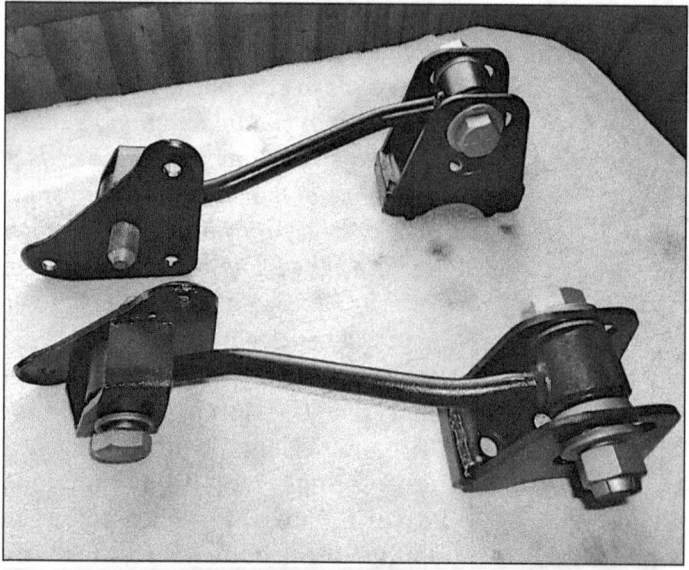

Torque links are similar to traction bars, and work well on short-wheelbase cars to reduce axle windup during hard acceleration. They were installed as standard equipment on every two-seat AMX, Hurst SC/Rambler, and V-8 Gremlin. Torque link assemblies were painted black, but were frequently covered over with undercoating.

Attaching the front of the leaf springs first makes installation of the rear axle assembly less difficult. Be sure that the placement of the jack stands doesn't interfere with the installation. Use folded towels to prevent the bottom of the springs from scraping against the garage floor. Because this is a 1968 AMX, black-painted springs are correct for this application.

Original rear leaf springs frequently have a keystone logo with part number and date code stamped on the bottom of the lower leaf. Like many other undercar parts, leaf springs were originally painted and then left bare, or possibly painted silver only on top in later years. After media blasting, protect the springs with clear engine enamel, which does not change the color of the rubber isolators positioned between the individual leafs.

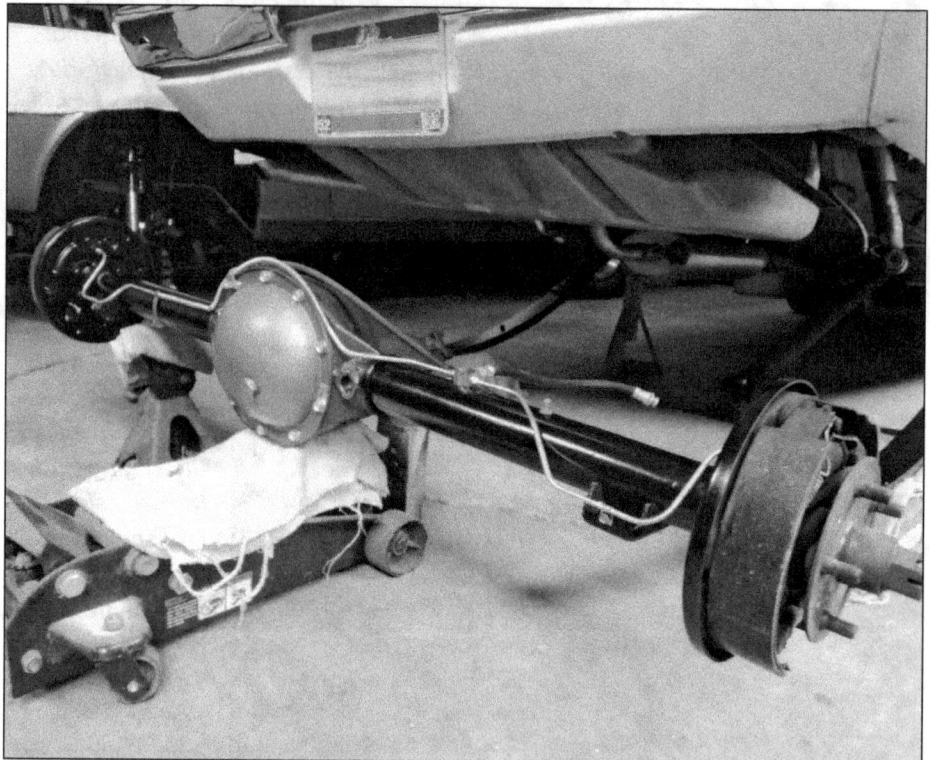

Carefully position the axle over the leaf springs. Raise the springs until the center bolt aligns with the hole in the spring perch, bolt the axle to the springs, and then lift everything together to install the rear shackles. Protect the axle and springs from coming in contact with each other or the garage floor.

later years in an effort to save money. Some 1970 springs were hastily painted silver, but only on the top surface. Many leaf springs were color coded at the front end, so be aware of these markings, which may be duplicated after refinishing the spring. The torque link assemblies were painted black originally, but were frequently covered by undercoating.

Most AMC muscle cars relied on the durable Dana model 20 rear axle, identified by its round 12-bolt rear cover. For better traction, a Twin-Grip differential was optional in most cases, such as when ordering the performance Go Package. Twin-Grip rear axles have an aluminum ring mounted to the hex-shaped filler plug; it indicates by AMC part number which rear axle lube is recommended. Complete axles fitted to 1968 model year cars were painted black before installation of the brake

The Dana model 20 rear axle common to most AMC muscle cars was not painted black starting with 1969 model year cars. The center section was coated with red primer, and then machined across the back where the cover fits, and included tabs for the inspection holes. Above and below these holes are welds where the bare steel axle tubes were attached to the center section. The rear cover also remained bare steel.

A white or light yellow paint daub is commonly found at or near the bottom of the center section, over the red primer. Although few people (including judges) will see this daub, this detail must be duplicated for an accurate 1969 or newer rear axle restoration.

A small yellow inspection mark is at the bottom of the passenger-side axle tube, near the backing plate. Although the axle tubes were bare steel, the brake backing plates were supplied in a black-painted finish. This makes for numerous different finishes on a typical Model 20 rear axle.

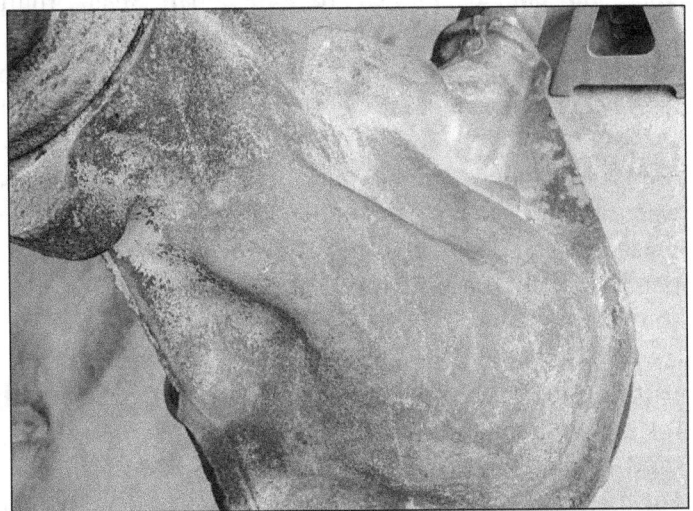

The top of this center section bears an "X," along with some other writing that cannot be deciphered now. These characters appear to have been written in white crayon on top of the red primer coat.

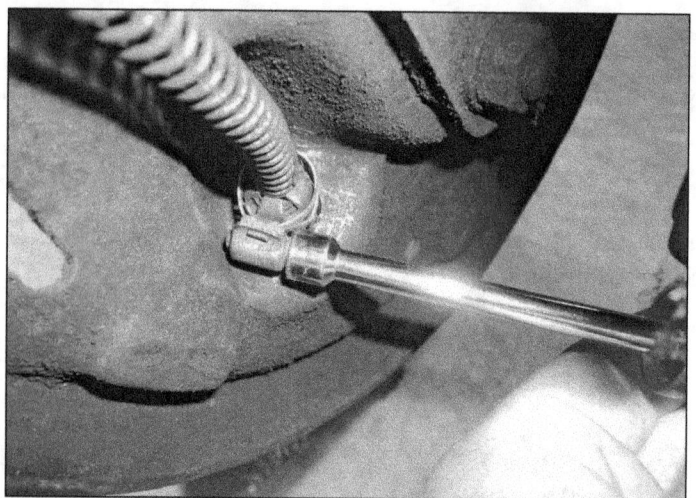

Releasing old parking brake cables from the rear axle backing plate is easy when a small hose clamp is used, such as a piston ring compressor, to squeeze the fingers holding the cable in place.

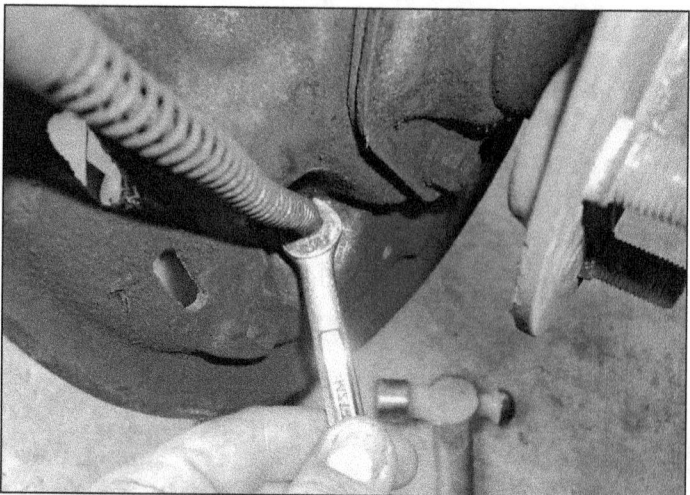

Once the fingers securing the parking brake cable are compressed, use a hammer and 3/8-inch open-end wrench to tap the cable end through the mounting hole. It's that easy!

If the brake cables are still in good operating condition, they can be cleaned up and reused. To reinstall, simply insert the cable end and open the fingers to hold it securely in place.

lines and cables. A rubber vent hose was routed between a fitting on the passenger-side axle tube and a similar fitting on the underbody above the axle.

In late 1968, AMC discontinued painting the rear axle assemblies, installing them in 1969 and newer models as received from the vendor. For these axles, the center section is coated in red primer, except for the machined rear surface to which the cover is mounted as well as the raised tabs on either side of the cover, which have round inspection holes where the axle tubes are inserted. The center section frequently had a white or very light yellow inspection mark at or near the bottom. Plug-type welds, both front and rear, are found where the axle tubes were attached to the center section.

The rear cover and mounting bolts, as well as the axle tubes, were bare steel originally, and are often heavily rusted as a result. The drum brake backing plates were painted black along with the brake drums themselves. The lower rear shock absorber mounts were also painted black for 1968, but left bare for 1969 and newer cars. Original shocks were gloss black and often had a small paint daub at the bottom.

Steering System

Most AMC muscle cars were offered with a choice of manual or power steering, and this variable did not affect the steering column. A tilt steering column was optional in most models (it was not available in the Hurst SC/Rambler), and tilt columns command a premium over standard versions today.

In many cases, AMC steering columns were assembled from parts that were already painted, so a variety of finishes can be found on a column that hasn't already been repainted. This includes a gloss-black portion underneath the dash, bare steel for the main shaft running through the engine compartment, and plastic parts that are also unpainted. The outer housing of the upper steering column is painted in a semi-flat finish to match the interior color.

The steering column shaft is connected to the steering gearbox with a rubber coupler incorporating studs that require two different size nuts. Pins opposite the nuts maintain a connection with the steering box in case the studs on the coupler break.

The steering gearboxes for both manual and power setups are Saginaw units with a cast-iron housing. Both the round end cover and rectangular top cover were aluminum;

UNDERCAR COMPONENTS

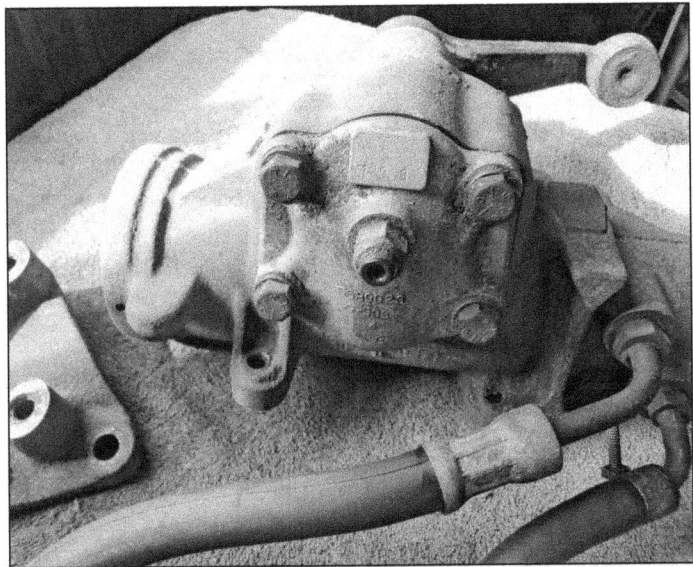

After a gentle degreasing and a washing with soap and water, this steering gearbox shares many of its original details, such as the bright orange inspection mark on the aluminum cover. Because there were so many variables when assembling these cars, finding original information while disassembling your particular car is the most accurate way to obtain correct restoration information.

A typical Saginaw power steering gearbox is made of cast iron with aluminum top and end covers. Black bolts are used to secure the top cover. A steering gearbox in good mechanical condition can be refinished while assembled after plugging the pressure and return hose ports. After glass-bead blasting the gearbox as a unit, refinish the aluminum covers and steering shaft connector. Allow time to dry, then carefully mask these parts and paint the housing with cast-iron-finish paint.

black bolts secured the top cover. A steering gearbox in good mechanical condition may be refinished without disassembly by plugging the hose ports for a power-steering box, then glass-bead blasting the entire unit. Apply clear paint to the aluminum covers and steel flange at the top of the box, allow to dry, and then after masking these parts, finish the body of the gearbox with cast-iron-finish paint. It's common to find a small paint daub on the aluminum top cover that can be recreated afterward.

The restored steering system on a 1969 or newer AMC car represents a collection of different finishes that include bare steel, cast iron, and plated hardware. Once installed, the subtle differences in color and sheen make for an attractive assembly that you will be proud to show off.

The bare-steel engine crossmember of this 1970 Javelin contrasts nicely with the cast-iron finish of the steering gearbox. Note also the light-colored end cover, and copper-colored splines where the pitman arm attaches to the steering gear.

Because the power steering pump is an engine accessory, its restoration was included in Chapter 7. Be sure to note the orientation of the power steering hoses at the gearbox prior to disassembly so the replacement hoses can be installed correctly.

Attached to the steering gearbox is the pitman arm, which was natural cast iron, along with the outer tie-rod ends, idler arm mounted to the passenger-side frame rail, and steering knuckles and spindles on 1969 and newer cars (1968 models still used black-painted spindles). The steel tie-rod adjusting sleeves were also left bare. Center links were treated with a darkened metal finish that is similar to gunmetal in appearance. Cast-iron steering parts may be replaced, bead blasted and clearcoated, or finished with cast-iron-finish paint. Carefully tape any rubber boots to prevent paint overspray.

Driveshaft

Driveshafts used on AMC muscle cars were bare steel with the exception of colored stripes used to identify them. In most cases three stripes were used for this purpose, running around rather than down the driveshaft. Natural-cast paint is a good choice for refinishing a driveshaft before duplicating the original stripes and installing new universal joints.

Braking System

Every AMC muscle car had drum brakes in the rear, with a choice of drum or disc brakes for the front. Early disc brake setups used Bendix four-piston calipers and solid, unvented rotors. These early brake parts are difficult to find today. For 1971, a switch was made to Kelsey-Hayes dual-piston calipers with vented rotors. Good front brake drums are also difficult to find; many are too thin to recut safely.

All early braking systems used a brass distribution block mounted to the passenger-side lower firewall. This block acts as an intersection, directing fluid to all four corners of the car. It also contains a pressure differential switch that activates the dash warning light if there is a difference in brake pressure between the front and rear brake systems. The brass distribution block, also found on 1971 and newer cars with front drum brakes, can be disassembled for cleaning, or rebuilt if badly corroded inside.

Cars with front disc brakes also employed a second brass valve located inside the passenger-side rear frame rail, just in front of the rear axle. This smaller valve regulated

The brass brake distribution block contains a pair of pistons that move to one side, and trip the dash warning light if there is a difference in front versus rear brake system pressure. This block has been painted over, and is full of dirt and corrosion. Replacement parts are available from Muscle Car Research. After cleaning, the brass housing and bracket can be glass-bead blasted, then smoothed with an extra-fine Scotch-Brite pad.

Completely rebuilt and protected by a coat of clear engine enamel, this distribution block functions like new. The mounting bracket was plated with a gold-cadmium finish originally, but reattaching the bracket to the valve after plating is especially difficult without damaging the brass.

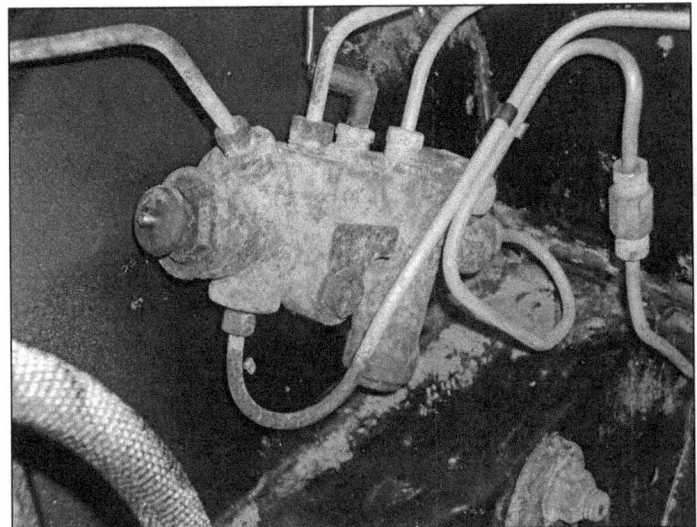
For the 1971 model year, a cast-iron combination valve replaced both the brass distribution block and smaller proportioning valve located in front of the rear axle on earlier disc brake cars. Cars with front drum brakes continued to use the brass distribution block incorporating the pressure differential switch.

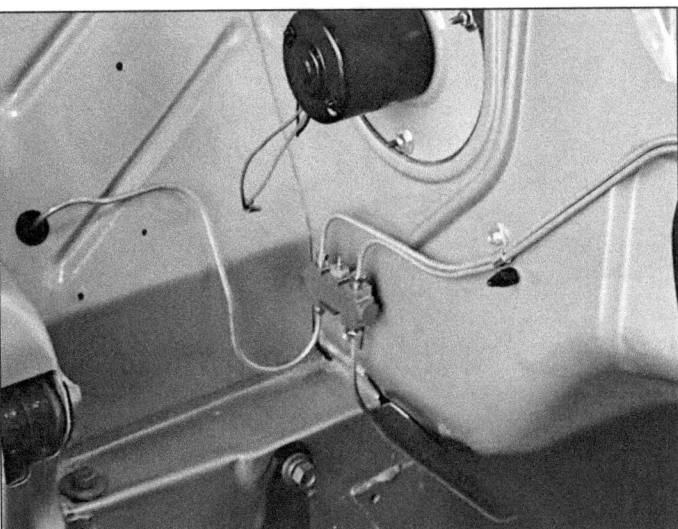
Pre-bent brake lines, such as these by Fine Lines, fit just like the originals and have correct oversized fittings where applicable so brass adapters are not needed. A bonus is the option of stainless steel tubing for permanent rust resistance. Here, the reproduction lines fit a restored brake distribution block perfectly.

front versus rear brake pressure to prevent the brakes from locking up during sudden stops. Model year 1971 saw a cast-iron combination valve that replaced both brass valves on cars with front disc brakes.

Steel brake lines differed depending on how the car was originally equipped, particularly near the master cylinder. Pre-bent reproduction brake lines are available from manufacturers such as Fine Lines, and include correct oversize fittings where required as well as protective spiral armor on the rear axle brake lines. This was used to prevent damage to the lines when the car was anchored to the car hauler truck for delivery, as well as from flying stones or other road debris. No other AMC brake lines used the spiral armor. The steel brake lines routed across the firewall on 1968–1969 models used bends that were more rounded than the crisper bends on 1970 and newer lines.

Front or rear brake drums were originally painted black, while disc brake calipers were generally natural cast iron (although some were reportedly painted black). Brake rotors were bare steel. It is recommended to replace the brake flex hoses even if they look fine because older rubber hoses can rupture or collapse without warning.

Exhaust System

Model year 1968 AMC cars still used ceramic-coated exhaust pipes that had a shiny blue appearance. These original pipes are almost non-existent today, so even most high-end 1968 restorations make do with standard steel or aluminized exhaust pipes. Pre-formed exhaust systems are available for many applications, or an exhaust system can be custom bent by a skilled technician for a perfect, rattle-free fit.

Conventional mufflers were used for most cars although the Hurst SC/Rambler was factory equipped with round Thrush mufflers. Inexpensive when new, finding a pair of NOS Thrush mufflers requires some luck today, along with several hundred dollars in most cases. Insist on authentic exhaust hangers and clamps for a high-end stock restoration. The unique original AMC exhaust tips were made from a straight section of heavy-gauge pipe finished with an angle cut; an attached worm gear clamp (like a parts store hose clamp) was included to secure it. The clamp was chrome plated along with the rest of the exhaust tip.

A popular performance option was the Trendsetter (or Sidewinder) system. This side-pipe exhaust system was bracketed to the car's underbody, and included slotted-aluminum heat shields. Trendsetters look great and sound quite a bit different from the standard dual-exhaust setup that exited behind the car.

CHAPTER 8

Early AMX and Javelin chrome-plated exhaust tips were made from straight, heavy-gauge pipe with an angled cut. They included a worm gear clamp welded in place to secure the tip to the tailpipe. The end of the tip underneath the clamp is slotted so it can be reduced in size for a tight fit. The clamp is chrome plated as well.

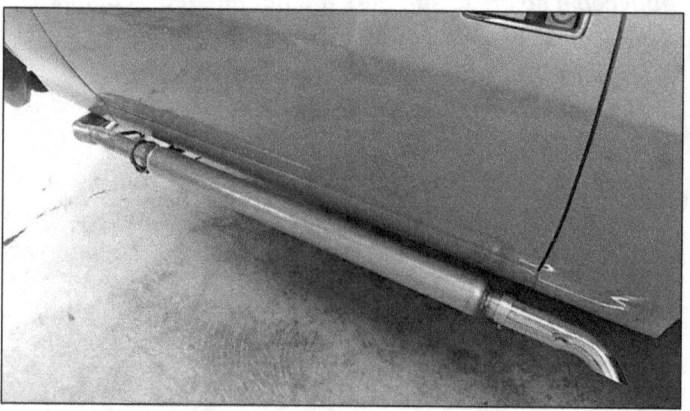

The Trendsetter side-exhaust system was a popular dealer-installed option on Javelin and AMX models. Because there is no flexible link in the system, the side pipes need to be able to move along with the drivetrain. Mounting brackets can be fabricated to include rubber bushings to reduce vibration and noise.

The completed Trendsetter side-pipe exhaust system includes slotted aluminum covers that slide into a channel attached to the rocker panel. Trendsetters replaced the original rocker panel moldings on Javelin and AMX models.

Wheels and Tires

Nothing changes the look and personality of a car more than its wheels and tires. That is why most muscle cars had optional steel rally wheels or even aluminum "mags" available straight from the factory. However, some owners preferred the look and low cost of hubcaps or wheel covers that were usually (but not always) fitted as standard equipment. Other muscle car buyers planned an upgrade to aftermarket wheels and tires right away, replacing the standard-equipment steel wheels.

The great thing about wheels and tires is that even a stock restored car can be significantly changed in appearance with the careful selection of styled wheels, without any alterations to the car. A popular practice today is to have a set of vintage wheels and tires for a trailered show car, with a separate set of wheels carrying modern radials for actual driving. Others keep a stock set of wheels for judged car shows, along with a set of custom wheels for less formal occasions.

Many AMC muscle cars, including Javelins and the 1968–1969 AMX, came with 14-inch steel wheels as standard equipment. Although a base model Javelin could have small hubcaps, SST models and AMXs were

UNDERCAR COMPONENTS

Not every AMC muscle car wore mag-style wheels from the factory. Many were equipped with optional full wheel covers, although few such cars are seen today. One drawback to this style of cover is that they are fairly heavy; they are heavier than the stamped-type wheel covers that were standard on the 1968–1969 AMX and Javelin SST.

AMC Magnum 500 wheels were chrome plated with black-painted inserts in 1968 only. The finish was changed in the following year to speckled paint on the spokes and flange, with the same black inserts. A brushed stainless steel trim ring was now clipped to the outer flange. Trim rings changed slightly during the 1969 model year. The "American Motors" inserts on newer replacement center caps are not recessed as deeply as on the originals.

equipped with full-wheel covers instead. Even with the larger covers it was a common practice to paint the steel wheels in the body color, making a nice color-keyed accent along the edge of the tire. Bias-ply tire choices changed by year, with redline tires generally used through 1969, and white-letter tires starting in 1970.

Certain models were only available with styled wheels, including the Hurst SC/Rambler, Rebel Machine, Hornet SC/360, and 1970 and newer AMX. Perhaps the most popular style of original-equipment wheel for AMC muscle cars was the five-spoke Magnum 500. In 1968, it was chrome plated with black accents. For 1969, the entire wheel was painted with a subtle two-tone effect, and a stainless steel trim ring was added. Hurst SC/Ramblers used the same wheel painted blue. Versions of the Magnum 500 wheel were offered into the early 1980s on rear-wheel-drive AMC models.

Magnum 500 trim rings were brushed stainless steel with a polished outer flange. Some replacements were made that are completely polished, and these can be carefully "brushed" with a Scotch-Brite pad used in a circular motion with the ring removed from the wheel. The earliest-style rings had four mounting clips secured to a steel ring, and used a nearly round valvestem hole. A change made early in the 1969 model year was to an oval-shaped hole that interfered less with the valvestem. Early- or late-style, all four trim rings should match!

The early 1970s saw the introduction of yet another type of ring, this one with a crimped "gripper" flange to hold it in place. This was an improvement over the four-clip rings that were difficult to install, especially if one of the clips happened to line up with a wheel weight. The later-style rings tend to scratch up the wheel rim.

Magnum 500 wheels originally installed on AMC cars were 14x6 inches, and included a simple chrome center cap with "AMERICAN MOTORS" spelled out on the insert.

Cars equipped with optional 15-inch wheels often used a five-slot–style steel wheel that has become known as the "Machine wheel" since it was standard equipment on the limited edition Rebel Machine. This wheel has become notorious for its crimped-on stainless trim ring that was designed not to be removed. Because it sealed tightly to the outer flange of the wheel, dirt and water collected inside, causing rust that eventually perforated the outer rim of the wheel. Using the proper technique, the crimped trim ring can be removed so the wheel can be restored, but without specialized skills it is very easy to destroy the ring.

Due to its complex nature and limited production, Machine wheels

CHAPTER 8

The 1969 Hurst SC/Rambler was outfitted with the same 14 x 6–inch Magnum 500 wheels as other AMC models, except these were painted bright blue over the entire face of the wheel. These wheels were manufactured by Motor Wheel Corporation, and are date coded, which is important to the serious restorer.

Legendary for commanding well over $1,000 per set, this styled 15-inch steel wheel has become known as the Machine wheel due to its standard-equipment status on the limited production Rebel Machine model. The stainless trim ring was designed to be permanent; it often caused rust to perforate the outer rim. The same wheel was optional on 1970–1971 AMX and Javelin models.

Replacing the Machine wheel for 1972 was this eight-slot–style steel wheel with removable stainless steel trim ring. It also incorporated the now familiar "volcano" center cap used on a variety of steel and aluminum wheels throughout the 1970s. A more common 14-inch version of the eight-slot wheel was used on Gremlin X and Hornet X models, among others.

in good condition are prized among AMC enthusiasts and very expensive to purchase, costing $500 or more per wheel. This same wheel was also optional on the 1970–1971 Javelin and AMX, and using a slightly different center cap.

Later 15-inch wheels were an eight-slot rally wheel trimmed with a clip-on trim ring and familiar AMC "volcano" center cap. This was a larger version of the 14-inch wheel found on Gremlin X and Hornet X models. These wheels, used beginning in 1972, were painted argent silver with a low-gloss black center. Although the 14-inch version is commonly found, 15-inch eight-slot wheels are more scarce, as are the trim rings, and are usually priced accordingly.

Currently, there are no accurate reproduction wheels available for AMCs in the aftermarket, and NOS replacements are pretty much non-existent. People often use chrome Magnum 500 Ford wheels, but it's not encouraged nor recommended because they are of a different size.

Brake Lines and Fuel Lines

Rounding out the undercar systems are the front-to-rear brake lines and main fuel supply line. All AMC brake lines are 3/16 inch in diameter; fuel lines are 5/16 inch in diameter. They were installed prior to application of the textured-black undercoating. The V-8 fuel line, which runs up the driver's side of the car, has a section of protective spiral armor located behind the front wheel, and requires one 3/8-inch mounting clip.

Pre-bent reproduction fuel and brake lines are available for AMC muscle cars in either the original tin-coated steel or long-lasting stainless. Because the stainless steel lines are not highly polished they are very similar in appearance to the originals. For this reason, stainless lines are generally considered more "preservation" than "modification," with no points deduction in stock class judging guidelines.

UNDERCAR COMPONENTS

Refinishing Galvanized Parts

Small shields protect the main fuel line from damage caused by front suspension travel, and also keep dirt and gravel from collecting on top of the front frame rails. As with other undercar parts, they were protected with a galvanized finish. However, in climates where road salt is used, these shields are frequently rusted and must be refinished. Here is a method to simulate the original finish with convincing results.

1 Although it originally had a galvanized finish, this part was rusted and required glass-bead blasting. The original appearance can be duplicated by dabbing argent silver paint on the surface using a piece of loosely balled-up tin foil.

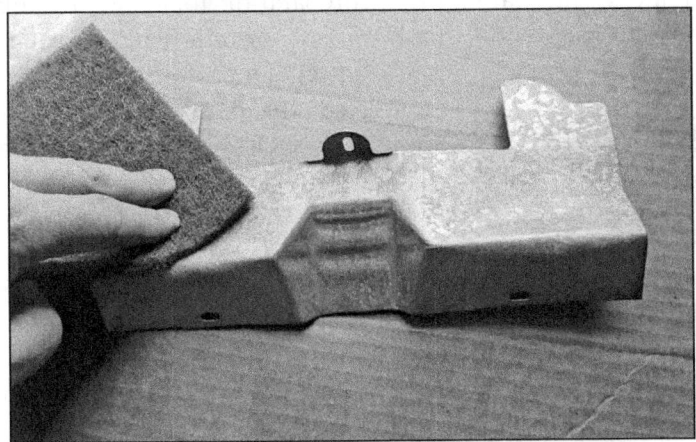

2 After allowing time to dry, blend and smooth out the paint with an extra-fine Scotch-Brite pad. Be careful not to actually remove any of the paint. After this step the surface should feel smooth, but the pattern will still be visible.

3 Next, apply a couple of thin coats of clear engine enamel to prevent the bare metal from rusting. Do not allow the paint to become too shiny; a semi-gloss appearance is just right. Now the part looks as good as new and is ready for installation.

Restore or Over-Restore?

Just as with the engine compartment, detailing the underbody can be done as neatly as you like, or more hastily with less precision for added authenticity. Carefully painting the underbody with the help of a car rotisserie likely produces much nicer results than factory original, as does the slow and deliberate application of undercoat with no overspray on the front or rear suspension parts. The choice is yours, although stock class car show judges are becoming more attuned to factory-original build techniques with each passing year.

CHAPTER 9

INTERIOR

Most AMC muscle car projects require at least some interior restoration, if not the complete replacement of the components. Seat covers, headliners, and carpet varied in quality depending on model year and application, often showing wear after only a few years. Decades of exposure to sunlight can degrade plastic dash tops and trim pieces, while deteriorated weather strips allow water to damage door panels and other interior parts. Even a car with a nice original interior may require some disassembly if rust repairs are needed for the inner rocker panels or floorpans. Removing the dash assembly makes it easier to remove the main wiring harness, and to change the heater core.

If you are fortunate enough to find a complete project car it may have an interior like this. Although serviceable, it needs carpet and seat covers, plus steering wheel and armrest restoration. However, the complete dash and door panels are nice; that's a big plus with replacement parts becoming harder to find each year.

Interior Removal

Removal of the seats should be done early on, especially if they will be sent out for new upholstery. With the seats out of the way, it is much easier to disconnect all of the wiring in preparation for removing the dash, or just for removing the main harness itself. Once everything is disconnected, the dash can be almost completely disassembled right inside the car. The gauges, radio pod, and overlays can be removed and safely stored for future use.

Once this is done, the main dash frame is reasonably easy to manage. Be sure to unbolt any braces underneath, the parking brake pedal bracket, and the steering column, then remove the chrome-plated screws on top, right below the windshield. After that, loosen the two side bolts and lift out the dash frame. With the parking brake pedal unfastened, the driver-side kick panel can now be removed.

Door Panels

Interior door panels and rear side panels are generally secured with clips and screws. After removal of the window cranks, armrests,

INTERIOR

With luck, your project car does not have a rat's nest of wiring issues hidden behind the dash. In the past, adding gauges or stereo equipment was not always done with the greatest of care. Thankfully, reproduction wiring harnesses are now available from AMC parts suppliers for popular AMC muscle cars.

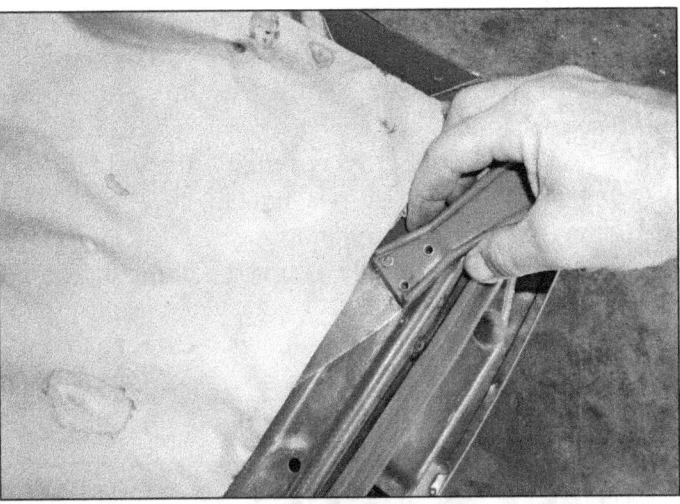

Underneath the door panel is the water shield paper, which is stuck in place using long beads of 3M Strip Caulk at either end. To remove the water shield paper, insert a dull putty knife to gently separate the paper from the inner door. If the paper tears, replacements are available, although most differ in appearance from the originals.

and remote mirror control bezel, remove all of the Phillips screws. If the panel is still firmly attached, and not merely hooked at the top, carefully check for clips along the sides. Remove these with a flat clip-removal tool, or by inserting your open hand behind the panel to support it while disengaging the clip from the door or bodyside.

Headliner

All 1968–1970 AMX headliners are a one-piece formed type made of a cardboard-like material, secured by the trim pieces that surround it. Removal of the headliner is typically accomplished by unscrewing and removing the plastic and metal trim pieces, then unhooking the headliner at the sides. The early-style AMX headliner with the crosshatch pattern has been reproduced, along with the smooth version that replaced it. The change to a smooth AMX headliner was a running change implemented throughout the 1969 model run.

Early Javelin headliners were made of formed fiberboard covered in vinyl. This type of headliner is problematic because the lightly padded vinyl did not adhere well to the fiberboard. Over time, the vinyl began to separate, something that was often accelerated by the turbulence caused from driving with the side windows open.

The longer Javelin headliners used a fiberboard shell covered in vinyl with foam backing. This type of headliner tended to separate over time, resulting in the vinyl covering sagging or falling. These headliners can often be repaired using 3M spray trim adhesive to carefully reattach the vinyl.

Although the original headliners for 1968–1972 Javelin models also tended to separate, they have not been regularly reproduced and new replacements are generally unavailable. An improved method of construction for newer headliners solved the separation problem, but these headliners cannot be used in 1968–1970 Javelins because of the center dome light hole.

Carpet and Underlayment

Carpeting can be removed right away to facilitate floor and rocker panel repairs, or it can be the last thing removed from the interior; it provides a nicer surface to sit or lie on while disassembling the dash or other parts. Carpet was another item that changed for the 1969 model year, from a loop type to cut pile. However, some carpet colors changed even earlier as the supply of loop carpet was depleted.

Both types of carpet were installed over underlayment and jute padding. Heavy, tar paper–like underlayment was installed in 1968–1970 AMX models from the firewall to the rear sill, lapping over into the forward portion of the trunk. This was used as a barrier against heat and road noise.

The current reproduction cut-pile carpet kits for early AMX models are not made exactly like the originals (with an inverted Y-shaped seam running up the center of the lower rear section). However, they are molded to fit the contours of the floorpan so most look good and fit well.

Just like the underlayment, factory original carpet has cutouts for ease of mounting the seats. Reproduction carpet kits do not, so with the carpet in place and secured with the chrome-plated screws used originally, locate the seat mounting holes by inserting a long needle through the bolt holes underneath the car.

INTERIOR

Start the front carpet installation by pulling it all the way forward so it reaches the hooks or plastic anchors on the firewall, being careful not to allow the carpet to slide back down. Next, fit the front footwell areas, using bricks or other heavy objects to keep it in place until the chrome-plated screws are installed. Some extra width can be hidden underneath the center console. Cars without a console must have adjustments made at the outer edges instead.

Underlayment is like the tarpaper used to insulate the passenger compartment from heat and road noise. It can often be removed carefully then reinstalled after floor repairs or other restoration work. Storing underlayment between sheets of wax paper keeps it clean and prevents it from sticking together.

Jute carpet padding makes the floor of the car feel more plush and comfortable. Padding is sometimes included with new automotive carpet, or can be purchased separately. Glue was used originally to keep everything in place.

AMC JAVELIN, AMX & MUSCLE CAR RESTORATION 1968–1974

If carpet padding becomes water soaked or has taken on an unpleasant smell, a few days in the sunshine does wonders. After plenty of time to dry and generally air out, store your jute padding in a new garbage bag until it is time for installation.

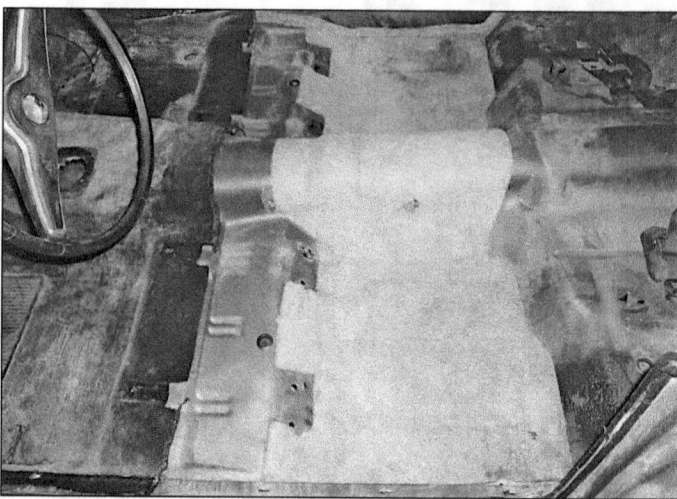

Unlike the 1968–1970 AMX, Javelin models used only carpet padding with no underlayment. Jute padding was only used where the carpet would be stepped on, so none was installed underneath the seats.

On top of that was thicker padding that was haphazardly glued in place underneath the carpet.

Also found underneath the carpet of a 1968–1970 AMX are cardboard fillers that level out the irregularly shaped rear sill. Without these "shoulder boards" the carpet sags at the ends near the wheelhouses. Transporting people or pets back there in years past often broke down these cardboard fillers with the same result. Reproductions are available from AMC parts suppliers; with careful measuring, the original screw holes can be reused for their installation because the placement of the screws was fairly random.

Early Javelin models used underlayment only for the front toe board, with jute padding installed underneath the driver's as well as the front and rear passengers' feet. The perimeter of the carpet was held in place by several chrome-plated Phillips-head screws, large plastic push-in retainers at the firewall, and metal hooks found underneath the instrument panel. The front kick panels and doorsill cover plates secure the carpet at the sides. The seats also do a fair job of keeping everything in place.

Doorsill Cover Plates

AMC doorsill cover plates were made of stamped aluminum. Javelin, AMX, and Hurst SC/Rambler models used identical plates that were drawn in a process before stamping, leaving faint stripes over the raised part of the plate. This striped effect, referred to as "etching," was not duplicated on subsequent runs of the sill plates that were available through AMC and (later) Chrysler parts departments. These later plates are completely polished, and although they function just fine, they have a distinct appearance that is obvious to car show judges.

As of this writing, doorsill cover plates have been reproduced for large AMC cars as well as newer small-body models such as the Gremlin and Hornet. However, because correct early-style sill plates have not been reproduced for Javelin and AMX models, rare NOS sets typically sell for $600 or more today.

Doorsill cover plates were made of stamped aluminum, which tended to dent and corrode. A second run of sill plates was manufactured but they lacked the subtle stripes and crisp details found on the originals. Currently, some AMC doorsill plates have been reproduced, but not for Javelin, AMX, or Hurst SC/Rambler models. For this reason, NOS originals typically sell for $600 or more per pair.

Window Glass

Side window glass may be removed for bodywork and paint, or to replace cracked or damaged weather strips. Fixed in position, 1968–1970 AMX quarter-window glass slides into a rubber channel where it is secured by two gold-colored Phillips-head screws. These are the same screws that retain the stainless steel roof-rail weather-seal channels, so that is a good place for a nice undamaged original screw for the lower quarter-glass mounting tab, which is the only one visible.

The Javelin quarter-glass and regulator is installed as an assembly. If infrequently used, these window mechanisms tended to become gummed up and difficult or impossible to work, so they benefit from a good cleaning and lubrication of the tracks and regulators.

Door glass removal is accomplished by removing the door panel, then following the procedure outlined in the factory TSM for your car. After removal, thoroughly clean and lubricate the regulators and window tracks, and replace any worn or broken parts.

The "shoes" that hold the side windows in place are glued to the lower edge of the glass and frequently come loose. The proper adhesive to attach these can be sourced from a glass shop, or use 3M weather-strip adhesive. Be sure to attach the shoes *exactly* in their original position, or they will bind and eventually come loose.

The front and rear glass is glued in position with a 3/8-inch-thick butyl seal that comes on a roll.

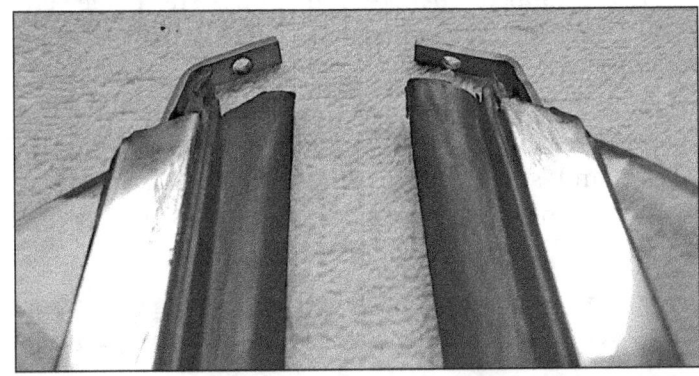

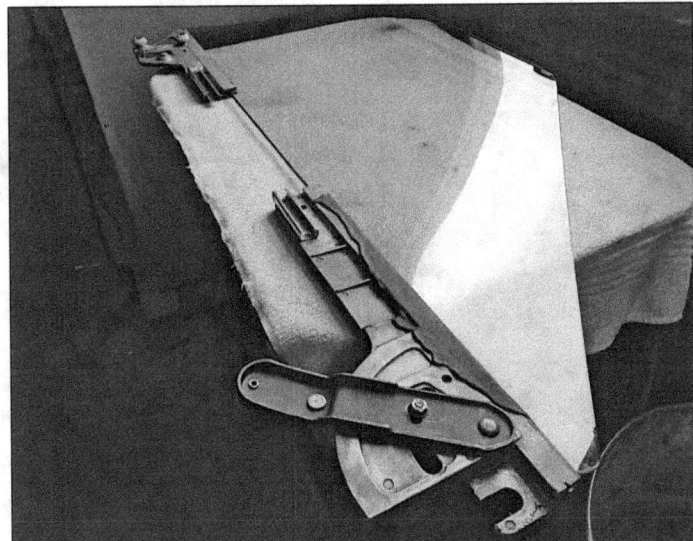

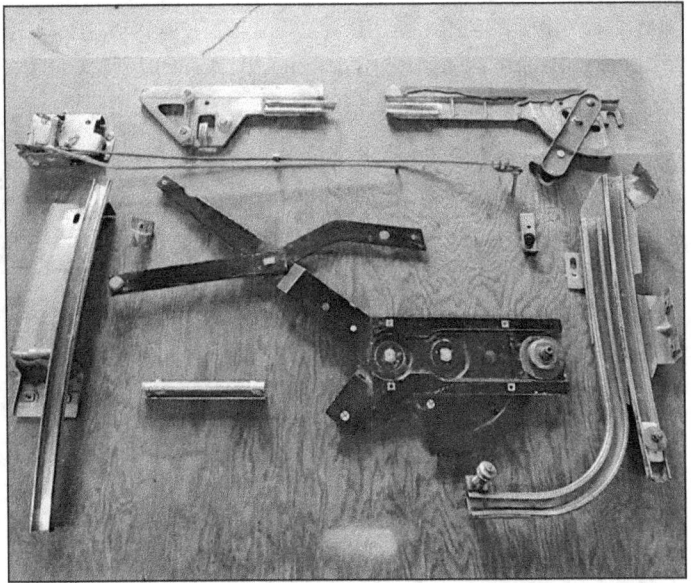

Quarter-window glass for 1968–1970 AMX models slides into a rubber channel formed by the roof-rail weather strip, then attaches with two Phillips-head screws using small tabs at the top and bottom of the glass. When replacing the roof-rail seal, first mark the location of the upper screw hole with a tape arrow because the hole will be completely hidden by the new seal. Then, install the upper screw through the rubber seal.

AMC door glass is glued to aluminum shoes that travel in the channels within the door. It is often necessary to reattach the shoes once they become separated from the glass. Be sure the shoes remain in exactly the original position (including the height of the glass in the shoe) or binding and eventual failure will occur.

Window and door-latch mechanisms changed slightly from year to year, but all benefit from a thorough cleaning and lubrication of the window tracks and door latches. Window adjustment procedures are outlined in the TSM for your particular model year.

Both windows are positioned with small, hard rubber blocks placed in the lower channel. New, tinted replacement windshields for most AMC models are readily available. Non-tinted windshields are not as easy to find; in most cases they are only available in good used condition. Although they look very similar, 1968–1970 Javelin and AMX rear windows are not the same size as 1971–1974 glass. Accordingly, the side/top exterior stainless moldings are a different length as well.

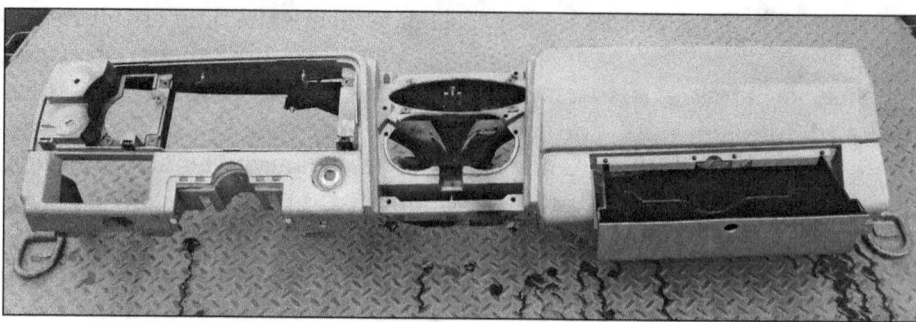

When stripped of most of its extra parts, the early AMX or Javelin instrument panel is easy to handle, but use care so you don't stress or crack the decades-old plastic. With the gauge cluster and radio pod removed, a good washing often brings back the original color of the dash. Badly faded or discolored parts can be repainted.

Dash and Console

Changes abound in AMX and Javelin instrument panels, even within the same model year in some cases. The 1968 Javelin was noted for its all-plastic dash, an industry first (although there is steel bracing underneath). Speedometers topped out at 120 mph for 1968, and black was one of the interior colors available. For 1969 models a 140-mph speedometer and larger tach was optional for the Javelin and standard in the AMX. Wood grain was added to the center speaker cover panel, and a passenger-side grab handle was added above the glove box. One mid-year addition was a molded-plastic visor installed over the three-hole gauge panel. Dark charcoal replaced black as an interior color for 1969 models only, with a switch back to black for 1970.

Dash Removal

Removing an early Javelin or AMX dash assembly is not as difficult as it appears. It can be almost completely disassembled right inside the car, leaving the main structure, which is fairly light and easy to handle. Begin by removing the lower radio housing, and either unbolting or removing the steering column.

1 *To remove the 1968–1969 gauge overlay, remove the three Phillips screws from the bottom, and then carefully tilt the bottom of the overlay to disengage the two plastic taps that hold the top edge. The center speaker cover is clipped in place and simply pulls straight away from the dash.*

2 *After reaching behind the dash to unfasten the speedometer cable, the instrument cluster can be pulled out to disconnect the electrical connection. The smaller pod to the left contains a clock, tachometer, or block-off plate. The main wiring harness can now be unscrewed from the dash.*

INTERIOR

3 Using a long screwdriver, remove the chrome-plated Phillips screws from the top edge of the dash structure.

4 Don't forget the long Phillips screws at both outer edges. These can only be reached after removal of the A-pillar trim pieces.

5 Next, loosen the 1/2-inch bolts supporting each side of the dash structure. These do not have to be completely removed because the side brackets only hook over them.

6 With the lower radio housing already removed, the complete dash can be rotated forward to disconnect any remaining electrical connections. Now the dash assembly is ready for removal from the car.

Model year 1970 also saw a completely new dash for the Javelin and AMX. Less sculptured and now incorporating a separate upper pad, Javelin SST and AMX models featured wood-grain overlays, while base model Javelins used silver-painted overlays that actually look fairly contemporary by today's standards. The narrow, padded dash top did not hold up well, frequently curling from exposure to the sun.

Reproductions are currently available if a good original dash pad is not available. Otherwise the plastic dashes held up fairly well. Minor warping or a crack is common on the top near the defroster vents, and 1970 models tended to crack near the grab handle located below the glove box.

Plastic Dash Repair

Minor cracks inherent to early AMX and Javelin instrument panels can be successfully repaired, as long as the backside of the crack is plastic welded, then reinforced to provide additional strength to the repair. Attempting to repair a crack working only from the front side does not produce satisfactory results.

1 The 1970 AMX or Javelin dash is similar to the earlier type but has a full-width removable pad on top. Cracks are inherent to this dash, particularly underneath the glove box where the grab handle installs.

2 A typical crack runs from one of the grab handle mounts down to a rivet that attaches the plastic body of the dash to a steel reinforcement. Luckily, minor cracks such as this can be repaired with excellent results.

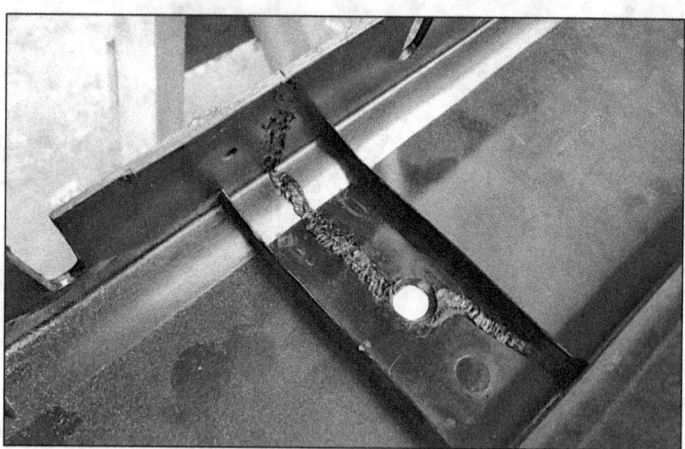

3 Use gentle pressure to close the crack, and then use a plastic welding process to melt it together, working on the backside of the dash. Be careful not to use too much heat, which may distort or even burn through the dash. Although kits are available for welding plastic material, using a small, pocket-sized screwdriver heated with a propane torch works well too.

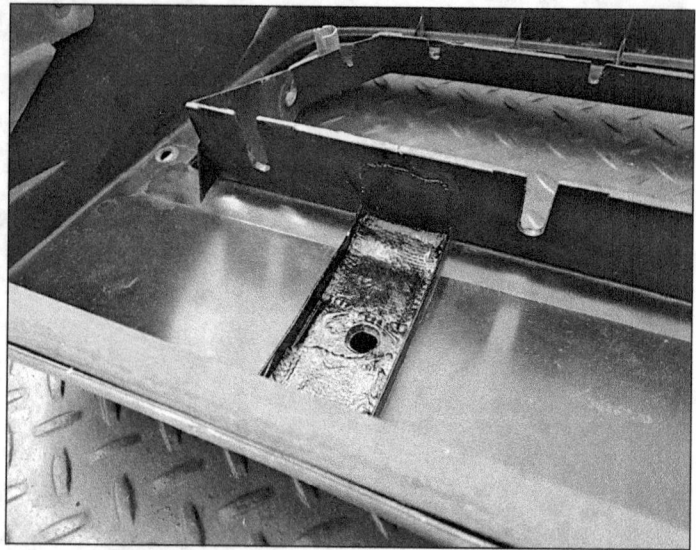

4 Next, reinforce the repair with small sections of fiberglass matting and resin or POR-15, which is available in a tube. With this area now stronger than original, the frontside can be sanded, prepped, and refinished.

For 1971, Javelin and Javelin AMX models received another new dash, this time styled like a cockpit for the driver while providing ample additional legroom for the passenger. Now the entire dash top was padded, and was manufactured with or without vents depending on whether or not the car was equipped with air conditioning. Javelin models had a small script located above the center glove box; the Javelin AMX did not.

Javelin and AMX consoles also changed frequently, and were only available with an automatic transmission for 1968–1970. A short console was used in 1968, which included only the shifter and slots to park the female ends of the front seat belts. For 1969 the center console grew to include a small storage compartment, magnets to hold the seat belts, and a courtesy light. Wood-grain overlays were now used as well. Changes for 1970 included the direction of the wood grain; it now ran side to side, to better match the dash overlays and also included the addition of a lock for the storage compartment.

Early Javelins with a column-shift automatic transmission could still be ordered with a console, minus the shifter and bezel, but they are extremely rare. The 1968–1970 cars equipped with a 4-speed manual transmission had the choice of a small optional storage tray or a fold-down armrest installed between the front seats.

Beginning in 1971, Javelin models offered a center console with either manual or floor-mounted automatic transmissions. The 1971 console was slightly different from those of 1972–1974; the difference was found at the front where it meets the lower dash. The top shifter plate for a 1971–1974 Javelin 4-speed console is particularly uncommon and expensive to purchase today.

Seats

Most AMC muscle cars were equipped with individual bucket seats; in fact, three distinct types were used between 1968 and 1974. The earliest type was a fully reclining low-back bucket, with headrest optional in 1968. Next was a non-reclining high-back bucket seat with hard-plastic back used in 1970–1972, followed by a slim-shell high-back bucket for 1973 and newer models. The handle used to tilt the seatback forward was located in the center of the seatback in 1973, and at the outer lower corner the following year.

Front seats are secured by two bolts at the rear of each seat track and one special Phillips-head screw at the front of each track. The Phillips screw doubles as a stop to limit the forward travel of the seat. These screws are typically difficult to remove when

Although foam cushions and reproduction seat covers are available from Legendary Interiors for many AMC muscle cars, one application not covered is a base model 1970 Javelin such as this one. You can be sure that the driver's seat is in even worse condition underneath that cover!

A skilled interior trim shop can create new seat cushions, and sew up replacement covers from original vinyl yardage available from SMS Auto Fabric. Minor puckers and wrinkles will disappear on the first warm sunny day.

CHAPTER 9

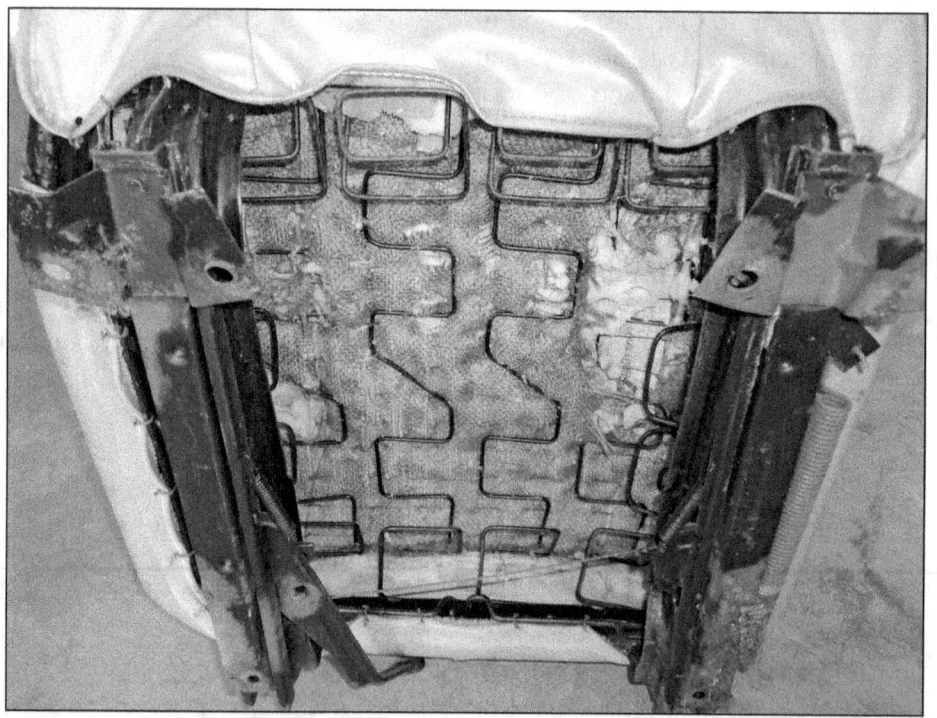

As the foam seat cushion breaks down, it falls in pieces to the floor after the burlap barrier deteriorates. Eventually, so much foam disappears that the steel springs begin to protrude through the top surface of the seat. Reproduction cushions and covers are available for AMX and Javelin recliners.

Hog rings attach the fabric border of a vinyl seat cover to the metal framework. Inexperienced installation often causes damage to brand-new seat covers. If you don't have upholstery experience, practice on some old seats before attempting to re-cover your good ones. Having the right tools, such as hog ring pliers, is a help.

Recliner mechanism cover plates were made of a chrome-finish plastic. Many were broken as passengers climbed into or out of the back of an AMX. Very nice reproductions are available from PG Classic. A curved-style recliner handle that is easier to grasp replaced the straight-style handle shown here.

rusted in place because the head is easily stripped with a screwdriver.

Should this happen, slide the seat all the way back and then carefully cut a slot into the head of the stop using a cutoff tool. A large flat-blade screwdriver can now be used to remove the stop, although it will now have to be replaced with a new one. If the flat-blade screwdriver does not remove the stop, the head can be completely ground off to free the seat; the threaded portion of the stop can be drilled out and the hole tapped if necessary.

Many popular AMC seat covers and foam cushions have been reproduced by Legendary Interiors, including foam cushions for early AMX and Javelin seats to replace the original ones, which tended to crumble and fall out of the bottom. Covers for applications not offered by Legendary can be custom sewn by a trim shop using original vinyl or cloth yardage available from SMS Auto Fabrics or other sources. Foam cushions that are not available from the aftermarket can be carved to shape by a skilled upholstery shop as well.

When restoring a car seat, strip it down to the bare frame and check for broken springs and other damage that must be welded. Next, clean and repaint the tracks and then install the foam cushions and covers. Getting everything to fit properly takes patience and a gentle touch so as not to tear the new covers. If you have never recovered a seat before, a trim shop can assemble them for you without risk of damage.

Early Javelin and AMX reclining seats have a chromed plastic cover for each recliner mechanism. Because of

INTERIOR

their vulnerable position, especially with the seat tilted forward, these mechanisms are commonly cracked and broken, or have had much of the chrome finish worn away from contact with the seat belt. Luckily, PG Classics offers excellent-quality reproductions. The shape of the recliner handle changed from a straight, tapered handle that was difficult to grasp, to a curved handle that extended farther outward from the seat and was easier to operate.

If your project car has a weathered, faded, or torn back seat, Legendary Interiors supplies new covers for many applications. Occasionally good, used, back seats come up for sale; they are salvaged from parts donors that rarely carried rear-seat passengers. If you find one that matches the back seat in your car, buy it whether you need it or not; they are usually very inexpensive and it's always good to have a spare.

Seat Belts

Two-point lap belts were standard equipment in the earliest 1968 models, with a separate shoulder harness as an option. Three-point restraints soon became standard equipment as vehicle safety evolved in the late 1960s and early 1970s. AMC seat belts saw other changes as well. The earliest lap belts usually seen in 1968 models were made of a coarsely woven strap with a small chrome-plated retractor attached to the outer belt. This retractor recoiled the belt to stow in the bell-shaped anchor cover when not in use.

Model year 1969 marked a change to seat belts with a finer weave that now incorporated a retractor built into the base of the outboard anchor. These belts still used a metal pull-type

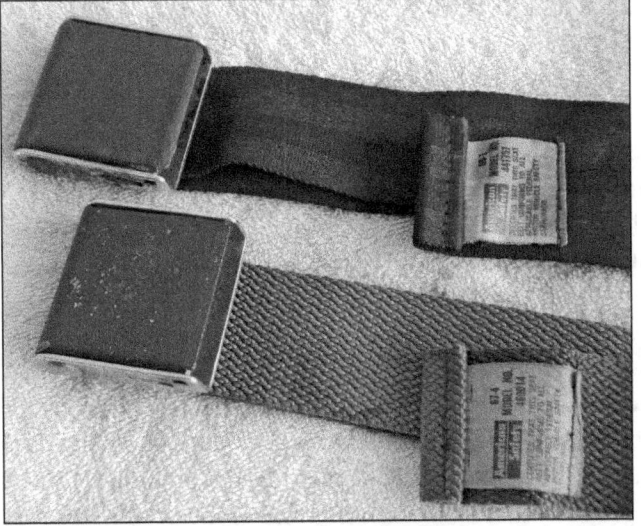

Early-style seat belts (bottom) were used in 1968 models. Straps with a smoother weave (top) were used beginning in 1969. The style of the front seat-belt retractors changed as well. AMC safety belts are date coded by year and quarter on the cloth tags.

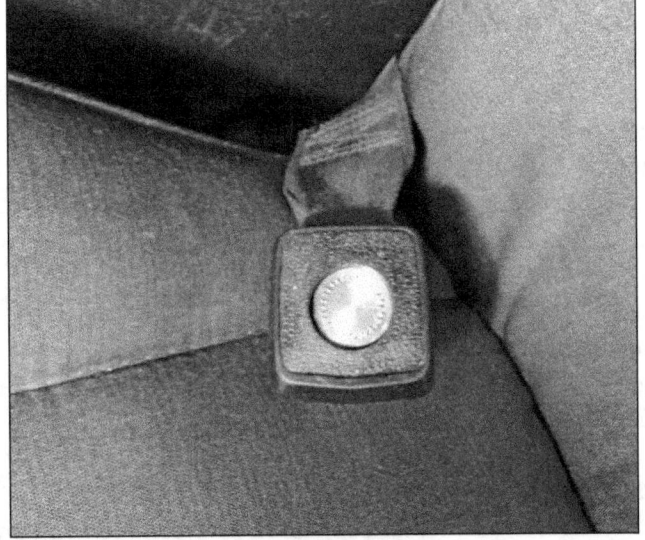

By the early 1970s, plastic push-button seat belts came into use, replacing the old-style metal buckles. Shoulder-harness belts were still separate from the lap belts in 1973, and stowed near the headliner when not in use. Three-point belts with built-in retractors followed.

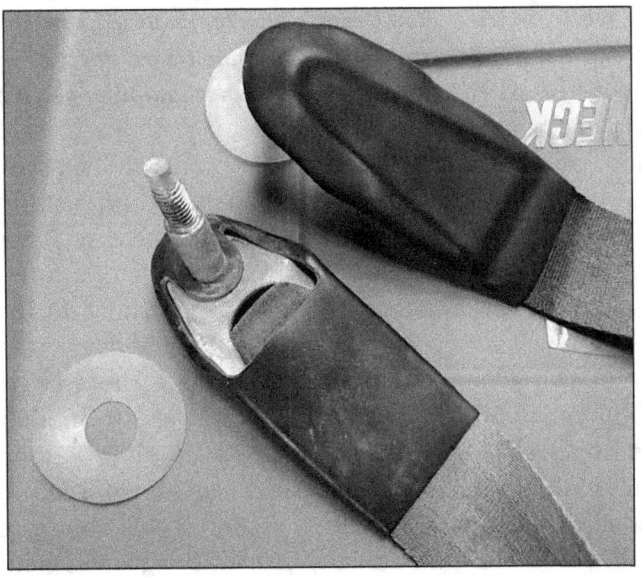

Early-style shoulder-harness belts were attached near the rear window. Because the vinyl cover actually loops around the mounting bolt, it may seem impossible to remove the belt without cutting the cover. However, the careful use of a heat gun softens the vinyl enough so it can be pulled to the side for easy removal of the bolt.

AMC JAVELIN, AMX & MUSCLE CAR RESTORATION 1968–1974

buckle as in 1968. Plastic, push-button buckles came later, along with shoulder belts that were permanently attached to the lap belts, becoming true three-point harnesses.

Federal law required the installation of a seat-belt interlock system in 1974 models. This required the front seat restraint to be secured if weight was detected on the seat; otherwise the car could not be started. Even a package on the passenger-side seat could be detected by the system and prevent the car from starting. Because of this as well as other problems, the seat-belt interlock was only used for one model year, and most systems were disabled early on.

AMC seat belts came in a variety of colors and types depending on model year, and finding certain combinations can be difficult today, especially if a particular date code is required for a specific application. Seat belts must be replaced if they are cut, frayed, or do not buckle properly. Companies, such as Ssnake-Oyl Products of Texas, can restore some belts.

Door Panels

Early-style door panels used on 1968–1970 AMX and Javelin models were made of cardboard stapled to a metal top piece, covered with embossed vinyl glued to the board. AMX and Javelin SST door panels for 1968–1969 included a wood-grain accent that was arrow shaped for 1968 but with a simple rectangle for 1969. Door panels for the 1970 AMX and Javelin SST could be keyed to the interior fabric; base model Javelin door panels were solid vinyl and completely different in appearance. Many early Javelin and AMX door panels have been reproduced by Legendary Interiors.

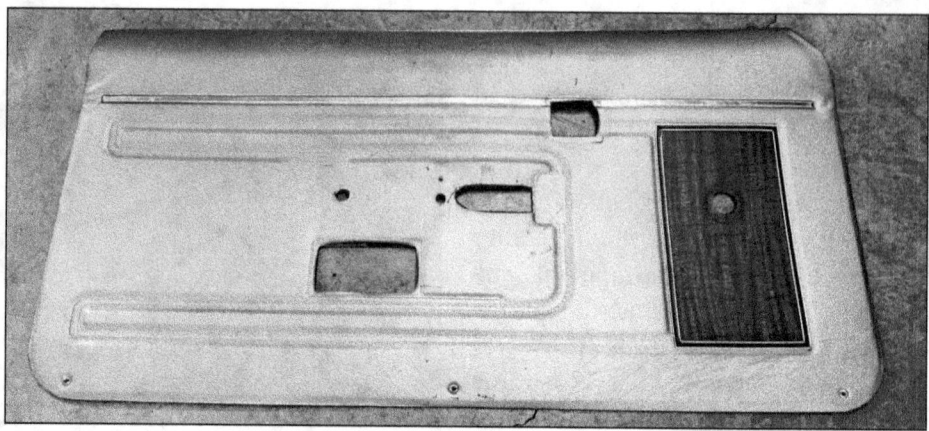

AMX and Javelin door panels used from 1968 through 1970 were made of cardboard stapled to a formed metal top piece. Repainting the panel with SEM interior paint can hide scuffs and discolorations. When not installed in the car, store the door panels face down on a firm, level surface, or let them hang freely so the board does not curl.

Water damage is fairly common on early AMC door panels. If the board is in good condition, except for warping caused by moisture, wet the backside of the panel, rest it on a firm surface, and then weight the entire board with bricks or cinder blocks. As the board dries it takes the new flat shape. If the vinyl has separated from the board at the edges it can be reattached with contact cement.

The vinyl covers on early, box-style armrests tended to shrink and curl, but these can be repaired if the vinyl is not cracked or torn. This style of armrest includes a plastic vent built into the bottom, which is frequently broken if the person removing the armrest is not aware of the center mounting screw hidden at the bottom. Plastic plugs fill the upper mounting screw holes on 1968 and base model cars, with differing wood-grain overlays used in 1969 and 1970.

Beginning in 1971, molded, hard-plastic door panels were used for all Javelin models, which included a narrow accent band determined by trim level; base, SST, AMX, or Pierre Cardin. A 1972–1973 Javelin AMX with a Pierre Cardin interior used the Cardin door panel inserts. These new door panels consist of separate upper and lower sections with a soft vinyl armrest/door pull built into the panel.

INTERIOR

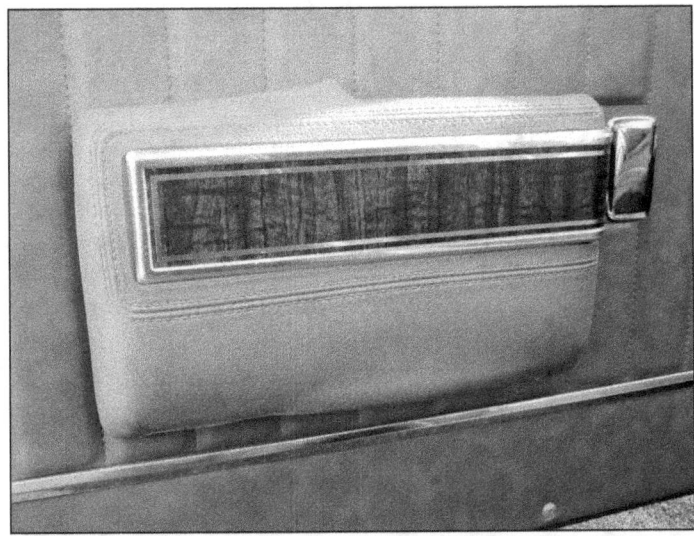

Early-style armrest curl is a common problem. If the vinyl is not cracked or torn it can be softened and reattached to the hard plastic backing. This wood-grain overlay is unique to 1970 models; the 1969 overlay does not have a bright silver edge, only a thin silver pinstripe.

Three styles of AMC window regulator cranks were used during the muscle car era. The earliest type (left) was used in early 1968 models only. It was replaced by a different style (center) and used from 1968 through 1973. The newest type (right) was found in 1973–1974 models.

For a uniform appearance when reassembling the interior doors, the window regulator crank should be positioned downward and pointed slightly to the front (the 4:00 position for the driver's door and 8:00 for the passenger's door) with the window glass in the fully raised position.

Steering Wheel

A three-spoke sport steering wheel with a simulated wood-grain outer rim was used in 1968–1969 AMX and Javelin SST models. They were great-looking wheels when new, but unfortunately tended to crack and separate in several places when exposed to seasonal climate changes. The texture of the wood grain also wore away as the car was driven.

The plastic front and rear portions of the outer rim expand and contract independent of the metal center, so once it is completely separated this wheel will crack again (even when properly repaired) as

Striking when new, but often the victim of environmental damage and wear, the AMC wood-grain steering wheel was installed in a variety of models through 1969. Good, uncracked wheels are seldom found for sale, and the rare NOS wheel is valued at more than $1,000. Changing the color of the backside is possible with careful masking and attention to detail.

The simulated–wood-grain AMC sport wheel was manufactured in various interior colors including charcoal gray, which was used in 1969 AMX, Javelin SST, and Hurst SC/Rambler models. An original wheel with no cracks or separations is a rare find to be treated with care.

CHAPTER 9

Refinishing the outer housing of a steering column is done in a low-gloss interior paint, as are other interior trim parts made of steel. The backside of the steering wheel should match in color, but have a glossier finish. Careful masking is crucial when refinishing this type of assembly.

Over time, using an AMC sport steering wheel may completely wear off the simulated–wood-grain finish, leaving behind a smooth plastic surface. Luckily it is fairly easy to replace the grain, as long as the rest of the wheel is in good condition. Begin by thoroughly washing the outer rim with a surface cleaner and allowing it to dry. Next, protect the back of the wheel and spoke ends with masking tape.

Follow up by using a coarse-grit sandpaper to replace the grain. Start with 36-grit paper, gently working around the rim of the wheel until the desired pattern is achieved. Follow that with 80-grit paper to add some finer scratches to the surface. When finished, wipe the surface with black paint using a paper towel, working it into the new grain. Before it dries completely, wipe off the excess paint with surface cleaner, leaving behind a freshly grained surface.

Model year 1970 saw the switch to a dual-spoke, rim-blow sport steering wheel. A soft-rubber switch ran around the perimeter of the wheel, allowing the driver to use the horn with his or her hands in any position. However, accidental honking was common, and the switch proved to be problematic, so this type of wheel was discontinued after just two model years. A Javelin center emblem is shown.

soon as it is exposed to cold weather. Large cracks found at the center of the wheel react similarly to cold weather. For this reason, a 1968–1969 wheel with no obvious cracks or separations is a rare find and commands a good price today.

Model year 1970 saw a switch to simpler two-spoke steering wheels, with a novel rim-blow feature optional. This was a soft-rubber horn switch running around the outer rim that made it possible to sound the horn with the driver's hands in any position on the wheel. The rim-blow feature was problematic, however, making it short lived on AMC cars.

Next came an attractive sport wheel with three brushed-aluminum spokes and a soft-vinyl outer rim. Available in a choice of colors, this wheel proved to be fairly durable and was used in one form or another in AMC, Jeep, and even some Avanti II and Bricklin cars through the late 1970s. Later-style

INTERIOR

A new, brushed-aluminum three-spoke sport wheel for 1972 proved to be the most durable yet, and it was produced in a variety of colors throughout the 1970s. After 1973, the center horn button changed to a simpler A-mark logo with "AMC" initials. Similar "Jeep" centers were also used.

wheels with a thicker vinyl or even a leather-covered outer rim directly replace the earlier ones for non-stock applications.

Interior Refinishing

Inside the car, the steering column, along with other interior metal parts, was painted with a special low-gloss paint that matched the interior color scheme. This included the exposed door tops found inside Hurst SC/Rambler, Gremlin X, and Hornet SC/360 models. Most hard-plastic interior pieces were molded in black, and then painted for use in cars with any other interior color. These parts can be recolored or merely freshened by using SEM interior paint, following the suggested cleaning and surface preparation procedures.

Vinyl seats, steering wheels, and other soft interior parts that see regular contact may not be successfully recolored. It's always best to replace these items with reproduction, NOS, or better-quality used parts in the correct color. Similarly, interior trim parts, gauge clusters, ashtrays, speaker grilles, etc. can be upgraded when NOS or better-quality used parts are located.

For ease of installation, assemble the interior in the reverse order that it was disassembled. Not having the dash or seats in the way makes it easier to position and install the headliner. Seats should be installed following the carpet and dash, and to prevent damage, door panels and doorsill cover plates should be the final interior parts installed.

AMC constantly changed suppliers so parts differed from one month to the next in some cases. It's highly recommended that you consult with fellow hobbyists who have build dates close to your car's for accurate, date-applied parts.

A desirable original accessory, and popular upgrade during restoration today, is the Rally Instruments setup added to early AMX and Javelin models. For 1968–1969 this included a unique center cover with a molded "eyebrow" over the gauges. This particular AMX is a radio delete car with an original-type block-off plate installed. These items are available from AMARK AMX/Javelin Parts.

A great period-correct accessory for cars not already equipped was a genuine "AM" script tachometer for the top of the dash. Rare and expensive today, original accessories such as this really add appeal to the interior of an AMC restoration.

CHAPTER 10

TRUNK

Excepting the V-8 Gremlin X, all 1968–1974 AMC muscle cars have a typical locking trunk area with no access from the passenger compartment. The trunk area of these cars was painted in the body color, followed by speckle-finish trunk paint on 1970 and newer models.

The underside of the trunk lid and the latch remained body color on these cars.

One important detail often missing on a 1968–1970 AMX trunk compartment is the tapered ends of the interior floor underlayment, which spills into the forward part of the trunk. If missing, new sections can be cut to fit and then attached with weather-strip adhesive. Because Javelin models did not have underlayment extending all the way back, none is visible from inside the trunk.

To provide some protection to the outer body's sheet metal from cargo shifting inside the trunk, a heavy coat of textured sound deadener was applied to the inner quarter panels prior to paint. Naturally, some of this often found its way onto the outer wheelhouses and, in many cases, even to the outer ends of the trunk floor. However, care was generally taken to prevent emblem or side-marker light holes from being covered over.

Sound deadener that has flaked off or has been removed by grinding or sanding for quarter-panel repairs can be replaced with plastic body filler, mixed with very little hardener, then applied with a small roller until the desired texture is achieved. Very early 1968 models had sound deadener sprayed inside the trunk as seam sealer as well. This practice was soon changed to a manual application of seam sealer around the driver- and passenger-side wheelhouse, fuel filler cover, and even the spare tire hold-down in many cases.

These are examples of original spare-tire tools and a hold-down removed from a 1968 AMX. Early inflator canisters were branded Chilton instead of American Motors, and indicated for use with size 7.35x14 tires. The scissor jack and the unique folding lug wrench were painted black before assembly.

TRUNK

The trunk area requires careful attention to detail just like every other area of the car. The components inside were originally installed and finished in a particular order that must be duplicated for an accurate restoration. Certain items and finishes also changed depending on vehicle build date.

When preparing for an overall repaint, first install and adjust the trunk lid. The entire trunk area, including the underside of the lid, jamb area, latch, and striker can then be sprayed together without risking chips and scratches later while adjusting the trunk lid.

Textured sound deadener was sprayed onto the inner quarter panels to offer some protection to the outer body sheet metal from shifting cargo in the trunk. If the original coating is flaking off, or must be removed for quarter-panel repairs, using body filler mixed with very little hardener can duplicate it. This allows time to apply the material with a spreader; roll it out until the desired texture is achieved.

The diagonal rear bumper brackets located inside the trunk were originally painted semi-gloss black. They were installed after the car was painted, including the speckled trunk paint beginning in 1970. By 1973, many of these brackets were coated with speckled paint, not body-color paint.

Underneath the trunk mat, a yellow wire is attached to the gas tank sending unit, which enters the trunk through a rubber grommet. It is protected by a section of asphalt-coated wire loom, and fastened to the trunk floor with black tape. Reproduction trunk mats are available for many AMC models if the original cannot be reinstalled; unfortunately, many do not match the cut and texture of the originals exactly.

Many cars had a fuel tank vent installed behind the trunk striker panel. It consisted of a loop of 5/16-inch-diameter fuel hose from the filler neck through a rubber grommet to a fitting on the fuel filler housing inside the trunk.

CHAPTER 10

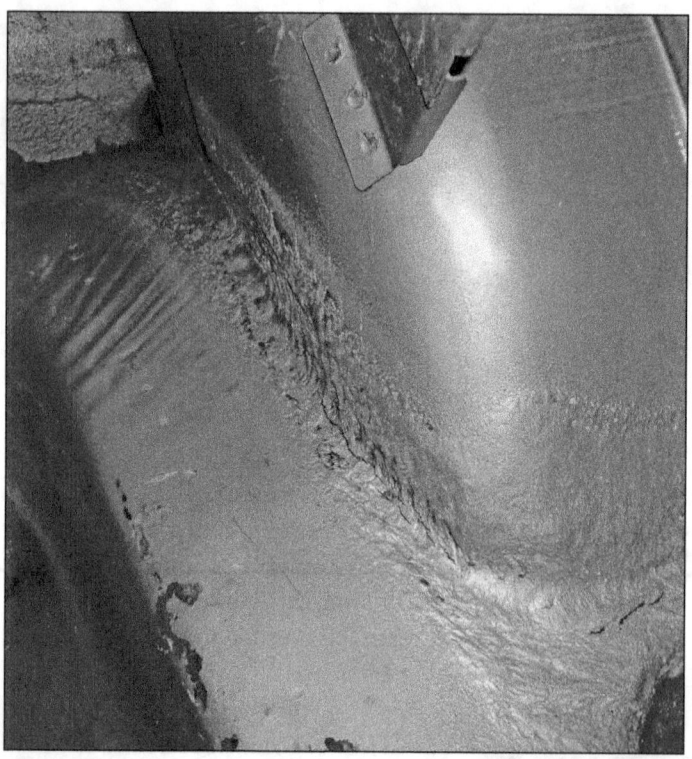

Some very early 1968 models used spayed-on sound deadener as seam sealer inside the trunk and passenger compartment. Sealer applied manually soon replaced this. Both types were then painted over when the complete body assembly was sprayed.

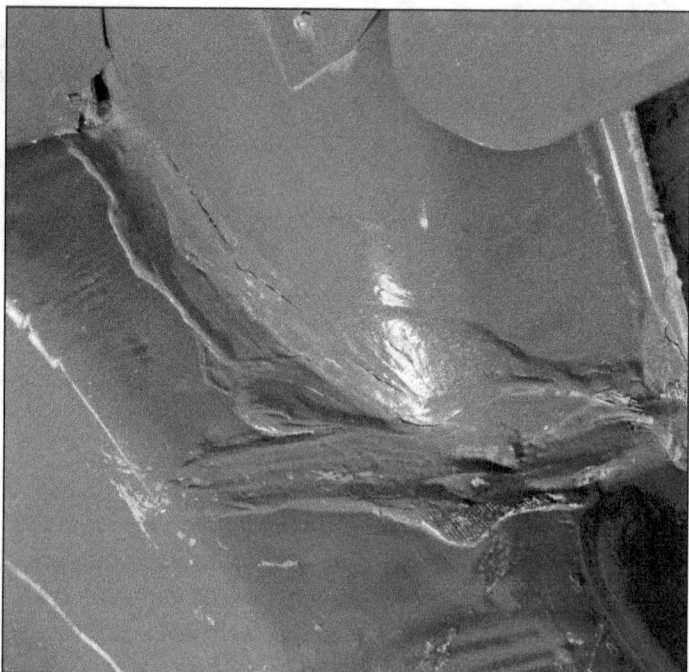

Most often the original seam sealer used on the floor-pans and around the wheelhouse panels in the trunk was not applied with a lot of care. This application can be preserved or duplicated for an accurate trunk area restoration. Using disposable latex or nitrile gloves, apply plastic body filler with two fingers to replace seam sealer inside the trunk.

As when new, reproduction trunk mats are the finishing touch that protect the painted trunk floor from scratches and other damage. Even with a new trunk seal installed, check underneath the mat after washing the car to be sure no water has leaked into the trunk. The lower corners of the rear window are notorious for water leaks.

The wiring harness for the rear lights was secured to the taillight panel with small studs that held plastic straps on some cars and bendable steel tabs on others. For 1970, a new taillight panel on Javelin and AMX models necessitated keeping the harness in place by using several foam rubber firewall grommets stuffed above the taillights.

Two-passenger AMXs, Go Package Javelins, as well as other AMC models included a Space Saver spare tire manufactured by BFGoodrich. Intended to save trunk space as well as weight, the Space Saver spare included a canister of compressed gas used to inflate the tire if necessary. Most canisters today, even brand-new ones, are empty and used for display purposes only; you do not want to inflate or attempt to use an original Space Saver spare because it will not return to its original compact form once inflated.

Cars originally equipped with a Space Saver spare tire have the spare tire hold-down welded in a position where a conventional tire does not fit.

The Space Saver spare tire was mounted on a standard steel wheel that was painted bright orange, apparently to discourage long-term use, or to remind the driver to replace it with an actual tire as soon as possible. To correctly refinish this wheel, the backside should be painted first in black, then with orange paint oversprayed onto the black through the slots between the wheel center and outer rim. Omaha Orange is a great match for the color used on these wheels.

Reproduction decals are available for Space Saver spares, including one issued to many owners after taking delivery of their car.

In addition to the tire-inflator canister, a novel folding lug wrench and scissor-type jack were provided as well. Both of these items varied slightly by year and application. Although the lug wrench was always painted black, the scissor jack could be either black or bright blue starting in 1970.

Storage of the spare tire and tools is shown on the jack instructions sticker affixed to the underside of the trunk lid. Many reproduction stickers lack sufficient detail to see this, but often an original jack instructions sticker can be photocopied, or even reproduced on peel-and-stick paper with excellent results. Jack instruction stickers changed as AMC replaced the early "AM" script with

Even a ratty factory-issued trunk mat is useful for determining the original size and cut of the mat. Some reproductions do not match the originals exactly. Here you can see some of the brown underlayment flaps that fall into the front part of the trunk in a 1968–1970 AMX.

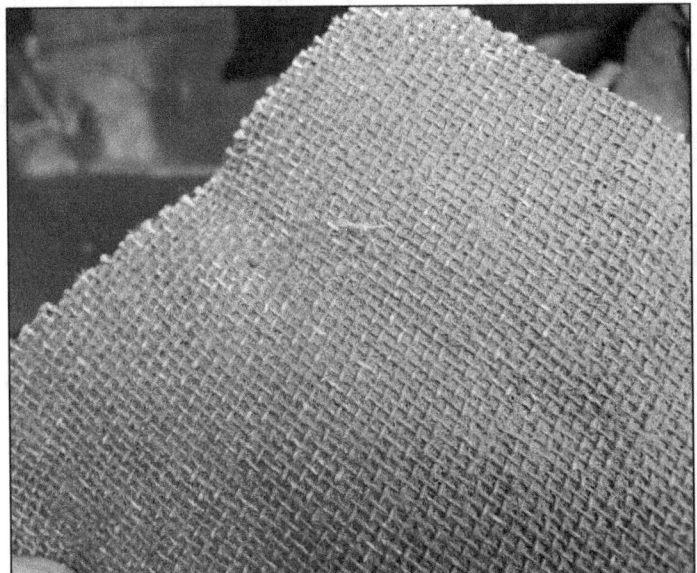
An original trunk mat from a 1968 AMX consists of a coated burlap-like material, and is rough to the touch. Good used trunk mats are hard to find, and unused NOS mats are extremely rare. Even a similar reproduction trunk mat is better than not having one at all.

Whether your car requires a full-size spare tire or compact Space Saver, the spare tire, inflator canister (if applicable), and tire changing tools must be stored as shown on the "jack instructions" sticker affixed to the bottom of the trunk lid. Space Saver spare tires were installed face down, pinning down the scissor-type jack. Clip the inflator canister to the lug wrench after tightening the hold-down wing nut.

This typical, unused BFGoodrich Space Saver spare tire still shows signs of wear, particularly from being mounted inside the trunk on top of the jack. Glass-bead blasting removes paint and surface rust from the wheel without damage to the rubber tire. Be sure to protect the valve-stem with duct tape before blasting the wheel.

The backside of this wheel was painted black first, and then the front was done in bright orange without any masking or other special care. Sometimes the orange paint even ran onto the backside of the wheel. Good enough for a new car circa 1968!

the new A-mark logo; the instructions often differed among cars equipped with a Space Saver spare versus conventional full-size spare tire.

Another label commonly found in the trunk is a silver-foil warning sticker for cars equipped with a Twin-Grip rear axle. It was (often crookedly) attached to the lower part of the passenger-side inner wheelhouse, near the spare tire. Also in the trunk were the angled rear bumper brackets that were installed after the cars were painted, including the speckle-finish paint on 1970 and newer models. These brackets were always finished in semi-gloss black.

A popular option ordered for many cars was a trunk light. This was secured inside the trunk lid bracing, near the latch, with a single silver-colored Phillips-head screw. This light was operated by a mercury switch, lighting the bulb only with the trunk lid in the open position. However, when displaying the car at shows, the trunk light can be unplugged via a single bullet connector found near the driver-side trunk hinge.

The rubber trunk seal fits tightly into a channel running around the trunk opening. Generally, some weather-strip adhesive was used at the corners to keep it in place. The seam where the ends of the trunk seal meet is at the rear part of the trunk opening where it is less likely to leak water, often several inches to the passenger side of center.

Once your trunk area is refinished, exercise care when hauling large items so that nothing comes in contact with the inside quarter panels, spare tire, or underside of the trunk lid.

After stripping the original paint, repaint the backside, and then apply the orange to the front. Omaha Orange, among other colors, is a reasonable match to the original shade. Be extremely careful to mask the valve and tire so they are not oversprayed. Reproduction stickers for Space Saver wheels are available.

TRUNK

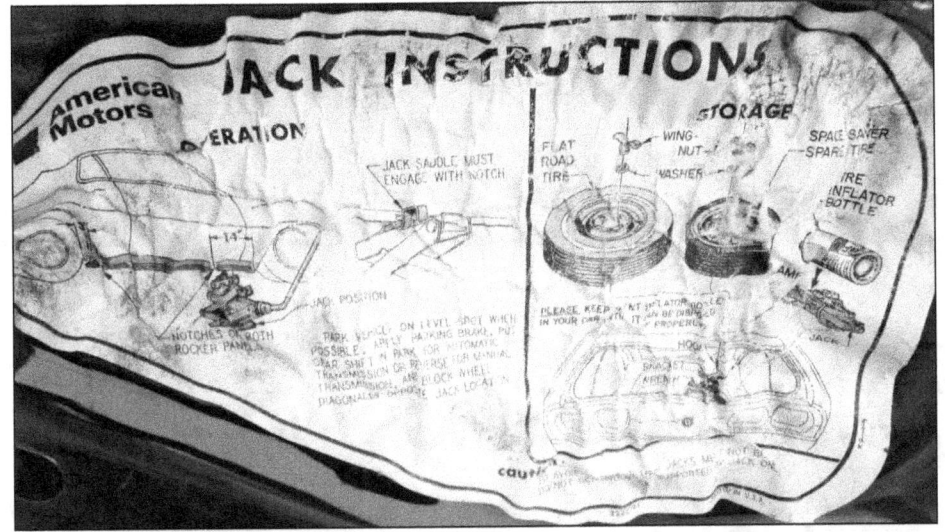

Because they were printed on paper, original jack instructions stickers frequently deteriorate after exposure to humidity. Instructions for the most popular applications have been reproduced; however, many are of poor quality, made of shiny film or missing important original detail.

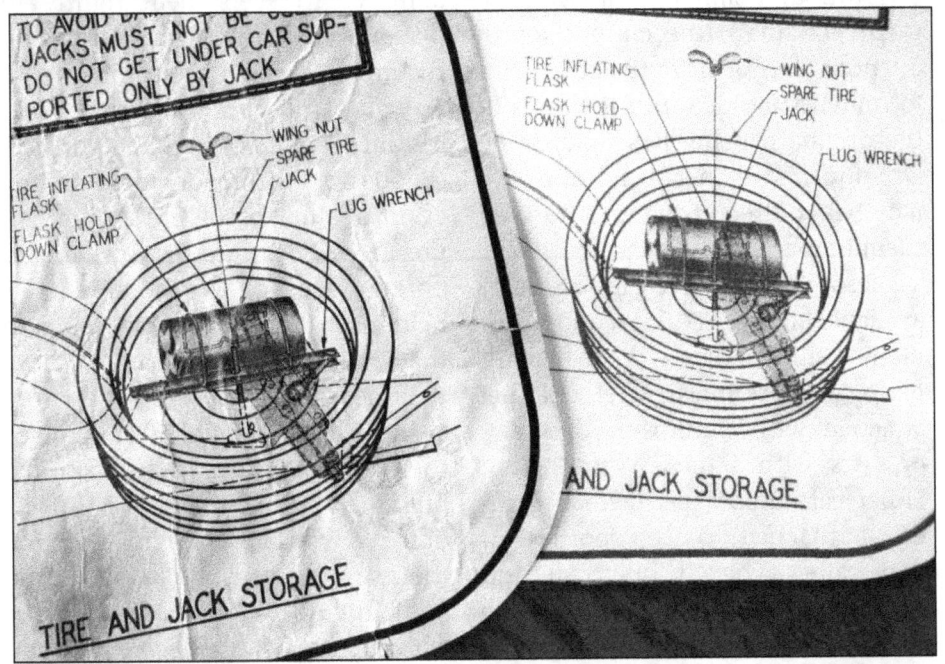

If an original jack instructions sticker can be removed without losing any of the printing, it can often be recreated at a print shop by digitally cleaning up a scan of the original. Then it can be printed on self-stick paper, or simply attached to the trunk lid using rubber cement.

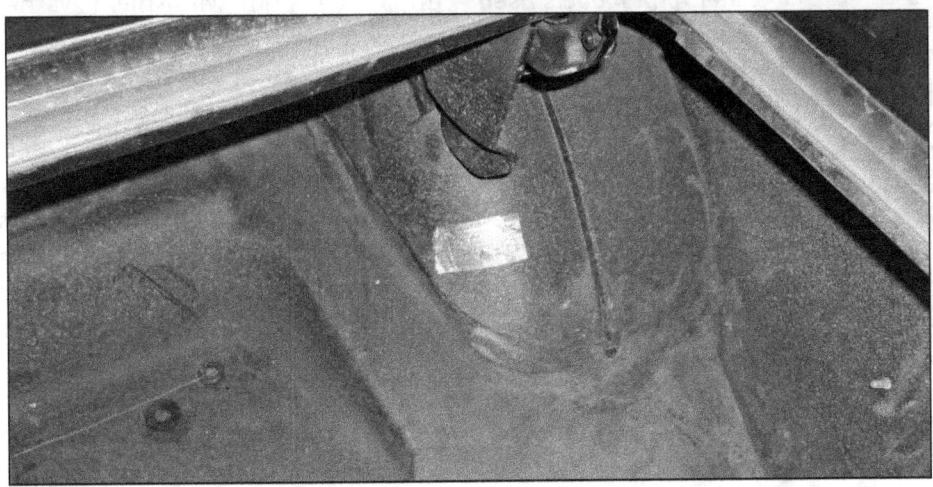

A foil sticker applied to the passenger-side inner wheelhousing indicates the presence of a Twin-Grip rear axle in this AMC muscle car. The sticker serves as a warning that even with one rear wheel elevated, the other still drives. That would be a bad situation in which to find yourself during a routine tire change!

CHAPTER 11

BODY TRIM AND FINISHING

Depending on the level of disassembly required for your particular restoration project, a car's return from the paint shop could mark the beginning of a bare-shell reassembly, or at the very least, the reinstallation of the car's weather strips, bumpers, lights, grille, and other exterior brightwork. A good place to start is with the rubber parts: door, window, cowl, and trunk seals plus the assorted rubber bumpers and stops found throughout the car.

Rubber Parts

Reproduction door seals are available for Javelin and AMX models. Although similar in appearance to the originals, the current reproductions do not have the steel reinforcements molded into the ends of the originals. Being less rigid, some additional weather-strip adhesive may be required at the ends to keep them in place.

Roof-rail weatherseals are also available from AMC vendors for many vehicles. These were held in place by a stainless steel channel attached with Phillips-head screws on cars with frameless side glass. Other cars used a perimeter weatherseal attached to the door's window frame. Typically, door seals and roof-rail seals require at least some adhesive to keep them tightly in place. In most cases, trunk seals also require adhesive at the corners.

The rubber cowl seal was installed to prevent the driver's vision from being obscured in the event of a major cooling system failure. It seals the upper cowl to the bottom edge of the hood, and is held in place by a formed steel band that was temporarily attached to the car before paint. For this reason, it should be body color, along with the two Phillips-head screws used to hold it. Typically, these were the second screws from the end although there are exceptions. For maximum authenticity, the remaining screws are slightly shorter and remain unpainted. Both windshield washer nozzles have a small circular seal where they pass through the cowl.

In addition to the round hood stops found on the upper core support (and hood latch support of 1971–1974 Javelin models), rubber side bumpers were also used; on first-generation cars they were originally installed with the higher side closer to the engine. A second-generation Javelin likely has these bumpers reversed with the higher side facing out. Also don't overlook the rectangular pads

Later AMX models used a one-piece nameplate, which had two mounting posts. Because it's a common practice to dress a standard Javelin as an AMX, be sure to position these emblems correctly. Base and SST trim-level Javelins have a small "Javelin" script above the small center glove box; AMX models do not.

BODY TRIM AND FINISHING

Reproduction door weatherseals available for AMC applications lack the steel reinforcements found in the ends of the originals. A bit of weather-strip adhesive serves to keep the ends in place without this extra support. Plastic retaining pins are often provided as well, but the originals can be refinished and reused instead.

The seam for the rubber trunk seal is always toward the back of the trunk opening, often to the passenger's side of the latch and striker. In most cases, some weather-strip adhesive is required at the corners to keep the trunk seal in place and prevent water leaks.

The cowl-seal retainer band was attached with two screws, and then painted along with the rest of the car. Typically, the second screw from the end was used during the paint process; however, there were exceptions (shown). The screws added when the rubber seal was installed are a bit shorter, and are not painted in the body color.

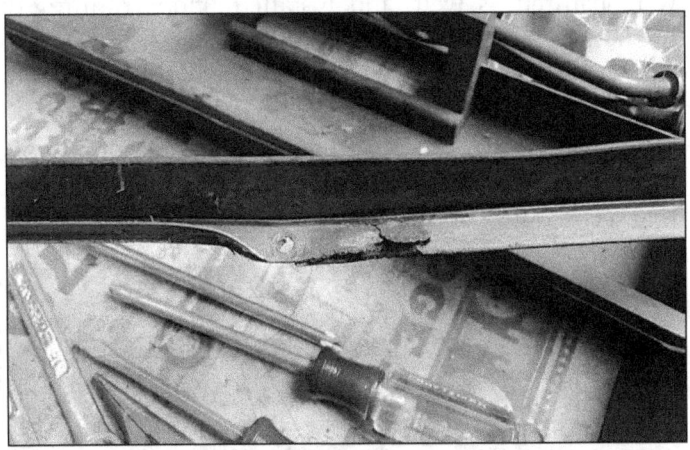

Over years of use, the unpainted backside of the cowl-seal retainer band invited rust, but reproduction bands are available from AMC parts suppliers. Unfortunately, a portion of the cowl behind the band was blocked from being painted, and is prone to rust damage.

placed at the highest part of the fender sill, which keeps the hood from making contact when closed and latched. These rubber bumpers and pads are available from American Parts Depot, Kennedy American, and other AMC parts suppliers.

Doors have cone-shaped rubber bumpers located near the latch, and a circular rubber plug sealing a small access hole on 1969 and newer doors. Exterior side-window sweeps clip into position at the door top. These should be installed following the side window installation. Interior window sweeps are part of the door panel on AMX and Javelin models, but separate on others.

Bumpers

Bumper rails were chrome plated on all AMC muscle cars, with 1969 AMX and Javelin models equipped with the Big Bad Colors option being the sole exception. These limited production cars had front and rear body-colored bumpers that included

A freshly plated bumper in proper alignment with the car body contributes to a great-looking restoration. Used soft towels taped to the bumper ends prevent paint damage until the bumper is aligned and bolted in place. With plenty of clearance between the bumper rail and body, the towels can then be easily removed.

a thin polished molding on the front rail, which completed the bright perimeter of the grille opening. If rear bumper guards were ordered they were painted as well, and installed using thin rubber gaskets to prevent paint chipping and rust.

Front bumpers typically used black-painted brackets bolted directly to the front frame rail. Different bracket combinations were used depending on model and year. Rear bumper brackets were a two-piece design with the main bracket bolted to the frame rail through the trunk floor, running diagonally to the taillight panel. A smaller bracket was located inside the rear bumper rail, and was sealed to the body with a small amount of black 3M Strip-Caulk.

Both front and rear bumpers for 1968 and 1969 Javelin and AMX models were identical; 1970 front bumpers were a one-year-only design, and 1971–1974 front rails were the same year to year with only changes to the bumper guards. Javelin and AMX rear bumpers changed slightly with the biggest difference being square versus later rectangular mounting holes. A quality chrome-plating shop can salvage a dented or twisted bumper rail, or one with extra holes drilled for a trailer hitch. However, due to industry regulations, expect to pay from $600 to $750 for replating an average set of bumpers, and possibly more if additional repair work is needed.

Installing bumpers on a newly painted car requires a great deal of care and patience. It is very easy to scratch or chip the surrounding paint if precautions are not taken. The best method is to attach all of the bumper brackets, guards, and hardware to the bumper rail, and then wrap the ends of the bumper with soft towels taped in place. This prevents the rail from

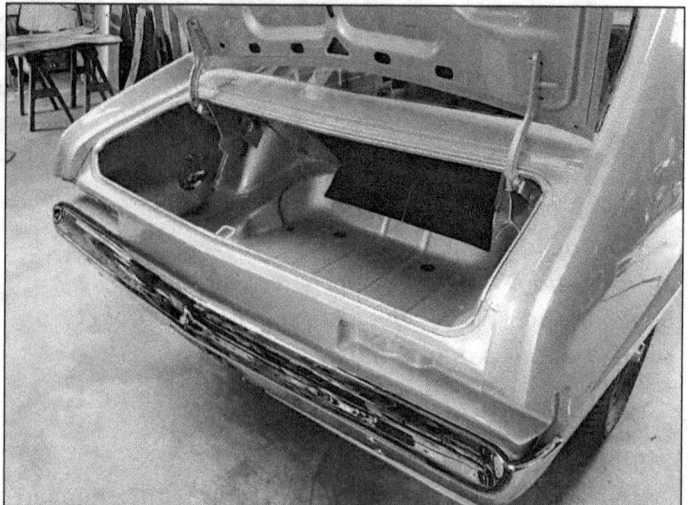

As when installing the front bumper, both ends of the rear bumper rail must be wrapped in towels to protect the surrounding paint during installation. The rear bumper has less adjustment, but still should be perfectly centered and level. It is safer to install the bumper before adding the taillights and center reflector.

The lower portions of the 1968–1969 AMX grille and headlight bezels fit behind the upper edge of the front bumper rail. Install these items before lifting the bumper into its final position. Early Javelin grilles do not fit underneath the upper lip of the front bumper.

making contact with the paint before the bumper is properly adjusted and secured. The towels can then be easily removed.

Bumpers should be straight and perfectly centered on the car. Spacing between the bumper end and fender should be even on both sides. On 1968–1969 Javelin and AMX models the bumper should not make contact with the plastic headlight bezels. Having a helper available to install bumpers is preferable, although it can be done by one person using a padded milk crate or similar stand to hold the opposite end of the bumper at its approximate mounting height.

Moldings and Trim

Installing outer body moldings and other brightwork requires the same care as used when mounting the bumpers. Otherwise, paint chips and scratches are a definite possibility. Even though the front and rear window molding clips are installed before outer body paint, using a strip of masking tape along the window opening protects the paint until the moldings are snapped securely in place. These and many other exterior trim pieces, including some rocker panel moldings, are made of formed stainless steel. Minor dings and scratches in these parts can usually be repaired, or sanded out and polished.

Stainless steel roof-rail trim is fairly easy to remove, but very difficult to reinstall without damage. Although some restorers report using a bottle opener to remove it, this task is best accomplished using a small block of wood and hammer to tap the molding outward from the underside, working from one end to the other until the molding is removed.

Bright stainless steel drip-rail moldings are fairly easy to remove, but difficult to reinstall without bending or denting. If there is no rust nearby, many restorers prefer to protect the moldings with tape and leave them in place rather than risking damage. Minor scratches and scuffs on the drip rail moldings can be polished out right on the car.

Replacing the drip-rail moldings must be done by hand, or by using a soft, well-padded mallet to gently tap them into position. Be aware that because of their very tight fit even an additional coat of paint on the roof rails may prevent the moldings from being installed. This, combined with their fragile nature prompts many restorers to leave the drip-rail moldings in place when repainting the car. Minor scuffs and scratches can still be polished out if necessary, even with the moldings in place on the car.

Most other moldings and trim require unique clips or fasteners for installation. Many plastic clips cannot be reused, but replacements are generally available from AMC vendors or from auto body suppliers. Solid cast moldings, such as early AMX rocker panel covers, require Phillips-head screws for installation.

AMC emblems are mounted using a variety of methods, including barrel clips for the AMX quarter-panel circles. These circles are curved slightly to conform to the contour of the quarter panel. When installing used circles, set them in place without the clips so you can check the fitment. If adjustment is needed, it can be done before snapping them in place.

CHAPTER 11

All AMC engine identification badges are interchangeable for ones of the same year without modification to the car. For 1968–1969 models, the badges are secured with acorn nuts on the inner quarter panel. These nuts should not be painted the body color when refinishing the trunk area because the badges were originally installed after paint.

Stainless steel screws work great for this purpose and never rust. Just be sure to paint the heads black to match the grooves in the moldings. The wheel lip moldings used on 1971–1974 Javelin models were also attached with small screws. No such moldings were used on earlier cars.

AMC emblems and logos are attached with a variety of fasteners including barrel clips, acorn nuts, and spring clips. If emblem- or trim-mounting holes need to be transferred to a replacement body panel, use paper to make a pattern of the holes.

Positioning New Holes

During auto restoration it frequently becomes necessary to transfer the position of emblem or trim-piece mounting holes to a replacement body panel. Never guess, especially when installing emblems that will forever look odd if crooked or even slightly misplaced.

1 Sometimes emblem or trim-piece mounting holes must be transferred to a replacement body panel, such as with this NOS 1970 Javelin hood, which is supplied without any holes. When using the front fenders or trunk lid from a different model year car, it is often necessary to replace original emblem mounting holes as well.

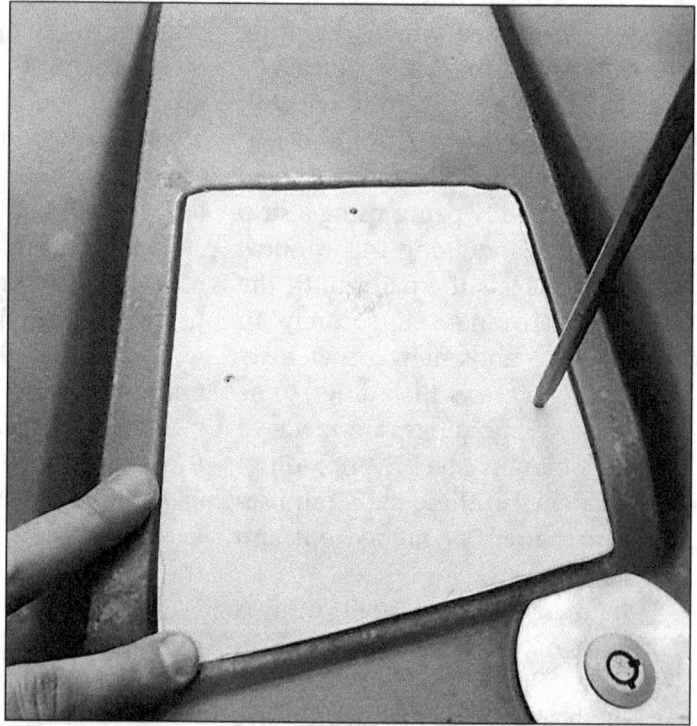

2 Using the original panel, or one just like it, make a pattern showing the position of the holes. The pattern should line up with the edge of the panel, or some other reference point, so that it can be positioned in exactly the same place on the new panel.

3 After transferring the position of the holes, use a center punch to dimple the metal before drilling. This prevents the bit from walking, even slightly, which would reposition the hole. Use only a sharp drill bit, and then deburr the new holes.

4 With the mounting holes in exactly the right position, the trim piece fits perfectly. This task is best accomplished before paint, but if it needs to be done afterward, carefully paint inside the holes to prevent rust from starting.

Grille and Lights

The late 1960s and early 1970s is when most automakers switched from stamped or cast-metal grilles to those made of plastic, and American Motors was no exception. Javelin AMX models for 1971–1974 actually used both. Although fairly durable, the plastic grilles originally used on AMC muscle cars generally took a beating due to their vulnerable position on the car. Bumpers provided little actual protection, and even minor taps generally resulted in damage to the grille. Others were damaged during engine swaps or other mishaps.

Decades later, NOS grilles are difficult to find and very expensive. Most used grilles have at least some damage, usually cracks or broken mounting tabs, if not pieces completely missing.

Many damaged plastic grilles can be repaired and refinished by a skilled specialist, after which no evidence of the original damage is visible. This process involves bonding breaks or even fabricating or transferring pieces from a donor grille that is in worse condition than the one being repaired. Refinishing a repaired or new unpainted grille is a multi-step process that varies by application. If possible, wash and closely examine your original grille for evidence of overspray of paint patterns that may indicate the original paint process.

For example, a 1968–1969 AMX grille was molded in black plastic. The finned area was then masked for the application of textured

The 1971 Javelin AMX outer grille screen included a silver mesh in the center. Screens used for 1972–1974 models were blacked out in the center but still used a bright outer frame. The flat "AMX" nameplate has a special base that matches the contour of the grille screen.

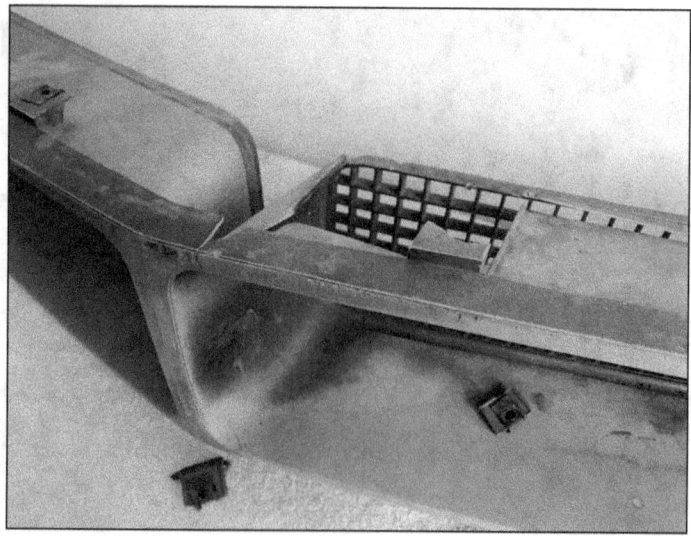

In the right hands, even this damaged Javelin grille can be restored to like-new condition. Skilled grille repair and refinishing is difficult and time consuming, so expect to pay accordingly. If your grille only needs freshening, merely duplicating the original finish is not as difficult.

A skillfully restored grille looks as good as, or even better than, an NOS grille. This 1968 Javelin grille even has reinforced mounting tabs that are less likely to break than the originals. Most AMC muscle car grilles have not been reproduced, and because unused NOS grilles are in short supply, the ability to repair a damaged original grille has become more important than ever.

The inner grille tub pressed into service for 1971–1974 Javelin AMX models started out as a standard 1971 Javelin grille, which was then modified to accept turn signals and the outer screen. Being suspended with inadequate support underneath often causes this grille to crack under its own weight.

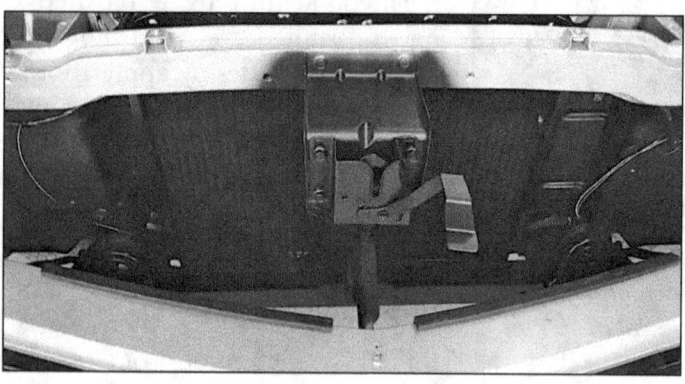

Look closely at the back edge of this AMX grille support panel. Two molded rubber pads hook to the edge, providing support for the plastic grille. Not using the three mounting tabs on the bottom of a 1968–1969 grille may save it from certain damage in the event of a minor front-end bump. If the bottom tabs are used, be very careful not to overtighten them, because this will eventually crack the grille.

Tung-Sol model 6012 sealed-beam headlight bulbs were used in AMC muscle cars with two headlight systems. There are early- and late-style bulbs; the original type shown here was used through the early 1970s. A later replacement had a more complex diffusor pattern.

For the 1968 and 1969 model years, AMX models used a clear turn-signal lens with amber bulb, while Javelins were equipped with an amber lens and clear bulb. The lenses use a small notch for correct positioning. Newer clear lenses installed on Hornets and Jeep models have additional numbering at the bottom of the lens. This can be carefully wet sanded and polished away.

silver. You can duplicate this finish by layering thin coats of charcoal gray followed by argent silver, sprayed from a distance for the textured, dry effect. Next, paint the front edge of the fins with bright silver paint using a solid-foam paint brush. Use as little paint as possible so it doesn't run between the fins. The final step is to attach the "AMX" nameplate after the paint dries.

Just as important to the appearance and safety of your car is the front, rear, and side lighting. AMC muscle cars were originally equipped with Tung-Sol sealed-beam headlights. Using a different brand, especially halogen lamps, may cost you points in judging. Taillights with chrome-plated housings should be free of pitting and other defects. Early AMX and Javelin housings have been reproduced, along with the lenses. A complete center reflector for a 1968–1969 model is a bit more difficult to come by, although the red plastic insert is commonly available.

For 1968, cars sold in the United States were required to have front and rear side-marker lights, or in some instances reflectors. American Motors came up with a nice-looking, recessed side-marker lamp for many of its 1968 and 1969 models; larger side markers were produced for the 1970 model year. The 1970 lenses had square corners, which were then rounded off for 1971 and newer cars. The amber lenses were installed on the front, and the red ones were for the rear; occasionally you see a car with these reversed! Replacement side-marker lamps are readily available from AMC parts suppliers. Be sure every light functions as it should for your restoration, including the rear license plate lamp.

CHAPTER 11

AMX over-the-top racing stripes were part of the performance Go Package, but could be deleted upon request. They were not available on cars equipped with the 290 V-8. These stripes should appear perfectly straight when viewed from the front or rear of the car. After applying vinyl stripes, park outside in bright sunshine for a couple of days to set the glue and allow any small bubbles to disappear.

Vinyl Top and Stripes

Applying a vinyl top or stripe kit should be done at least 30 days after application of the outer body paint, allowing adequate time for the paint to fully cure. Reproduction vinyl tops are available for Javelins and other popular applications. Many pre-cut vinyl tops require some trimming, so be sure that the vinyl is not sliced along its edges by someone using a razor knife directly against the painted car body. Scratching or cutting all the way through the paint at the edge of the vinyl quickly produces rust around and underneath the top.

Vinyl stripe kits are less difficult to install, and can be handled by almost anyone with some auto restoration skills. Stripes can be installed wet or dry; however, it is recommended that beginners use plenty of soapy water so the stripes can be repositioned as needed. When in place, the excess water is squeegeed from underneath the stripes and then allowed to dry in the sun.

Dry installation requires fitting the stripes to the car, marking their location with pieces of tape, and then applying each section in one take. Burnishing the stripe with a cloth as you apply it keeps bubbles to a minimum. For the few bubbles that may appear, park the car in bright sunlight for a couple of days and most will disappear. Any that still remain may be carefully pierced with a pin and gently smoothed out using a soft cloth.

Stripe Application

Excellent-quality reproduction stripe kits are available for most AMC applications. Before applying stripes, dust the entire car, then wash the areas to be striped with surface cleaner. Always work inside, away from wind or bright sunshine until the installation is complete.

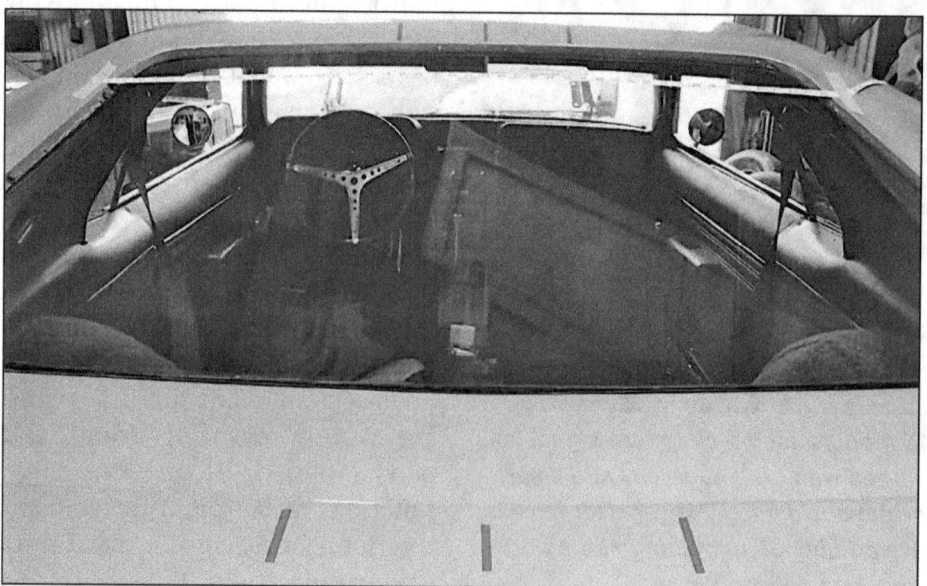

1 *Installing 1968–1969 AMX Go Package stripes takes some patience because they must be positioned exactly down the centerline of the car. With few places from which to measure on the roof, it takes some time to lay them out. Once the centerline is found, mark it with small pieces of pinstriping tape as a reference point.*

BODY TRIM AND FINISHING

2 Mark the edge of the backing paper as well, not the edge of the stripe because it could end up slightly overlapping the temporary guide tape. With the center and outer edges marked at both ends of each body panel, it is easy to perfectly apply the stripes.

3 Splitting the backing paper at the front of the hood and at the back of the trunk lid allows the stripes to be applied parallel over the compound curves of the panels. Be sure to work in a warm setting, because cold vinyl stripes are much less workable and can tear if tugged too hard.

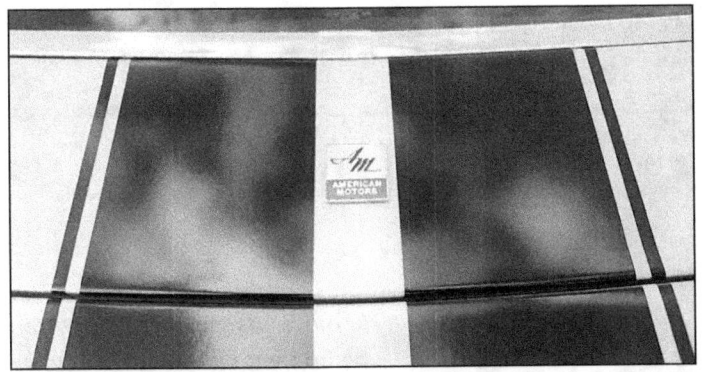

4 Be sure that the hood and trunk lid are latched before applying these sections of the stripe kit; the adjustment of the latch or striker could reposition the panels slightly, misaligning the stripe. Don't panic after installing the window moldings; unlike the square AMC emblem, the joints for the rear window molding are frequently not centered, especially at the top.

1 Likely because of the new hood scoop, 1970 AMX stripes changed to a C-shaped motif applied to the sides of the car. After trimming the backing paper to within 1/4 inch of the stripe, tape each section in place, then mark their position with additional pieces of tape. With the tape as a guide, remove the backing paper and apply the stripe, starting at one end.

CHAPTER 11

2 It helps to have a second person to hold the other end of the stripe and prevent it from attaching itself to the car. Be sure to loosen the paper from the front of the stripe at the end of each section before wrapping the stripe around the edge of a body panel. Peeling it off afterward is much more difficult and usually removes the stripe as well.

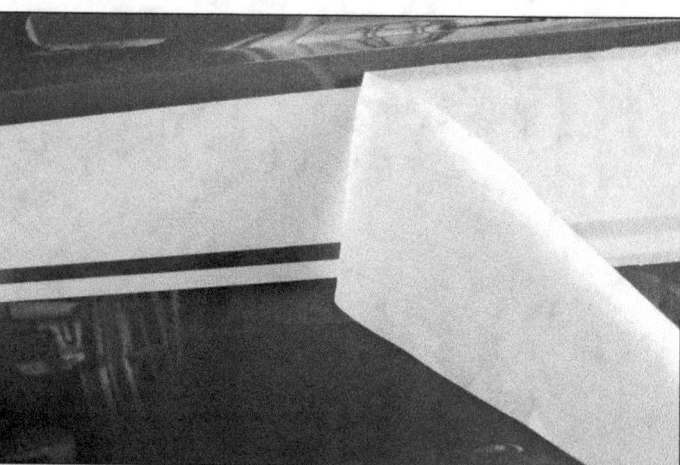

3 With the help of an assistant to hold the other end of the stripe, carefully peel off the top layer of paper, keeping it flat against the stripe. With the paper removed, burnish the stripe with a soft towel to work out any large bubbles. Any small bubbles that remain will disappear after parking in bright sunshine for several hours.

4 In most cases, vinyl stripes can be applied either wet or dry. Using soapy water allows some adjustment of the stripe before the glue sets. Any bubbles that remain will have water in them and may take longer to dry and flatten out. Applied wet or dry, an occasional bubble may require a tiny pinhole before it can be flattened out.

Many narrow pinstripes were originally painted on. Painting on racing stripes instead of using tape is another choice when restoring an AMC muscle car. The fact is that it's easier to mask and paint over-the-top AMX stripes than to properly install a tape kit, because at both ends the parallel stripes tend to merge due to the compound curves of the hood and deck lid. However, painted stripes could cost valuable points in stock class judging, especially if they are perfectly smooth by being buried underneath several coats of clear paint.

Before deciding whether to paint on stripes, be aware that few things look worse than stripes that are close, but not quite right. When laying out the stripes, consult several photos of original stripes taken from different angles. Better still, have a similar car nearby with the same style of stripes that you can measure and compare. Take your time and be sure the masking job is perfect before painting.

CHAPTER 12

Performance Upgrades

You may be surprised to find a chapter about performance parts and street machines in an auto restoration book. But during the original muscle car era of the late 1960s and early 1970s, many high-performance parts were available through American Motors as part of the Group 19 performance program. Items available over the AMC parts counter included camshaft kits, Edelbrock aluminum intake manifolds (single 4-barrel or a dual 4-barrel cross ram), performance gear sets, upgraded ignition systems, torque link kits for models not so-equipped, forged crankshaft and connecting rods for 290- and 343-ci engines, Doug's exhaust headers, disc brake kits, front and rear spoilers, etc. These parts, many of which carry AMC part numbers, are considered era correct because many were installed at the dealership even before the original owner took delivery of the car. Few people who bought muscle cars left them completely stock!

Named for the performance section of the AMC parts book, original Group 19 parts are fairly rare and expensive today. However, some items remain in production, or have been reissued or reproduced in recent years. Nothing beats leaving a car the way it was driven and enjoyed since it was new. If you compete in stock class judging, however, be prepared to provide original documentation for any non-stock parts found on your car. Using Group 19 parts exclusively to upgrade the performance of your AMC muscle car is a great way to enhance its performance while still keeping it legal for stock-type drag racing events.

Today, aftermarket manufacturers such as Edelbrock offer many performance parts suitable for an AMC, allowing your build to have a more modern feel.

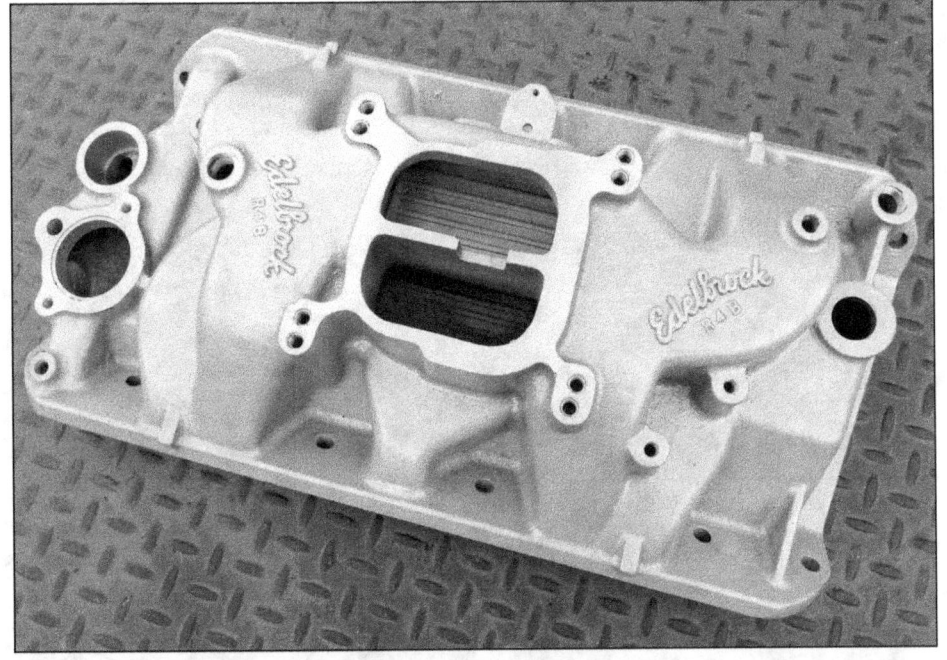

Many name-brand speed parts were available directly through AMC parts departments as part of the Group 19 program. Some were identified with AMC numbers on the parts, including the Edelbrock R4B intake manifold. This is the aftermarket equivalent, which is identical except for not having the AMC part number cast into the top.

Performance heads such as these from Edelbrock can be applied to your 343-, 360-, 390-, or 401-powered AMC. (Photo Courtesy Edelbrock)

Edelbrock's Air-Gap intake manifold features an open air space that separates the runners from the hot engine oil for a cooler, denser charge with more power. (Photo Courtesy Edelbrock)

Designed for 290- to 401-ci applications, Edelbrock's Performer-Plus camshaft offers durations of 204 degrees for intake and 214 degrees for exhaust with .420-inch intake lift and .442-inch exhaust lift. It is intended for high-performance street applications. (Photo Courtesy Edelbrock)

Made of heavy-gauge sand-cast aluminum, these Classic Series Edelbrock valve covers can provide that vintage look and feel. (Photo Courtesy Edelbrock)

If you are less concerned with having a factory-original appearance, a movement gaining momentum is restoring muscle cars to a "Day 2" appearance. This is the use of period-correct visual and performance enhancements typical of the way many owners modified their cars soon after taking delivery. Subtle modifications could include nothing more than a set of Cragar S/S or American Racing Torq-Thrust wheels and a set of custom valve covers under the hood. Or you can go all out and jack up the rear end with air shocks and shackles, add some side pipes, and put on an old-school hood scoop!

Chrome-plated Rocket Racing Wheels were a Cragar S/S knock-off available in a variety of sizes. Because this model is long out of production, finding a nice set, or even a pair, is a rewarding challenge when building a period-correct AMC street machine.

PERFORMANCE UPGRADES

Decades ago mismatched wheels and custom paint were the order of the day. Although not up to the standards of today's digital photography, vintage street machine photos may provide inspiration while you plan your own street machine project. Internet search engines and certain Facebook groups are great sources for finding photos of modified muscle cars from back in the day.

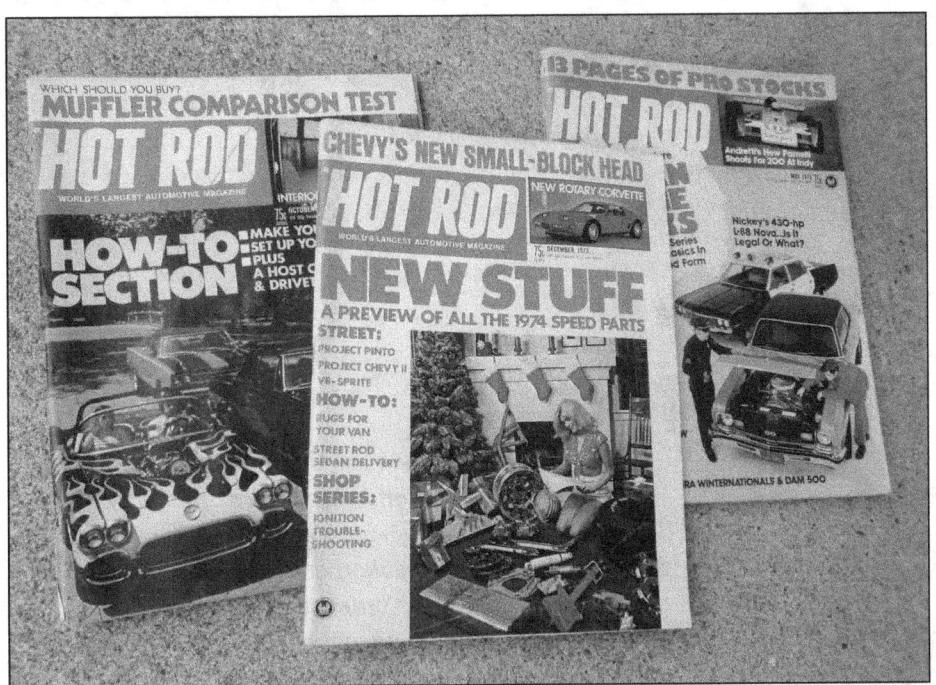

Another great source for period-correct information is old copies of car magazines such as Hot Rod *and* Car Craft. *Studying the featured cars as well as the advertisements for performance parts reveal how cars were modified in the late 1960s and early 1970s. If you don't have any old car magazines in your collection, pick up a few copies at the next swap meet or on eBay.*

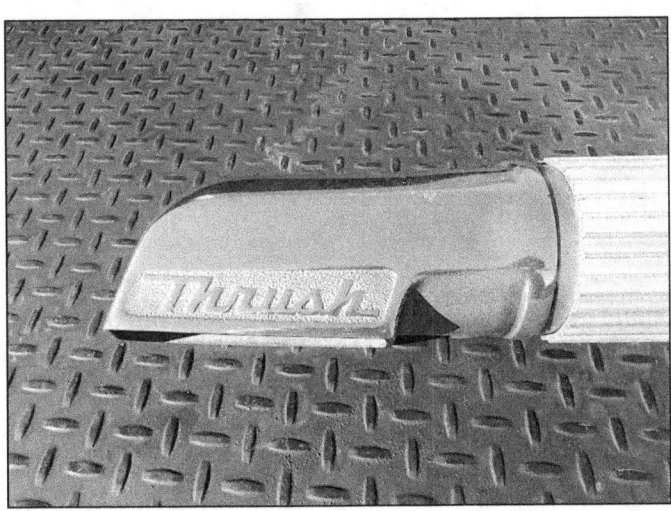

Thrush side pipes were inexpensive when new, and are pricey when found in good condition today. The end pieces often need to be polished before installation. Special mufflers, which fit inside the tubular side-pipe covers, are available from Speedway Motors.

Custom paint was very popular in the late 1960s and early 1970s, and back then some wild paint jobs could be seen cruising the strip. Panel painting, murals, stripes, and heavy metal flake were all popular paint schemes that can be duplicated by skilled painters today. For inspiration, you can consult almost any 1968–1974 issue of *Hot Rod* or *Car Craft*, or visit a 1970s Street Machines group on Facebook.

The challenge (and fun!) of building a period-correct street machine is locating era-correct parts rather than modern equivalents. Automotive swap meets, eBay, and Craigslist are great places to find unusual vintage performance parts, often at reasonable prices. Also check with friends who have been building cars for a long time, and people restoring a former street machine back to its factory original appearance. Very often, vintage speed parts are thrown in a box or left to collect dust on a garage shelf once a car is returned to stock.

Unfortunately, new tire choices are somewhat limited, especially in 14-inch-diameter sizes. A 245/60R14 tire is the widest 14-inch street tire currently available, so although vintage wheels in 14 x 9– or 14 x 10–inch sizes are fairly easy to find, locating tires to fit them is not so easy. Vintage bias-ply tires can be found but are best used for display purposes only, rather than driving. A workable

AMC JAVELIN, AMX & MUSCLE CAR RESTORATION 1968–1974

CHAPTER 12

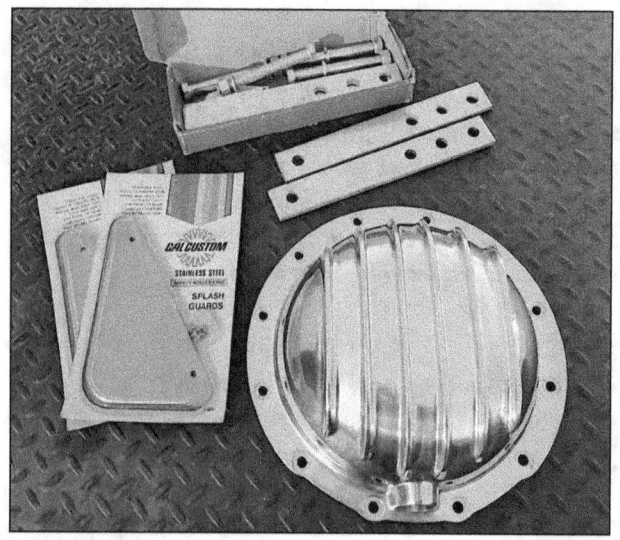

Underneath, you can install a finned-aluminum rear-end cover on your AMC model 20 axle. Adjustable spring shackles allow you to set the height only as high as required for rear tire clearance. Air shocks alone should not be used to lift the back end. And be sure to protect that 1970s custom paint job with some vintage stainless steel splashguards.

solution is to have a set of wheels and tires for shows, and a modern set of radials mounted on similar wheels for driving duties.

The bodywork of a 1971–1974 Javelin accommodates larger tires than earlier models, and to increase the width of the rear rolling stock even more, a popular swap is the narrower 1968–1970 AMX or Javelin rear axle. A direct bolt-in, the early axle is shorter between the spring perch and backing plate, allowing even more tire width when used with a wheel having an appropriate offset.

A popular street machine detail was painting the brake drums red so they stood out when viewed through a spoked or slotted mag wheel. This practice fell out of favor with the advent of front disc brakes that didn't lend themselves to custom painting quite as well as the drums. Large-diameter front brake drums are becoming hard to find for AMC muscle cars.

Engine dress-up items include valve covers and a variety of custom air cleaners. These Edelbrock AMC valve covers have been reissued, but it's the originals that have "RAMBLER" cast inside. Some vintage air cleaners, such as this Cal Custom "fly eye," typically sell for hundreds of dollars when in new condition.

PERFORMANCE UPGRADES

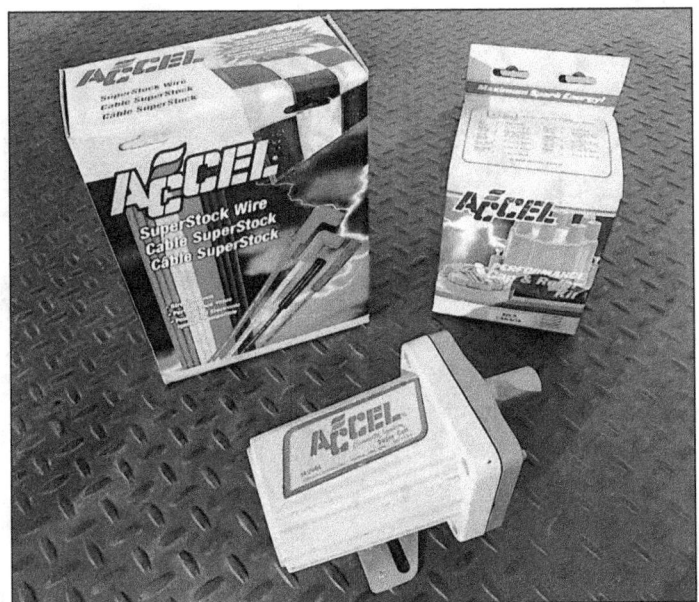

A modern Accel distributor cap and yellow spark plug wires from Summit Racing Equipment can be used and still have a vintage look. The classic yellow Super Coil, however, has been produced with a different label since the early 1980s. Finding an original, yellow-label Super Coil in good condition is a challenge, but it can be done.

The interior of your street machine can be personalized with the addition of a Superior Champ 500 genuine wood steering wheel. This may also be a solution for your cracked or separated original wheel. Be sure to pick up an AMC horn kit as well. Adding a couple of vintage gauges helps to keep tabs on the engine, plus they add to the early 1970s vibe for your vintage street machine project.

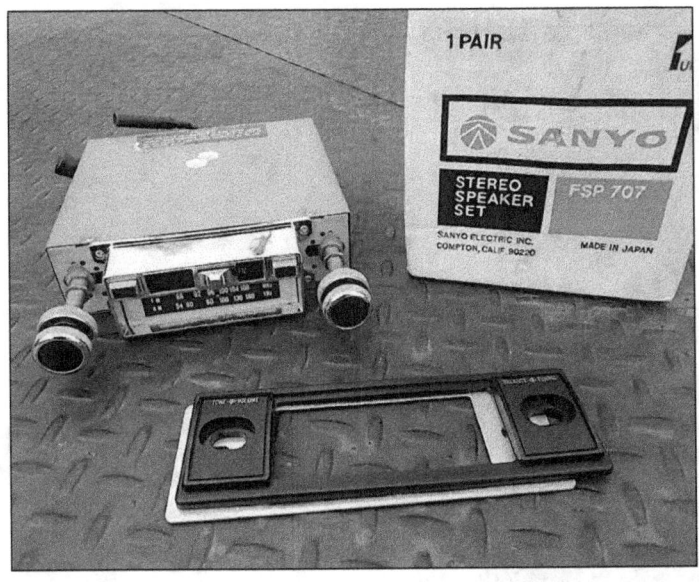

Vintage 8-track car stereo equipment is fairly cheap and easy to find. Even original speakers are available for a period-correct installation. Once in place, grab a few original 8-track cartridges, which are readily available at flea markets, swap meets, or on eBay.

Underhood modifications may include chrome-plated or finned-aluminum valve covers, a variety of aftermarket air cleaners or velocity stacks, exhaust headers, an Accel Super Coil and yellow spark plug wires, a Holley carburetor, and other vintage speed parts. A few original racing stickers (again, not their modern equivalents) can be the finishing touch; eBay is a great source for finding these.

A set of period-correct gauges can be installed underneath the dash using a two- or three-hole chrome-plated mounting panel. Locate a nice 8-track stereo and some vintage speakers too. And don't forget the foot-shaped gas pedal (although I've heard that these may not be safe to use) and genuine Champ 500 wooden steering wheel.

Wheel choices abound for a 1970s-style street machine. In addition to the Cragars and Torq-Thrusts, the Keystone Klassics and Ansen, E-T, or Fenton aluminum slots were popular, along with more uncommon wheels such as Motor Wheel Spyders. Cragar knock-offs manufactured by Rocket or Appliance make a bigger impact today due to their obsolete status. Similarly, the solid-styled Cragar SS/T is a wheel that provides a classic 1970s look.

Because the hot rod and custom car scene is constantly evolving, most modified cars can be dated to their

CHAPTER 12

Vintage Ansen Sprint slotted-aluminum wheels shod with vintage Goodyear Polyglas tires look great on this Gremlin street machine. Even the center caps are correct; it's attending to the details such as this that makes creating an era-correct street machine so much fun!

Appliance's Wire Mag wheels were another popular model in the early 1970s. Decades-old tires such as these BFGoodrich Belted T/As should be reserved for show duty only! If your street machine is not trailered everywhere, have a second set of modern radials for driving on the street.

You can't go wrong with chrome-plated Cragar S/S wheels; they are still sold today and provide a classic look for any street machine. Lifting the rear of the car with longer spring shackles and air shocks allows plenty of clearance for tires that are too wide to fit underneath.

AMC JAVELIN, AMX & MUSCLE CAR RESTORATION 1968–1974

PERFORMANCE UPGRADES

respective decade by the style of the car, as well as the custom parts that were used in the build. Keeping a muscle car faithful to its original build era is both challenging and rewarding because so many vintage-style high-performance parts are no longer made, or are now slightly different than when produced in the late 1960s or early 1970s. Showing up at the next car show or cruise-in with a period-correct AMC street machine will generate lots of positive attention for your car, no matter what else is present.

It's a little rough and unrefined, but this is how they were built. After decades of storage, this AMX was brought back to life, still displaying its vintage street machine look. As a rare and valuable car, it would be a difficult decision whether to restore this one to stock, or to leave it the way it is.

CHAPTER 13

PRESENTATION AND SHOWING

You've made all of the sacrifices needed to finish your AMC muscle car restoration project, including the investment of time, money, and skinned knuckles. Now it's finished, and it looks great! It's finally time to enjoy your car instead of just working on it. This chapter includes some tips for optimizing the appearance and presentation of your car, especially if you plan to compete for awards.

If you only participate in car shows to hang out with other "car guys," and for the opportunity to show off your pride and joy, you are a winner every time out. However, winning an award and the recognition of your efforts by your peers is not only a lot of fun, it can actually add value to your car if you ever decide to sell it. Certain awards, especially those earned at prestigious automotive events, definitely serve to document your car's status as a proven show winner, and therefore one of the best of its kind.

Detailing

This is an area crucial to the success of your car, yet one that is largely overlooked by many owners for a variety of reasons. To successfully compete on a national or even local level, each area of your car must be as clean as possible. However, there is a tendency to breeze over this step if it is too hot outside, the competition isn't as strong as expected, or the car was driven to the event rather than trailered. Don't use these excuses to justify a lack of preparation, and then be disappointed with a poor performance at the show.

It's no secret that cleanliness and presentation are just as important as condition, even more so in some cases! Sweat the details and the rest will take care of itself; this applies to every part of your car.

Following are some suggestions that may help to set your car apart from the others, and ensure a positive outcome.

Unless you have a trailered car competing in stock class judging, modern radials ride and handle much better than original bias-ply tires. Not everyone prefers a shiny "wet" look for their tires, especially when some tire dressings can turn brown and sticky. It's hard to beat the look of tires prepped only with Bleche-Wite tire cleaner.

PRESENTATION AND SHOWING

You have finally completed your AMC muscle car restoration. Now what? You take it to car shows, of course! Maintaining your car's "just finished" look is just as important as correctly restoring it to begin with. And going along with this special care are ways to optimize the display and promotion of your car. Many magazine feature-cars are discovered while being displayed at car shows.

Tires and Wheels

Starting at ground level with the tires and wheels, safety dictates that all of the tires be in good condition without excessive wear, cuts, or dry rot. All of the tires should be the same size unless purposely staggered. Tire brand and style should be consistent on all four corners. For stock classes, cars that were not available with radial tires generally lose points for having them.

Black Magic Bleche-Wite used with water and a scrub brush works great for cleaning any tires, even blackwall tires and redlines. Using tire dressings that produce a "wet look" is a matter of personal taste. If this is a look that you prefer use only a high-quality rubber dressing, never sprayed directly on the tire because it usually ends up on the wheel as well as the pavement next to the tire. Instead, apply the tire dressing with a clean, lint-free cloth.

For tires with a clean, dry look simply towel dry the tires after washing, then follow up with a second lint-free towel to "buff" the sidewalls to a dry shine. If this regimen is followed from new, most tires develop a pleasing shine that does not turn brown or greasy to the touch. Be sure to remove any obvious pebbles from the tire tread once you arrive on the show field.

Wheels or wheel covers should be clean and free of rust, corrosion, dents, and curb rash. Most quality tire shops can balance your wheels without putting any weights on the front side. If you ask nicely, they may even index your white letters in relation to the valvestems, which should be the proper length with matching caps. For stock classes, leave the valve caps that look like skulls, dice, or eight-balls at home. Align the center caps as well, when possible; it's the smallest of details that really add up.

Damaged wheel trim rings or hubcaps should be repaired or replaced if available. Steel wheels should be nicely finished without painted-over wheel weights or, worse yet, ghost images left from old weights. Aluminum wheels can be polished or refinished as required. All lug nuts should be present, matching, and in good condition. Do yourself a big favor and replace any questionable nuts if they're rusted or rounded off. Changing a flat tire on the side of the road is not the time to discover a problem.

Trunk or Cargo Area

The trunk area is often overlooked. It's convenient just to keep it closed, or use it for storing your extra chairs or cleaning supplies. But the trunk does matter at a judged car show. Some were originally sprayed the body color and others were finished with speckle paint. If you plan to compete in a stock class be sure to replace the original finish.

Be certain the trunk seal is in good condition and that the trunk light works if your car has one. Install the correct jack instructions for your particular car in its proper location. Reproduction trunk mats are available for most popular models. If unavailable for your car, locate a good original or make your own from a larger mat intended for a different model.

If you're lucky, you still have your original spare tire, jack, and tools; these items are becoming quite expensive, especially the early compact spares. These items should be mounted in their original location, usually shown on the jack instructions. Carefully strip and repaint any scratched or rusted tools in their original color.

Hatchbacks such as the Gremlin X also benefit from a clean cargo area. If the carpet or spare tire cover is faded it should be dyed or replaced. Use a product such as Lifter1 for tough carpet stains that resist ordinary cleaning products.

CHAPTER 13

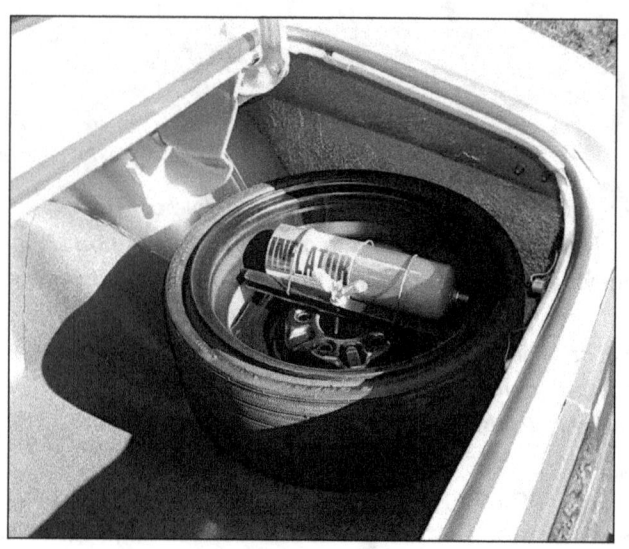

The show field usually has great lighting that spotlights every part of the car. This includes the trunk area, which should be kept just as clean as the interior. Stow all of your gear and cleaning supplies underneath your chairs behind the car. The trunk is also a great place to display an album of "before" photos, or your latest magazine feature.

Be very cautious about chairs or other cargo coming in contact with the sides of the trunk or the underside of the trunk lid. Folding canvas chairs that store in matching cloth bags are trunk-friendly if you take the time to return them to their bags for the drive home. For your chairs, select a neutral color or one that complements your car. Pack as lightly as possible, especially for local shows. The less you bring the less you have to pile up behind your car on the show field. Car shows are not campgrounds.

Once at the show, your trunk is a great place for a tasteful display of memorabilia, your car's latest magazine feature, or an album of "before" pictures. Just don't overdo it; moderation comes into play here.

Engine Compartment

Because it has become the custom to show off your engine at any car show, or even the local cruise-in, your engine compartment presents an opportunity for detailing that can make or break a show car. I discussed the correct refinishing and assembly of the engine bay in Chapter 7, so here are some tips for its presentation and upkeep.

Be sure to replace the hood insulation if originally equipped, and be sure it is not installed upside down. If a reproduction battery is unavailable for your particular model or year make your own by installing a reproduction sticker or even painting a new battery. Old-style battery caps can be used on a new battery if it isn't a sealed type. Cast-iron exhaust manifolds can be sandblasted and coated with POR-15 Exhaust Manifold Coating for an authentic "Day 2" appearance (which occurred once the engine enamel burned off). Attention to minor details such as having the fan belts readable from the front of the car should not be overlooked.

Once your engine compartment is finished, spend as much time as needed to keep it clean. Dust the topside after every drive with a wax-treated car duster and keep those chrome accessories polished. Stay on top of those pesky fluid leaks and with reasonable care your engine bay will look just as nice in 20 years!

The same rules apply to the underside of your show car. Invest as much time as necessary to keep it clean, especially one that is driven regularly.

Exterior

Bodywork and paint separate the truly great cars from the rest. If you are fortunate to have nice, factory-original paint, cherish it because cars are only original once. But be careful because older paint can become thin at the edges and elsewhere and can easily be buffed through to the primer coat. Brand-new paint can also be ruined this way if you are not skilled with a buffer.

If you have never buffed paint before, practice on your daily driver

For a restored car that is driven any distance, keeping the engine and engine compartment as clean as the day it was completed is an ongoing challenge. Keep the topside dusted and stay ahead of any leaks that may appear. Bugs on the radiator core can be safely removed with a stiff-bristle brush.

PRESENTATION AND SHOWING

Your paint job's best friends are a California Car Duster to remove the dust and grit and a quality detailing spray, such as this one from Meguiar's, to deal with the bugs and road grime. Used after every drive, these products enable you to forego washing your car with water, unless you are caught in the rain.

When the occasional car washing is required, use only high-quality liquid car wash soap; never use dish detergent unless you are planning to reapply the wax anyway. Wax should be applied at least once a year if your car is outside at all.

Wax the car inside a garage or storage building after using a car duster to eliminate any grit from the surface. Be cautious around trim and emblems that can trap wax or be snagged with the soft towel used to buff off the wax. Take your time and use care; there shouldn't be a speck of wax visible anywhere when you are finished.

For this reason, do not use a spray wax that may end up inside your cowl vents and in other inaccessible areas. Use only bottled liquid or paste-type car wax without a cleaner, which can dull your paint. Generally, any car wax that is safe for clearcoat paints is the one to choose. Excellent products are available specifically for vinyl tops as well.

No matter how nice your paint job is, dull, pitted, dented, or faded trim pieces can ruin the whole effect. Upgrade these items as they become

or even a parts donor car to develop your skills before attempting to color sand or buff your collector car. Otherwise, contact your local detail shop for professional results.

With some luck and planning you may not need to actually wash your car for years at a time. Washing your car with water should be avoided. The reason for this is that every car traps water somewhere: inside the doors, underneath the rubber weather strips, or in the window channels. And water breeds rust and rot. In addition, it takes a lot of time to properly dry the engine compartment after a car wash.

Instead, the frequent use of a California Car Duster, along with Meguiar's or a similar spray-on car detailer to handle the bugs and road grime, will keep your car looking great all season long. Use the hose for washing your car only after unexpected encounters with wet roads or a muddy show field.

You can be sure that the car show judges will be checking down here, so be sure that the lower quarter panels are just as clean as the rest of the body. To maintain a paint job this shiny, use only a high-quality liquid car wax without a cleaner that can dull the surface of the paint.

Damaged or pitted body or interior trim pieces detract from the look of a car, no matter how nice the rest of it is. Stainless steel body moldings can be straightened and polished for a like-new appearance. Some emblems and other small trim pieces have been reproduced, or can be upgraded as better-quality parts are found.

available because most have not been reproduced for AMC cars. Ask for referrals for chrome plating; some shops do excellent work and some do not.

Be sure that your bumpers are straight and centered on the car. Dented or scratched aluminum or stainless trim can be straightened and polished to look brand new again. Many painted emblems or engine identification logos can be refinished by carefully masking them, or by thinning the paint and applying it with a small brush, letting the paint flow into the emblem.

Many stock class judges don't like aftermarket mud flaps or splash-guards. For cars that are driven to the show, these can be temporarily installed with spring clips and removed after you arrive.

Be sure that all interior and exterior lights as well as the horn are operational. Cracked or weather-checked lenses should be replaced with reproductions or good originals when available. Plastic lenses can be polished if they are dull. Be sure your headlight bulbs are the correct type, and that the bulbs match. Halogens headlights will likely cost you points on an older car entered in the stock classes.

Don't overlook your license plates; many states allow year of manufacture license plates for historical cars. Be sure that your plates are not bent, rusted, or crooked. Avoid license plate frames that say something on the front of the car, but an original AMC dealer frame for the rear plate is a nice period-correct detail. Be sure that the license plate screws are matched and not rusted. Again it comes down to the smallest details.

Window glass should be free of defects, and proper cleaning is crucial for competition. For excellent results use your favorite glass cleaner along with balled-up newspaper for no streaks or lint left behind; just be careful with the newspaper ink if you have a light-colored interior. If your windshield is cracked, chipped, delaminating, or scuffed from using the windshield wipers, install a new one at your earliest opportunity; your view will be greatly improved. And, for a show car, it will likely stay that way forever. For your new windshield, install new wiper refills, even if you don't plan to use them; apply a coat of Rain-X just in case.

Passenger Compartment

Your car's interior is another area where it can outshine the others if you take the time to do it right. Interior plastic parts require special care. If these parts are in good condition wash them with soapy water, allow to air dry, and then apply a quality plastic protectant. Broken pieces can be upgraded with better ones, NOS parts, or reproductions if available.

Faded trim can often be recolored using SEM products; always follow the product directions for the best results. Seats, the steering wheel, or other severe-use parts, however, should be replaced with parts manufactured in the correct color for lasting durability.

Clean the instrument panel regularly including those dusty air conditioning vents. Use a lint-free cloth or damp cotton swab (such as Q-tips) here. After cleaning, align all of the vents in a uniform direction. A California Dash Duster works great for quick interior touch-ups.

Faded carpeting should be dyed or replaced. To maintain its new appearance, vacuum the carpet until there isn't a speck of foreign matter on it or the floor mats. Genuine accessory floor mats, with their AMC logos, are a great addition to a show car. Door panel care is the same as for the dash. Keep the chrome parts polished, including the window cranks, which should be a mirror image of each other, generally facing down and slightly forward when the glass is in the raised position.

Use a premium-quality leather and vinyl dressing containing a UV blocker on the interior soft trim. On the show field, your seat belts should be stowed properly or arranged uniformly on both sides.

Presentation

This aspect of your car show display goes beyond the car itself; it even includes how you park in a particular situation. When displaying your car, straighten the wheels if it is parked straight, as in a parking spot.

PRESENTATION AND SHOWING

A show-quality interior requires more than a quick visit with the vacuum cleaner. The seats should be adjusted evenly on both sides with the seat belts neatly stowed or placed uniformly on the seats. No personal items should be visible, including keys, a cell phone, or a garage door opener. At the show, your steering wheel should always be straight, regardless of the position of the front tires.

If parked at an angle you may angle the wheels slightly to one side for effect, but be sure the steering wheel is in a straight position even with the wheels turned to one side. This is something you can practice every time you park.

I have touched on traveling as lightly as possible so you avoid having a pile of personal items in the trunk or stacked up near your car. Two chairs set up behind your show car is appropriate, and should provide enough room underneath to stow all of your gear and cleaning supplies. Refold any towels you may use for cleaning; it just looks better that way. And if you happen to be parked near a crushed beverage can or other piece of litter, take a second to pick it up and dispose of it, if only to make your car look that much better. This is all part of presentation.

Car Show Props

Just like shiny tire dressing, car show props is another area that is subject to individual taste. As a rule they should be avoided, or at least displayed in moderation and with good taste. Avoid stuffed animals, drive-in restaurant trays with plastic food, crybaby dolls, or those gas-oil-water cans that only detract from the car.

Keep photo albums off the radiator support and in the trunk where they can be viewed without spoiling the front view of your car. If you require a show board with historical information or "before" photos, limit the size so you don't block any more of the car than necessary. Your show board should look professional, never be hand lettered, and not be taller than the headlights. Anything higher can become a hazard should it blow over and hit your car or someone else's. And there is absolutely no point in having a show board containing only current photos of your car, with the same car parked right there to look at.

Be a good ambassador for the AMC brand and community when displaying your car at multi-make car shows. Cheerfully answer the same questions as many times as they are asked. Many people have never seen a car like yours; take time to educate them on its unique features and qualities. Most of all, enjoy your car show experience; this is what you have worked for!

Excellent presentation at a car show includes positioning the car and front wheels in an attractive manner. This AMX prototype's keepers have set up camp well behind the car, and left the important historical information inside rather than blocking the front or side views of the car. The entire car is clean and detailed yet the tires aren't as shiny as the paint job. And no stuffed animals either!

CHAPTER 14

CARE AND STORAGE

Your freshly restored AMC muscle car is a thing of beauty, and the envy of your friends and neighbors. Because cars of this type are seldom used for regular transportation, you can expect it to look great indefinitely; that is, if certain precautions are taken beginning on the very first day.

Driving and Parking

Careful driving is obviously the most important factor for keeping your car looking like new. Be careful with all of that V-8 power. It may be more than you, your friends, or your adult children are used to. Always park with care. If you need to take your car to the shopping center, park far from the stores in a safe, isolated spot away from other cars and shopping carts.

If possible never leave your car unattended. When staying out of town for a car show, park with other participants in a secure, well-lit parking lot. Entire truck and car trailer rigs have gone missing during car show weekends. Do whatever you can to make your car or tow vehicle difficult to remove. This could include using an alarm system or a kill switch, or simply blocking in your vehicle with another one. When at home, keep your car garaged at all times; many classic car insurance policies insist on this.

Weather Conditions

Environmental forces work continuously to reduce every man-made

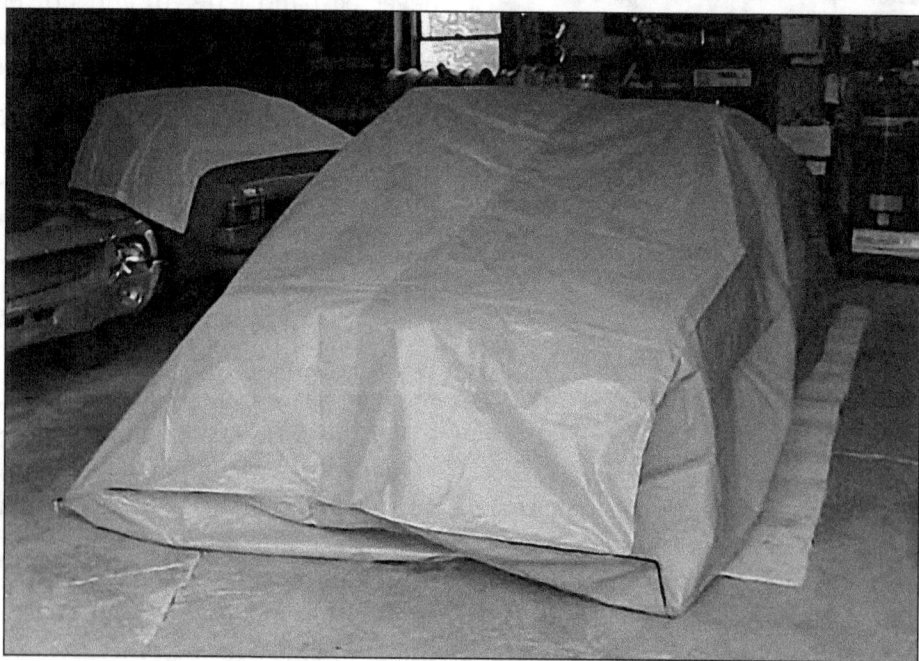

Even bare-steel parts such as brake rotors do not rust while stored inside the CarJacket. Rodents and other pests cannot survive inside, and the car is even protected from dust or overspray while stored inside the bag. The desiccant crystals can be dried by baking, and used again and again.

object to its basic elements, gradually returning them to the earth. Consider the abandoned dragstrip, shuttered building, or long-neglected vehicle reduced to little more than glass and stainless trim in an overgrown field. Sunlight and humidity have exactly the same effect on a freshly restored muscle car. One key to maintaining your automotive investment is protection from the elements.

Even in arid climates, damaging rays of sunshine destroy paint, soft trim, and interior parts, as well as vinyl tops, often leading to rust problems underneath. For this reason, avoid prolonged exposure to direct sunlight unless you are at a car show.

If your car is stored next to a garage window, be sure the curtains are drawn to block the sun's rays, as well as the prying eyes of strangers. If you need to park your car outdoors for an extended period, invest in a high-quality *outdoor* car cover, or at the very least cover the dash and seats with sheets or blankets.

Maintain a coat of wax on any exposed paint, preferably one with a UV blocker. Be sure to apply a similar protectant to vinyl tops, rubber bumper strips, etc. When you drive your collector car on sunny days, never leave it parked with all of the windows rolled up. Allow at least an inch for heat to escape, rather than being trapped inside where it will bake your interior.

Potentially even more damaging than sunlight is humidity. Moisture allows the formation of rust and corrosion, which attacks most metal parts of the car, including the body and frame rails. After driving in the rain, or washing your car with a hose, allow plenty of time for the car to air dry both inside and out before replacing the car cover. Even when a car *looks* dry, water may still be pooled inside the doors and window channels, underneath the trunk seal, etc.

In climates with seasonal temperature changes, rapid warming can produce condensation inside an unheated garage or storage building. Chrome, as well as other plated parts, can be permanently damaged as a result. In extreme cases, brake parts can seize and a clutch disc can even rust to the flywheel. Other less serious cosmetic damage is also common thanks to moisture and condensation including surface rust, mildew, and staining.

Storage Tips

Putting down plastic sheeting or even carpet underneath your garaged collector car does little to keep it dry. In fact it can trap water underneath the car, which would ordinarily evaporate sooner. But there are ways to protect your restored muscle car from the ravages of moisture when in storage for the off-season.

A coat of WD-40 works well to protect chrome-plated parts from rust. And because of its light consistency, cleanup is easy in the spring. The entire exhaust system can also

The CarJacket encloses the entire vehicle in an airtight bag that contains desiccant crystals to maintain a perfect low level of humidity. Simply remove the battery and cover the car with soft blankets before zipping up the jacket like a giant sleeping bag.

CHAPTER 14

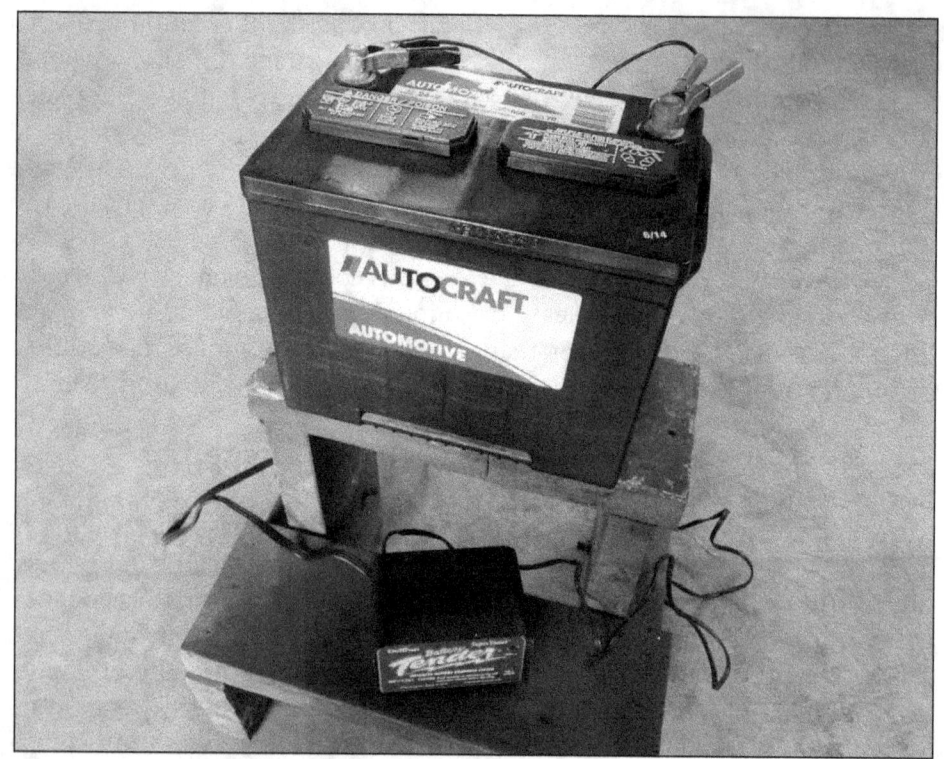

A Battery Tender greatly extends the life of the battery while your car is in storage. Better than just keeping your battery inside where it's warm, it monitors your battery and maintains a full charge, just as if you were regularly driving your car. For a battery used only part of the year, a Battery Tender will likely double the life of your battery.

be coated with WD-40, and most of it will burn off quickly at spring start-up. Your chrome exhaust tips will likely be the only parts that need to be washed.

A constant temperature, such as an even 50 degrees F, prevents the formation of condensation. If you do not have access to heated storage space there is still a practical solution for keeping your car perfectly clean and dry. Products such as the CarJacket are like an airtight sleeping bag for your car. By sealing a perfectly dry car inside the bag, along with the desiccant crystals provided with the kit, your car remains at a constant state of low humidity until the bag is opened. Dust or even paint overspray from other projects cannot reach the car. An added benefit is that because the car's fuel tank vents into the CarJacket, no pests can survive inside, so there is no chance of insect or rodent damage.

Use blankets or a soft dust cover inside the CarJacket to keep the material of the bag from contacting your finish. These can also be used to protect your car when stored in a heated garage or storage facility.

Always remove the battery before long-term storage of your car. To prolong its life exponentially, an attached Battery Tender maintains a full charge without the constant attention and danger of overcharging with a trickle charger.

Protect the fuel system of any car that is idle for more than a couple of months by adding Sta-Bil or a similar fuel stabilizer additive. Be sure all of the other fluids are fresh and topped off before long-term storage.

Tires, especially bias-ply tires, benefit from additional pressure before sitting unused for a long period.

By following these tips, spring startup and spring cleanup isn't a big deal. Install the battery, check all of the fluids, adjust the tire pressure to the recommended spec, and you are ready for another season of car shows and cruise-ins!

CHAPTER 15

FUTURE COLLECTIBILITY

When compared point by point to their direct competition, AMC muscle cars are, for the most part, a terrific value. Not as popular as comparable GM, Ford, or Chrysler models when they were new, or now, AMC cars have been slower to gain momentum and status as collectibles. While most Big Three muscle cars gradually gained value through the early to mid-1980s, the value of a typical good-quality 1968–1970 AMX remained around $5,000 to $7,000 for years. Even in the late 1980s, with the first wave of renewed muscle car popularity, values for other domestic muscle cars increased while AMC prices stayed pretty much in place. That was good news for the AMC faithful who were not yet priced out of the market for Kenosha-built muscle cars.

However, in the past couple of decades things have changed. Perhaps because many collectors were left out financially from the Big Three muscle car camps, many mainstream car collectors began buying AMC muscle cars, as did some celebrity collectors. Muscle car magazines have featured countless restored cars as well, exposing a new audience to some of the finest AMC cars. Many of the automotive TV shows have featured an AMC or two as well. Finally, with this new exposure came value, and before the muscle car market crashed in 2010, premium regular-production AMC muscle cars commonly traded in the $30,000 to $60,000 range.

Although the values of all muscle cars have cooled off since then, AMC values have lost a smaller percentage, likely because they were not artificially inflated to begin with. The current values of upper-echelon AMC muscle (two-seat AMX, Hurst SC/Rambler, and Rebel Machine) have brought up the value of other models, such as the 1971–1974 Javelin AMX and 1971 Hornet SC/360.

Collectors and enthusiasts are also discovering models such as the 343-powered Rambler and the 1971–1973 Matador two-door sedan as lower-priced alternatives to an

With the rising costs of AMC muscle, it's not uncommon to find an unrestored Gremlin or Hornet needing minimal work for a nominal price. This 1972 Gremlin has the look and feel of a bona fide muscle car, yet is a fraction of the cost of its stablemates. (Photo Courtesy Colin Comer)

CHAPTER 15

Fans of larger AMC muscle cars have long embraced the 1970 Rebel Machine. There were also just a few 1971 Matadors produced with a Machine Go Package, but they are seldom seen today. A lower-priced alternative is a 1971–1973 Matador coupe. These have the same basic body style with a choice of V-8 engines. And with less collector status there is no guilt about making some changes to suit your particular taste.

As the values of the most collectible AMC muscle cars have continued to increase, second-tier models such as the Javelin AMX have been dragged upward in price as well. In addition, as these models become too expensive for entry-level collectors and enthusiasts, even "image" cars such as the 1977 Hornet AMX will become a valued commodity in the collector car market. These models had the look, but not the punch of earlier models, and depended largely on styling and handling enhancements to attract buyers.

SC/Rambler and a Rebel Machine, or a 360 V-8 Hornet X Hatchback instead of a costlier SC/360.

As non-mainstream models increase in popularity and value, the market drives up the value of low-performance "image" cars, such as the third- and fourth-generation AMX variants known for their flared wheel openings, rear window louvers, and spoilers. The 1977 Hornet AMX and similar 1978 Concord-based AMX were offered with nothing larger than a 2-barrel 304-ci V-8, which was continued for the Spirit-based 1979 AMX. The 8-cylinder engines were discontinued from AMC car production for 1980, leaving the final AMX with only a 258-ci 6-cylinder engine available.

Despite a lack of serious muscle, the great styling combined with over-the-top graphics and competent handling continue to win over fans, making the 1977–1980 AMX a bona fide collectible today. Current values top out around $8,000 for one of these models in good condition.

Another newer model worthy of consideration is the 1974–1978 Matador Coupe, especially "X" package models with the 360- or 401-ci V-8. These cars look like nothing else on the road, and could be optioned with bucket seats and console, including a T-handle automatic shifter. Limited production makes finding some replacement parts difficult. Expect to pay upward of $7,500 for a nicely preserved Matador X.

Hornet X and Gremlin X models are also in demand, especially V-8 cars, and those with the unique Levi's interior. Although produced in greater numbers, their lower initial cost and eventual low resale value attracted younger buyers, meaning that most of these cars have been

FUTURE COLLECTIBILITY

Even without a 390-ci V-8 under the hood, or any V-8 in some cases, sporty newer models, including the Hornet AMX and 1978 Gremlin GT, can still be interesting collectibles. One example is the Levi's edition 1977 Hornet AMX; with just 100 units produced it has the same original production as the 1970 Trans Am Javelin, but in the case of the Hornet-based special edition, only three are known to exist today.

The fourth and final generation of the AMC AMX was based on the Spirit body shell for 1979 and 1980. The good news was the return of a 4-speed transmission behind the 304-ci V-8 in 1979, but the bad news was the discontinuation of the V-8 option for 1980. Third- and fourth-generation AMX models already enjoy a moderate collector following, but values remain relatively low and reasonably priced examples are frequently offered for sale.

used up and scrapped. The scarce low-mileage survivor commands a decent price in the collector car market, even with a straight-6 engine residing under the hood. A Hornet Sportabout X makes a practical collectible with enough room for a weekend getaway to your favorite car show.

One Gremlin variant already in demand is the 1978 GT, a final-year Gremlin decked out with fender flares, a front spoiler, and other sporty features. With its newly restyled dash with silver-colored overlays, this model was a preview of the fourth-generation AMX introduced the following year. Few Gremlin GTs were built and even fewer survive, making one a rare sight today, even at AMC car shows.

As the prices of even these models increase, base model Hornets, Gremlins, Spirits, and Concords, once nothing more than a cheap set of wheels, have now become entry-level AMC collectibles. Examples of AMC's revolutionary four-wheel-drive Eagle can still be found at reasonable prices as well, but watch out for frame-rail rust because most of these cars were driven in snowy climates where road salt was used every winter.

Pacers have a strong and loyal following, with low-mileage, heavily optioned cars already selling for five figures. Sporty Pacer X and 1978–1979 V-8 Sport models are especially sought after today. With AMC cars out of production for more than a quarter of a century, there will be fewer and fewer bargains to be found in the years to come.

Expect the most collectible AMC muscle cars, including the 1968–1970 AMX, Hurst SC/Rambler, Rebel Machine, Mark Donohue and Trans Am edition Javelins, Hornet SC/360, and the 1971–1974 401-powered Javelin AMX to eventually rebound to their pre-2010 values. Increased collector interest will continue to drive second-tier models upward as well, including base Javelin and SST models, as well as V-8 Gremlin and Hornet X models.

Third- and fourth-generation AMX models will gradually gain value as well, especially as the earlier versions become too expensive for new collectors entering the hobby. However, despite their great styling and other charms, a lack of factory-installed muscle will forever hinder their status and value when compared to earlier AMXs.

Although the prices for rare performance parts generally remain stable, anytime the market is in a downturn is a good opportunity to buy a restored collector car or even a project car. But the secret is out; AMC muscle cars will not be overlooked forever. With increased media attention and exposure at high-profile car shows worldwide comes new respect and increased value. Buy one *now* before it's too late!

Conclusion

The ever-increasing interest and resulting rise in the values currently being enjoyed by AMC muscle cars (and for that matter many other AMC models) ensures a bright future for these long overlooked and often disrespected vehicles. No longer the butt of jokes, AMC cars are holding their own against Big Three competitors, whether at an all-make car show, on the dragstrip, or in a collector car auction. Serious collectors are already investing real money to own and restore the finest examples of AMXs, Javelins, SC/Ramblers, Rebel Machines, and Hornet SC/360s.

For decades, many people have claimed that there is no *right* way to restore an AMC because "every car was different," or "they used whatever parts they had to keep the assembly line running." Although there is a tiny amount of truth to these Kenosha urban legends, the fact is that most models were regular, mass-produced vehicles with no special instructions or handling, bolted together exactly the same way as the ones before and after. Slight variations or running changes can be attributed to parts that were reengineered to function better, ones changed in appearance by an outside supplier, parts or hardware acquired from multiple suppliers, or simply assembly mistakes.

In most cases there is a consensus of what is *most correct* for a particular model produced within a certain period of time. As an example, you won't find an original 1969 AMX with the Big Bad Colors option, introduced mid-year, along with a black-painted front suspension and rear axle. It's time to get serious about restoring these cars, and doing it right!

Because of the multitude of subtle differences in hardware, equipment, finishes, and other variances that can be found from year to year, a book like this could be written for each model year covered, just as the factory TSM was updated and rewritten every year. But the basics are here, enough information to get you started and heading in the right direction with your own AMC muscle car project. Challenge yourself to research and restore your particular model as authentically as possible.

I cannot stress enough to carefully inspect and document any *original* car *before* starting a restoration. A particular detail that is exactly the same on ten other similar cars may be different on yours. However, if your car has already been "restored" once or twice, or is obviously assembled from the parts of several different donor cars, it is always best to follow the accepted formula for restoring each component so that they appear most correct for your particular application. Going by the recollections of an uncle's friend who worked at a dealership in 1970, regardless of how well intentioned, is a sure way to get bad information, and ultimately refinish parts of your car incorrectly.

For optimum resale value, stock is always better. Limit changes to custom wheels or other parts that are easy to remove if you need to. Avoid modifications that cannot be undone easily; even changing to a different paint color requires extensive disassembly if you or a subsequent owner wants to replace the factory-original color. Never create a reproduction door tag making your car appear to be something that it never was.

With more collectors and enthusiasts entering the AMC hobby each year, there is no end in sight to the popularity of AMC vehicles, especially the muscle cars; demand is already outpacing the supply of surviving cars. This popularity, combined with an increasing number of reproduction parts being introduced, spells a bright future for the products of American Motors.

Drive and display your AMC muscle car with pride!

Source Guide

3M Chemicals
St. Paul, MN 55144
888-364-3577
3m.com

AMARK
6501 Firestone Rd.
Jacksonville, FL 32244
904-777-1675
amarkamc.com

American Motors Owners
   Association
1615 Purvis Ave.
Janesville, WI 53548
amonational.com

American Parts Depot
409 N. Main St.
West Manchester, OH 45382
937-678-7249
americanpartsdepot.com

APS Tower Paint
2120 W. Nordale Dr.
Appleton, WI 54914
800-779-6520
apstowerpaint.com

Battery Tender
801 International Speedway Blvd.
DeLand, FL 32724
877-456-7901
batterytender.com

Blaser Auto
3200 48th Ave.
Moline, IL 61265
309-764-3571

Bleche-Wite Tire Cleaner
6925 Portwest Dr.
Houston, TX 77024-8042
855-888-1990
blackmagicshine.com

California Car Duster
818-998-2300
calcarduster.com

California Classic AMC
977 Florida St.
Imperial Beach, CA 91932
619-423-0364
californiaclassicamc.com

Car Jacket
13165 Center Rd.
Bath, MI 48808
800-522-7224
carbag.com

Craftsman Tools
craftsman.com

Detroit Muscle Technologies
23624 Roseberry Ave.
Warren, MI 48089
586-777-7167
detroitmuscletechnologies.com

Dupli-Color Products Group
Cleveland, Ohio 44115
800-247-3270
duplicolor.com

The Eastwood Company
263 Shoemaker Rd.
Pottstown, PA 19464
800-343-9353
eastwood.com

Fine Lines
127 Hartman Rd.
Wadsworth, OH 44281
800-778-8237
finelinesinc.com

Galvin's AMC Rambler Parts
634 E. Lockeford St.
Lodi, CA 95240
209-365-6315
ramblerparts.com

Kennedy American
7100 State Rte. 142 SE
W. Jefferson, OH 43162
614-879-7283
kennedyamerican.com

Legendary Auto Interiors
121 W. Shore Blvd.
Newark, NY 14513
800-363-8804
legendaryautointeriors.com

Lifter-1 Carpet Stain Remover
833 Melrose Dr.
Lenexa, KS 66214
800-543-8371
lifter1.com

LORD Fusor Products
877-275-5673
lord.com

M&H Electric Fabricators
13537 Alondra Blvd.
Santa Fe Springs, CA 90670
562-926-9552
wiringharness.com

SOURCE GUIDE

Meguiar's Car Care Products
meguiars.com

Milwaukee Paint
3532 W. North Ave.
Milwaukee, WI 53208
414-445-1500
match-it.net

Muscle Car Research
Box 247
Burke, VA 22009
571-262-1612
musclecarresearch.com

NAPA Auto Parts
800-538-6272
napaonline.com

Ohio AMX Restorations
234-788-1839
CarNutDirect.com

Phoenix Graphix
400 S. 79th St.
Chandler, AZ 85226
800-941-4550
phoenixgraphix.com

PG Classic Reproduction Parts
10305 Rte. 144
Saint-Andre, NB, E3Y 3H7 Canada
888-473-5855
pgclassic.com

Preval Paint Sprayers
1300 E. North St.
Coal City, IL 60416
877-753-0021
preval.com

POR-15
38 Portman Rd.
New Rochelle, NY 10801
800-457-6715
por15.com

Rain-X
6925 Portwest Dr.
Houston, TX 77024-8042
855-888-1990
rainx.com

SEM Products
1685 Overview Dr.
Rock Hill, SC 29730
866-327-7829
semproducts.com

Seymour Paints
917 Crosby Ave.
Sycamore, IL 60178
800-435-4482
seymourpaint.com

Shelby Coleman Grille Restoration
808 Putnam St., Apt. C
Findlay, OH 45840
419-701-8461

Skat-Blast Cabinets
7075 State Rte. 446
Canfield, OH 44406
800-321-9260
tptools.com

Speedway Motors
340 Victory Ln.
Lincoln, NE 68528
800-979-0122
speedwaymotors.com

Ssnake-Oyl Products
114 N. Glenwood
Tyler, TX 75702
800-284-7777
ssnake-oyl.com

Sta-Bil
sta-bil360.com

Summit Racing Equipment
P.O. Box 909
Akron, OH 44309
800-230-3030
summitracing.com

Strip Master
2746 Ohio 44
Rootstown, OH 44272
330-325-1050

TP Tools & Equipment
7075 State Rte. 446
Canfield, OH 44406
800-321-9260
tptools.com

WD-40
P.O. Box 80607
San Diego, CA 92138
888-324-7596
wd40.com